Mike Shanahan is a freelance writer with a doctorate in rainforest ecology. He has lived in a national park in Borneo, bred endangered penguins, investigated illegal bear farms, produced award-winning journalism and spent several weeks of his life at the annual United Nations climate change negotiations. He is interested in what peo ple think about nature and our place in it. His freelance journalism includes work published by *The Economist*, *Nature*, *The Ecologist* and *Ensia*, and chapters of *Dry: Life without Water* (Harvard University Press, 2006); *Climate Change and the Media* (Peter Lang Publishing, 2009) and *Culture and Climate Change: Narratives* (Shed, 2014). He is the illustrator of *Extraordinary Animals* (Greenwood Publishing Group, 2007) and maintains a blog called Under the Banyan.

Ladders to Heaven

Mike Shanahan

Heaven

How *Fig Trees* shaped our HISTORY,
fed our imaginations
and can ENRICH OUR
FUTURE.

unbound

This edition first published in 2016

Unbound
6th Floor Mutual House, 70 Conduit Street, London W1S 2GF
www.unbound.co.uk

Text Design by Ellipsis Digital Limited, Glasgow

A CIP record for this book is available from the British Library

ISBN 978-1-78352-236-1 (trade hbk)
ISBN 978-1-78352-237-8 (ebook)
ISBN 978-1-78352-302-3 (limited edition)

Printed in Great Britain by Clays Ltd, St Ives Plc

1 3 5 7 9 8 6 4 2

For Charlotte and Noah

Then the trees said to the fig tree
'You come and be our king!'
The fig tree replied,
'Must I forgo my sweetness,
forgo my excellent fruit,
to go and sway over the trees?'
  Judges 9: 12-13 (Old Testament)

'I have not cut down any fig tree . . . why then does
calamity befall me?'
  Ravana, the ten-headed demon-king of Lanka, in
  The Ramayana (c. 500-400 BCE)

'Every fruit has its secret. The fig is a very secretive
fruit.'
  DH Lawrence

Dear Reader,

The book you are holding came about in a rather different way to most others. It was funded directly by readers through a new website: Unbound. Unbound is the creation of three writers. We started the company because we believed there had to be a better deal for both writers and readers. On the Unbound website, authors share the ideas for the books they want to write directly with readers.

If enough of you support the book by pledging for it in advance, we produce a beautifully bound special subscribers' edition and distribute a regular edition and e-book wherever books are sold, in shops and online.

This new way of publishing is actually a very old idea (Samuel Johnson funded his dictionary this way). We're just using the internet to build each writer a network of patrons. Here, at the back of this book, you'll find the names of all the people who made it happen.

Publishing in this way means readers are no longer just passive consumers of the books they buy, and authors are free to write the books they really want. They get a much fairer return too – half the profits their books generate, rather than a tiny percentage of the cover price.

If you're not yet a subscriber, we hope that you'll want to join our publishing revolution and have your name listed in one of our books in the future. To get you started, here is a £5 discount on your first pledge. Just visit unbound.com, make your pledge and type **ladders** in the promo code box when you check out.

Thank you for your support,

Dan, Justin and John
Founders, Unbound

Contents

List of Illustrations   xiii

Chapter 1: Snakes & Ladders and Tantalising Figs   1
Chapter 2: Trees of Life, Trees of Knowledge   11
Chapter 3: A Long Seduction   27
Chapter 4: Banyans and the Birth of Botany   43
Chapter 5: Botanical Monkeys   53
Chapter 6: Sex & Violence in the Hanging Gardens   63
Chapter 7: Struggles for Existence   77
Chapter 8: Goodbye to the Gardeners,
    Hello to the Heat   93
Chapter 9: From Dependence to Domination   105
Chapter 10: The War of the Trees   122
Chapter 11: The Testimony of Volcanoes   136
Chapter 12: Once Destroyed, Forever Lost?   148
Epilogue: A Wedding Invitation   159

Acknowledgements   165
Sources   168
Supporters   197

List of Illustrations

Deadly Embrace	10
Forest Takeover	16
Eden's Figs	21
A Figure in a Fig Tree	34
Tree of Enlightenment	38
Beneath a Banyan	47
A Banyan's Blessing	50
All Shapes and Sizes	56
Journey's End	67
Life in a Dead-End	69
Ancient Allies	79
All Hail the Sky King	86
Strangler's Heart	96
Figs in the Family	109
Heaven's Gate	115
Crowning Glory	127
Volcano in Recovery	138
Night Gardeners	143
Robots in the Rainforest	157
Nature versus Structure	164

LADDERS TO HEAVEN

ONE:

Snakes and Ladders and Tantalising Figs

The figs were big orange beacons that lured me from afar. The snake was lime green and venomous and just centi-metres from my face. I found them both near the top of a tall tree in a Bornean rainforest. While the snake was safely coiled on a sturdy branch, all I had were some sweat-soaked fingers to save me from a fall. My heart raced. The snake's unblinking eyes looked as patient as time.

The year was 1998 and I was falling headlong into a fascinating story. The stars of the story are the fig trees – the 750 or so *Ficus* species. Over millions of years these trees have shaped our world, influenced our evolution, nourished our bodies and fed our imaginations. The best could be yet to come. Fig trees could help us restore rav-aged rainforests, stem the loss of wild species and even limit climate change. They could build vital bridges between scientific and faith-based world views. Their story reminds us of what we all share. It warns us of what we could lose.

In Greek mythology, a branch laden with sweet figs was among the temptations that teased the demigod Tantalus during his punishment in the Underworld. Each time Tantalus reached for the figs, the wind wrenched the tree's bough beyond his reach. This tale gifted English the verb 'to tantalise'. Those dull orange figs in Borneo, with their guardian snake, seemed certain to elude me too. I craved them, though I had no desire to eat their flesh.

The figs adorned the stubby branches of a *Ficus aurantiaca*, a species that starts out in life on the rainforest floor and climbs up the trunk of a big tree, growing as straight as a charmed snake. As it rises it paints its host tree's bark green with thousands of little leaves. This species relies heavily on primates to eat its figs and disperse the tiny seeds within them. But in this particular forest *Ficus aurantiaca* was a plant with problems.

First, few primates remained in the area. The National Park I was in was an island of ancient forest, at whose edges lapped a biting tide of oil palm plantations, farms and logging concessions. These man-made habitats posed dangers to primates and other wildlife. Like the National Park itself, they were often visited by shotgun-toting hunters for whom a monkey or a gibbon would be a prize kill. But even if primates had been abundant, something else was wrong. Like all fig species, *Ficus aurantiaca*, depends on tiny wasps to pollinate its flowers. That year, however, an intense drought had stricken the National Park. By forcing *Ficus aurantiaca* to stop producing figs, the drought had driven these insects into local extinction.

Across the National Park many other *Ficus* species faced the same problem. Without figs and fig-wasps, the plants could not reproduce. The many bird and mammal species that rely on figs as food faced a serious fruit shortage. And that would have knock-on effects for the other plants whose seeds these creatures dispersed. That's why I was so interested in the *Ficus aurantiaca* figs I spotted that day. They were a sign that life might be returning to normal. But to be sure, I needed to know what was going on inside them. All that lay between my curiosity and the answers I sought was that venomous snake and the risk of a long fall.

I was hanging from the last of seven ladders that some-body had lashed, toes-to-shoulders, flush to the tree. I had not brought a safety harness but climbed nonetheless. Those figs had banished security from my mind. As I tried to maintain my grip on the metal rungs, an intense wave of vertigo paralysed me. For a moment I could no longer sense my own body. It was as if my mind was all that existed of me, and it scrambled to process the sudden danger. I held my breath. Solid ground was a long way down, but I needed those figs and that meant I had to let go of the ladder with one hand to reach past the snake.

My obsession with figs had long since taken root. In the years ahead it would take me to temples, mountaintops and into the crater of an active volcano. It would stay with me long after I stopped studying biology. It would take solid form in the pages of this book. It has been a long and fruit-ful journey.

I first encountered these plants in my childhood home. One lived inside in a plastic pot and inched its way toward whatever light it could find. Just a metre high and spindly of limb, it would fall over if my sister or I ran past it too quickly. I was the youngest member of the family, so the periodic task of cleaning the tree's leaves fell to me. As I stroked each dark green leaf with a soft yellow duster so it shone, I couldn't fail to notice the label that stood upright like a tombstone in the soil. The exotic words there – *Ficus benjamina* – made no sense to my young eyes. Years would pass before I understood what those words meant and before I learned that this frail plant was a mere baby.

As one of the most common houseplants in the world, *Ficus benjamina* is seen more often indoors than out. But in the forests of Asia this species can reach 30 metres in height. Its reddish pea-sized figs sustain dozens of wild animal species. My mum referred to the plant in our hall-way as 'the fig tree'. This confused me, as outside, in our next-door neighbours' garden, there was another plant she gave the same name though it looked utterly dissimilar. Despite their differences, both plants were indeed fig trees, distant cousins with a common ancestor. This was my first exposure to the rich variety of fig species that has kept biolo-gists busy for more than 2,300 years.

The leaves of the plant inside were small and smooth, but those of the tree outside were rough to touch and wider than my dad's handspan. Unlike the tiny tree inside, the one outside was big enough to peer down at me from behind the two-metre tall wall that separated our garden from our neighbours'. And unlike the barren houseplant, the one outside often tempted me with its fruit – soft and tasty figs. It was *Ficus carica*, the so-called edible fig. The ancient Greeks valued this species so much they believed it to be a gift from the gods.

These fig trees sowed in my young mind some seeds that would long lay dormant. In time they germinated into a garden of fascination. Fig trees would show me the world through different eyes and different taste buds – those of diverse cultures from the present day and the distant past, as well as those of bats and birds, monkeys and much stranger beasts. This germination began in 1994 at the University of Leeds, in a lecture by biologist Steve Compton. He would later list his research interests on the university website as including 'Anything to do with fig trees and fig-wasps'. I had never heard of a fig-wasp. Steve changed my life when he taught me their story. It's a story to which D.H. Lawrence alluded in his poem about the 'Wicked fig tree' with its 'self-conscious secret fruit'.

Lawrence hinted at the trait that characterises all *Ficus* species and explains why they matter so much. It relates to sex. For any species of flowering plant to reproduce sexually, male pollen must fuse with female ovules – just like the sperm and eggs of mammals. The fertilised ovules turn into seeds. These are plant embryos. They develop inside their mother flowers until they are ready to disperse and take their chances in the game of life.

Some plants rely on the wind to transfer their pollen, but the vast majority need help from animals. Many rely on insects such as beetles, bees and butterflies, which spread pollen as they wander from flower to flower. More rarely, birds or mammals provide the service. Bats that feed on nectar pollinate the flowers of the blue agave, the succulent plant that is the source of tequila. Their pollen-dusted noses fit into the agave flowers like hands into gloves. Figs and their fig-wasp pollinators have an even tighter relationship, but have you ever seen flowers on a fig tree? I think not.

Sit under a *Ficus* tree every day of your life and you will see it produce crop after crop of figs but never a single flower. The mystery of this apparent virgin birth has endured for millennia. It is why ancient Hindu and Buddhist texts use the phrase 'seeking flowers in a fig tree' to describe a hopeless search. It's why a Bengali saying describes someone who has become 'invisible like a fig flower'. And why the Chinese characters for fig – 無花果 – mean 'the flowerless fruit'. The ancient phrase-makers never looked closely enough.

A proverb in the Tamil language of southern India comes close to solving the mystery. It refers to the way a fig tree's 'flowers bloom secretly and fruits flourish visually'. Here is the secret: the fig is not a fruit at all. It is a hollow ball whose entire inner surface is lined with tiny flowers that never see daylight.

The mystery of the hidden flowers arose as many as 80 million years ago when fig trees and fig-wasps forged a fortuitous bond that became biological shackles for them both. Fig flowers were once out in the open but, as the ancestors of today's *Ficus* and fig-wasp species developed their co-dependence, the plants evolved to exclude many other species from their flowers. Over generations, the platforms upon which the flowers stood developed into urn-like figs that hid the blooms away. Since then figs and fig-wasps have spread across the planet and diversified into an astonishing variety of species.

Today, every one of the 750 plus *Ficus* species is pollinated by just one or more tiny wasp species that can only feed and breed in their fig partner's flowers. The *Ficus* and fig-wasp species cannot survive without each other. Their destinies are bound together, and many more species gain as a result. I know because I counted just one group of beneficiaries and it took me years. To find out which animals eat figs, I trawled through hundreds of scientific papers, recorded my own observations and begged biologists to share unpublished data. The list that emerged was more motley than I could have imagined.

It included elephants and opossums, bearded pigs and spectacled bears, mongooses, bandicoots and tree kangaroos. I found records of 90 species of fruit bat and 80 species of primate eating figs. Deer, cattle and antelopes eat them. So do rats, mice and more than 30 species of squirrel. I even found records of fig-eating by giant tortoises and jackals, kingfishers and seagulls and several species of fish. The list included hundreds of species of birds, from pheasants to orioles, ostriches to woodpeckers and more than 120 species each of parrots and pigeons. In all, I found that figs feed at least 1,274 species of birds and mammals

– far more than any other types of fruit. These animals in turn disperse the seeds of thousands of other plant species. So figs help to sustain life across entire landscapes and it is because of this that I came to be in Borneo, hanging from a ladder high up a tree.

Tantalus never got his figs, but I got mine. As I plucked each one and shoved it into my pocket, sticky white latex oozed from the wounds I inflicted. This gummy sap is common to all fig species. It deters insects from feeding on them and it speeds recovery from injuries. For millennia, people have found ways to make fig latex work for them too. They have smeared it on branches to catch birds, curdled milk with it to make cheese, processed it to make rubber and used it as an aphrodisiac. I was glad of the latex that day. It covered my hands and strengthened my grip as I lowered myself down the chain of ladders and entered the murky forest again. The snake had not moved a single scale.

Back at my workbench in my research station in the National Park, I picked up a sharp scalpel and sliced into each fig. One by one they opened like mouths with nothing to say – they were barren hollows. Their flowers were unpollinated. They bore no seeds. Their pollinator wasps had not returned. My climb had been in vain.

It may seem strange to take risks in search of rare figs, but by the time I met that snake in 1998 I had come to understand three things: that fig trees play important roles in rainforests; that they have influenced diverse human cultures; and that today we are both destroying the former functions and forgetting the latter. Back then the science was fascinating enough. But I was learning too about a chain of reverence towards fig trees that coils back in time for many thousands of years and encircles the globe.

Fig trees appear in mythologies in the Amazon and in Africa, across the Mediterranean and the Middle East, and from the foothills of the Himalayas to the islands of the South Pacific. They feature in some way in every major religion, starring in the stories of Krishna and Buddha, Jesus and Muhammad. But these are all just recent examples. Fig trees were inspiring, sustaining and even protecting our ancestors long before they invented writing or domesticated the dog. They were among the first plants people cultivated and their figs are among the most nutritious of foods we eat today. Thanks to their curious biology, arguably no other group of plants holds as much ecological importance, evolutionary interest and cultural value.

Our shared story stretches back beyond the birth of our species, back to before our ancestors descended from the trees and walked upright for the first time. It is a story of life and death and of a deal undone. Its cast includes kings and queens, gods and prophets, flying foxes and 'botanical monkeys'. It features scientific and religious wonders born from biology that seems almost impossible in its elegance. Most of all it is a story about our relationship with nature. The story stretches back tens of millions of years to the age of the giant dinosaurs, but is as relevant to our future as to our past. As our planet's climate changes and reminds us that nature really does matter, the story has important lessons for us all.

Mike Shanahan

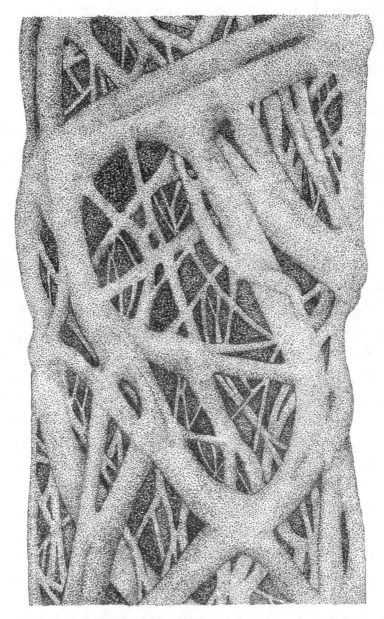

DEADLY EMBRACE:
A strangler fig imprisons its host tree with its rampant aerial roots

TWO

Trees of Life, Trees of Knowledge

On a July morning in 1860, Alfred Russel Wallace woke beneath a ceiling of woven palm fronds in what was little more than a shed, his temporary home in a rainforest just south of the Equator. Wallace was on Waigeo, an island in what is now eastern Indonesia. As the forest creatures called forth the new day, Wallace sipped his morning coffee and focused his gaze on a tall fig tree. And then he saw it: a telltale flash of colour. Within seconds he had abandoned his drink, grabbed his shotgun and charged through the humid forest to the base of the tree. A hunt was on. Many birds came to gorge on the ripe figs that day, but Wallace coveted one species above all others.

The fig tree towered over him. High up in its crown, the bird flapped between branches as it feasted on the figs. Down below, Wallace could spy none of its splendour. A mantle of yellow feathers flowed from the bird's crown to its shoulders. Its throat, cheeks and forehead shone metallic green. A highwayman's mask of black feathers hid its eyes. The only drab thing about it was the chestnut brown of its wings and belly. But this sombre tone was just the background for the bird's bright red display plumes, which peeked out from under each wing, waiting for an occasion to show off. To complete the costume, two long black twisted tail feathers trailed behind the bird as it moved.

Down below, gun at the ready, Wallace plotted the beauty's death. But first he had to find it. The crowns of lower trees crowded his view. Leaves shook. Figs fell all around him, as the feasting animals knocked them from branches or let them drop half-eaten from their mouths. Wallace spotted his target again. The bird was oblivious. He took aim, raising his shotgun until it was almost vertical. But before Wallace could shoot, the bird had flitted off into the forest. Just as it would do the next day and the day after that.

Wallace later wrote: 'It was only after several days' watching, and one or two misses, that I brought down my bird – a male in the most magnificent plumage.' It was a red bird of paradise. This prize catch was virtually unknown to the wider world. For Wallace, who planned to ship the bird to a trader in London, it meant a payday that would help fund his travel and studies.

Wallace was working his way across the region with his gun, a butterfly net and a mind pregnant with revolutionary ideas about life on Earth. A mix of adventure and misfortune had led him to that fig tree on Waigeo. He was born in 1823, the seventh of nine children, and he grew up in Hertford, a town 20 miles north of London. When Wallace's father was swindled out of a large sum of money, the family fell into poverty. This forced young Alfred out of school and into work at the age of 14. For several years he worked as a land surveyor, and his eyes and mind opened to admit the beauty and mystery of the natural world. But the office work was drudgery he intended to escape, so, in 1848, he engineered an adventure to South America.

In the Amazon rainforest Wallace collected thousands of specimens of species that were new to science. Four years later he set sail from Brazil with a great cargo of preserved beetles, butterflies, bird skins and more. Not everything was dead. For the next 28 days, the calls of Wallace's caged monkeys and parrots accompanied the wild songs of the Atlantic's wind and waves. Ahead lay a triumphant return to England.

But it was not to be. On August 6th, the captain came to Wallace's cabin and hit him with a blunt message: 'I'm afraid the ship's on fire.' Wallace and the crew crowded into a pair of leaking lifeboats in time to watch it sink. They drifted for 10 days, sunburnt and sodden, before a passing ship rescued them. Wallace had lost everything but a small case of notes and sketches. His collection had been worth a small fortune – tens of thousands of pounds in today's money. To science, it was priceless.

The disaster would have crushed the spirit of many a traveller. Wallace, however, later called it the 'most fortunate thing' to have happened to him. Without it he would have returned to the Amazon. Instead, in 1854, he headed east to the Malay Archipelago, 'a perfectly virgin country, which hardly any naturalist had then properly explored'. These islands ignited in him ideas that would illuminate the world.

Over Wallace's eight-year stay there he shot, trapped, bartered for and bought more than 125,000 animal specimens. Glittering in this trove were more than 5,000 species that no scientist had described before, including 212 types of bird. The more Wallace explored the forests the more he saw patterns in the diversity and distribution of plants and animals. But he was puzzled by the number of distinct yet clearly related species.

The prevalent view among both religious and scientific minds back home in Western Europe was that God had created each species in a fixed form. Wallace, though, was not convinced. He had plenty of questions about the origin of species and how they were so well-suited to the lives they led. Why were species present in some places but not others? Why did the intermediate forms die out, leaving only the distinct species? The forests of the archipelago thrust answers at him. The strangler figs Wallace encountered on every island he visited, and which impressed him more than any other trees, had a part to play. Their roots reached into his mind.

It was in 1858, when a strong fever gripped Wallace that he hit upon his big idea. He envisioned a 'struggle for existence' among individuals that vary in how well they can survive in their physical and biological surroundings. This variation, thought Wallace, could be the mechanism through which species evolve. It was sacrilegious stuff.

Wallace scribbled down his ideas and sent them by steamboat to his friend and fellow naturalist Charles Darwin. By weird coincidence Darwin had developed an almost identical idea, but had been scared to share it for close to 20 years because it so thoroughly contradicted the Bible. Wallace's letter prompted Darwin to go public. Within weeks, and without Wallace's knowledge, the two men's work had been presented as a joint paper to England's premier gathering of learned naturalists, the Linnean Society of London. The theory of evolution had arrived.

Fifteen months later Darwin published *On the Origin of Species* and changed the world. While Darwin became a household name, Wallace dallied in Asia, in thrall to its forests. In July 1860, he arrived on Waigeo, where he sought birds of paradise. He later wrote of these creatures that: 'Nature seems to have taken every precaution that these, her choicest treasures, may not lose value by being too easily obtained.' But in Waigeo, Wallace had an ally. He had chosen the site for his hut there in part because it was near the tall fig tree whose leaves would soon feel his gunshot. Six years into his odyssey across the archipelago, he knew he could count on big fig trees to reward his patience.

Wallace's tree was a kind of strangler fig, a group he called 'the most extraordinary trees of the forest'. They lurk in forests throughout the tropics where they can grow into colossal forms. It is not only their size that seizes the attention of anyone who sees them. It's also their shape. They look less like plants than primeval creatures that have

FOREST TAKEOVER:
A strangler fig colonises, embraces and replaces its host tree

frozen in time, their bodies a hulking mass of once-writhing limbs that dangle matted strands of dark hair.

The illusion comes from the tens or even hundreds of false stems that make up a strangler fig's trunk. These stems are in fact roots, for the stranglers don't grow up from the ground but start out in life as seeds that germinate high up another tree. The strangler's roots flow down their host tree, fusing and splitting and fusing again like the molten wax that cools as it courses down a candle.

There's something almost erotic in the way a strangler fig's roots meet, embrace and meld. For this, they feature in a myth among the Wayampi people from the Amazonian rainforest of French Guiana. According to the story, a man learned that his wife had been unfaithful. To take his revenge he smeared her and her lover with a magical oint-ment that glued their bodies together. He then threw the adulterers to their deaths from the roof of his house. A giant strangler fig grew out from their bodies, its roots and branches entwined like the lovers' limbs. The Buddha is said to have made a similar comparison, warning that sen-sual pleasures can leave human bodies 'bent, twisted and split' like the trees that fall victim to a strangler fig's encir-cling roots.

What Wallace saw in those roots was evolution in action. He noted how strangler figs gain a great advantage over plants whose seeds germinate on a dark forest floor. By contrast, strangler fig seeds germinate high in the canopy and so are immediately immersed in the abundant light they need to grow. After producing their first leaves to capture energy from the sun, and using their first tiny rootlets to absorb nutrients from the hollow in which they find themselves, the strangler seedlings send roots downwards in search of solid ground. When these aerial roots enter the earth they grow in girth and begin to draw moisture upwards. In a short space of time, these plants have all the advantages of light from the canopy as well as moisture and nutrients from the soil – a very successful short cut. 'Thus,' wrote Wallace of the strangler figs, 'we have an actual struggle for life in the vegetable kingdom, not less fatal to the vanquished than the struggles among animals which we can so much more easily observe and understand.'

A strangler fig's roots can create a mesh that encloses the host tree, limiting its ability to grow. It can be a deadly embrace. In some cases, the host tree dies and rots away, leaving behind a hollow core. With the host dead, the basketwork scaffold formed by the strangler fig's roots can still support the growing crown of delicate green leaves and keep the fig alive. Yet, even as the stranglers exert their brute power they show another side to their majesty. They both destroy and sustain.

Once or more each year they can display as many as a million figs that attract and nourish a stunning variety of birds and mammals. The influence strangler figs have on other species is disproportionate to their numbers, and this makes them important components of many forests. If you want to find wildlife in the tropics there are few better places to wait than beneath a strangler fig with a ripe crop.

Animals will throng there like devotees to a temple, and Wallace knew this.

So Wallace got his red bird of paradise because of the figs. His work – not least because it brought Darwin out of his shell – would set the stage for later scientists to show just how and why fig trees are so special. These trees have provided textbook examples of the beauty and complexity of evolution. This is because the destiny of each fig species is bound to that of various animals, from the partners that pollinate its flowers and disperse its seeds, to the predators that grow fat at the expense of future fig trees.

Ficus species exemplify variation – that key trait Wallace identified as enabling evolution. And so they should. Every day for the past 80 million years, fig trees around the world have been combining their DNA and packing it into trillions upon trillions of seeds. Thus, they have tested a staggering number of genetic combinations, each one an experiment in the struggle for existence. It's a struggle fig trees make look easy.

Not only did these plants survive the cataclysm that saw off the giant dinosaurs and many other species. They flourished. As they spread around the globe, they formed hundreds of new species and became the most varied group of plants on the planet. The side effects have been profound. These plants fed our pre-human ancestors and offered other gifts to the creators of the first great civilisations. Our predecessors rewarded these trees with roles in some of the oldest of our stories.

Judaism, Christianity and Islam all agree, for instance,

that figs trees have been part of the human tale since Day One. In the creation story these three religions share, a fig tree was present in the Garden of Eden along with the first people, whom English speakers call Adam and Eve. God had given the couple all they needed and the freedom to do what they liked, but with one proviso – they must not eat the fruit of the Tree of Knowledge of Good and Evil. In Western Europe we are often told that this fruit was an apple. However, this may simply be because of the Latin bibles that began to spread in the Middle Ages – although they sound different, the Latin nouns for an apple and evil are the same: malum. Some Jewish rabbis have concluded that the forbidden fruit was in fact a fig. It was a fig that Michelangelo portrayed when he painted the scene on the ceiling of the Vatican's Sistine Chapel in about 1510.

The story says Eve ignored God's rule and swallowed the fruit. Adam followed suit. They were suddenly aware of their nudity. According to the book of Genesis: 'The eyes of them both were opened, and they knew that they were naked; and they sewed fig leaves together, and made them-selves aprons.' A fig tree had come to the rescue, but Adam and Eve's lack of clothes was the least of their problems. God banished them from the Garden of Eden, so preventing them from eating the fruit of the Tree of Life and gaining immortality. This, these three religions agree, is where all of our promise and our problems began.

Like hundreds of millions of people around the world I heard the story of Adam and Eve at a very young age. Decades later, and after years of studying the biology of fig

EDEN'S FIGS:
Eve and Adam eat figs from the Tree of Knowledge, in an image first drawn
by a Spanish monk in the year 994

trees, the story took on new meaning when I started to learn how fig trees were central to other creation stories too. I learned about Mithra, a Persian deity and 'Judge of Souls'. Some versions of his story say he was born out of a rock beneath a sacred fig tree. Naked and hungry, Mithra hid himself from the howling wind in the branches of the tree, ate figs for his first meal and made himself garments from fig leaves. Then I heard about creation stories from thousands of kilometres away in Africa's Congo Basin. They describe how the first hunter was born from a species of fig tree. Cold and naked, he peeled the tree's bark away and fashioned clothing from it to protect himself.

It may sound uncomfortable but barkcloth is a real thing. Cultures in Africa, Asia and South America have independently worked out how to turn the bark of local fig trees into a malleable material they could wear or write on. People in Uganda still produce cloth from the bark of fig trees. The United Nations has classified the process they use as a 'masterpiece of the oral and intangible heritage of humanity'. Researchers and designers around the world now put the material to new uses, in everything from furniture and high fashion to yachts, cars and aircraft.

Figs feature in other origins too. The Kikuyu people of Kenya have a grove of sacred fig trees at the centre of their creation story. A story from Indonesia describes how two gods formed the first couple from a fig tree, carving horizontal slices of wood to create the woman and vertical slices for the man. A myth told by the Kutia Kondh people in Odisha, India, says the goddess creator Nirantali formed the first human's tongue from the ever-quivering leaf of the sacred fig (*Ficus religiosa*). Another story says Nirantali provided the first people with seeds of another fig species (*Ficus benghalensis*) to plant. The resulting trees provided shade with their thick leaves and, on Nirantali's orders, also fed the first people with their milky latex until grain appeared in the world.

Ficus species don't only feature in creation stories. They also represent gods and serve as abodes for spirits. They can be symbols of divine sustenance or ethereal bridges that link heaven and earth. In East Africa, Maasai people tell stories that say when the earth and the sky became separated, all that connected them was a sacred fig tree. It was via this tree's aerial roots that the Maasai god provided cattle to the people. Among the Akan people of Ghana, on the other side of the continent, one of the first traditional duties of the ohemaa – a female ruler also called a queen-mother – was to create a sacred place by planting a fig tree. Figs are also cosmic trees in Candomblé, a religion that originated in north-eastern Brazil when slaves taken there from West Africa found fig trees just as impressive as the sacred figs from which they had been separated.

In Hong Kong, where people say *Ficus microcarpa* fig trees are home to spirits, two of these trees have become famous as 'wishing trees'. For many years, people would come to throw oranges into the trees' crowns. They had written their wishes on strips of crimson paper, which they attached to the oranges with string. If a wishing tree's branch caught hold of the missile, their desires could dangle and be blown by a breeze up to heaven. But, in 2005, when the weight of all those wishes caused a branch to break off and injure a man and a child, the government banned the practice.

Far away on the Indonesian island Sumatra, the Batak people have a fig for their 'world tree'. This is a mythical *Ficus benjamina*, the same species whose leaves I dusted as a child. The Batak say their tree grows among the stars and that its roots reach down to earth. Mortals can clamber up them to reach heaven. On the island of Borneo, the Iban and other indigenous peoples traditionally prohibit the cutting of strangler figs, because spirits dwell among their roots. In Myanmar, for a millennium before Buddhism became the main religion, people worshipped spirits called 'nats' including Nyaung Bin, an old man who lives in a fig tree. In the Philippines, fig trees are said to be home to supernatural beings such as giant tree demons, goblins and the half-human, half-horse tikbalang.

To the north-east, on the Japanese island of Okinawa, folk stories feature short, red-haired spirits called kijimuna that inhabit fig trees. Far to the south, in Timor-Leste, the Sun god Upulevo is said to have settled on a fig tree to impregnate his wife, the Mother Earth. In the Sepik River area of Papua New Guinea, people consider fig trees to be an abode of crocodile spirits. Meanwhile, in Australia, aboriginal communities warn of the yara-ma-yha-who, a blood-sucking manlike creature that lives in fig trees and preys on unwary travellers. And on the Pacific Ocean island of Guam, thousands of kilometres from the nearest sizeable land mass, ancestral spirits called taotaomonas are said to live among the roots of fig trees.

These are just snapshots. There are bigger, better and much more profound stories to tell. Search for these stories and you will find them across a great swathe of the planet. They are ancient stories. They come from a time when nature formed the foundation of faith, and when science had yet to ask its first questions. What science has since shown is that there are good reasons for the preponderance of fig trees in diverse religions. This points to lessons for our modern world, and to potential bridges between sceptical and romantic minds.

Wallace saw no contradiction between spirituality and science. In his first major scientific paper on evolution, he found space to write of the wonder he felt when he set foot in the great forests of Borneo. 'When, for the first time, the traveller wanders in these primeval forests, he can scarcely fail to experience sensations of awe . . . There is a vastness, a solemnity, a gloom, a sense of solitude and of human insignificance which for a time overwhelm him.'

Psychologists Dacher Keltner and Jonathan Haidt have suggested that awe is something we evolved to feel. Such sensations may have given our ancestors an advantage in their struggle for existence, they say – by making them respect more powerful entities or pay attention to their environment, for instance. If so, perhaps this helps explain why *Ficus* species have become embedded in so many diverse cultures. Tropical forests are indeed awesome and giant fig trees are among the most awesome things within them.

Their power and fertility demand the attention and respect of every human eye that sees them.

My time to feel the awe Wallace described came in 1994 when I followed Charles Darwin's advice that: 'Nothing can be more improving to a young naturalist than a journey to distant countries.' I went to Sri Lanka. There I encountered *Ficus religiosa*. This species of strangler fig includes one of the most famous trees in the world, a tree that has travelled thousands of kilometres, has been made a king and has helped spread a philosophy of peace.

THREE

A Long Seduction

The Buddhist monk's robe sang out loud saffron over the rainforest's muffled tones of brown and green and grey. The monk walked fast. He was a tall tree's length away when he paused on the path and turned to face me and my friends. Sunlight cut through the forest canopy and shone hard off his shaved head. With one hand he raised aloft a black umbrella. With the other he beckoned: come, follow.

It was 1994 – four years before I found myself hanging from that ladder in Borneo. I was in the Udawattakele Nature Reserve in deliciously named Kandy, a historic city nestled in the highlands at Sri Lanka's heart. I had gone there with three university friends during our summer break and for me, the biology undergraduate, it was paradise. I had blown my student loan on the plane tickets and I had no regrets. It was my first time in a tropical forest. It changed me.

Overhead, golden-backed woodpeckers shot like painted

arrows between the trees. Other animals chuckled, cooed and coughed from hideaways high above me. Butterflies fluttered by and flirted in the sunbeams. Dragonflies, big as teaspoons, patrolled coffee-coloured ponds where turtles gazed lazy-eyed, secure on semi-submerged logs.

But all these things seemed insignificant in the presence of the forest itself. It hugged all it contained in a humid, humming gloom. The outside world seemed remote now, the sun an intruder. It sneaked peeks through breaks in the leaves but caught only glimpses of the life that throbbed below. The trees towered over us, viscerally alive yet so alien to our animal ways. Their breath sweetened the air we inhaled. It is hard to explain, but I could feel the concentration of life around me, as if its great density there had somehow reached into me physically. What struck me was the neutrality of that force. There was no malice or love there, just existence.

The monk smiled liked the Mona Lisa and we decided to follow. He strode in silence and led us through the forest to a clearing and a rock overhang that formed a shallow cave. The cave had been enclosed by a whitewashed wall, in whose centre was a wooden door. The monk unlocked the door and disappeared behind it, only to return seconds later with a broom. He swept the flat area outside the door, scattered some scraps of bread there, then sat down on a large slab of rock. He had yet to say a word.

The sun blazed and all around the forest crowded in on that little clearing. Within a minute the closest trees began to shake. Leafy branches crashed against one another. It was a mob of monkeys, more than a dozen of them. They poured down the tree trunks to feast at our feet on the torn bread. The monk watched in silence and smiled.

The monkeys were toque macaques, a species that lives only in Sri Lanka. Figs are among their favourite foods and it is thanks in part to the Buddha that they have a steady supply. For the monk, a fig tree meant much more than mere food. I realised this when he broke his silence to invite us through the wooden door. Beyond it was a small cave whose cool walls shone white with paint. He said monks had lived and meditated in the cave for the past 2,000 years. There was no furniture, just a small cushion, some books and a plastic-wrapped painting of the Buddha, sitting cross-legged and deep in meditation beneath a fig tree. The Buddha had wandered for six years before he found that tree. When he found it he also found enlightenment.

The man in the picture hadn't always been at peace. According to Buddhist lore, he was born into royalty around 563 BCE in what is now Nepal. The young prince, whose name was Siddhārtha Gautama, grew up insulated from the hardships of life. But he grew unhappy after he witnessed sickness and death, poverty and the decay that time inflicts on once-strong bodies. These senseless things disturbed him. At the age of 29 he left his home and his riches, his wife and his child, and went off to wander the world in search of meaning.

Gautama studied under wise men and lived for some time in a forest as an ascetic, but still he found no answers. On he trekked. Six years after he left home he arrived at a forest near the city of Gaya in what is now the Indian state of Bihar. There he found a fig tree. When he sat beneath it to meditate he pledged not to leave until he had liberated his mind.

The tree belonged to a species scientists today call *Ficus religiosa* – the sacred fig. This species grows up to 30 metres tall and has smooth grey bark and small red figs. Its hand-sized, heart-shaped leaves are shiny and stiff, with long pointed tips and long slender stalks. When the wind blows, the leaves tap against each other and create a sound like the wing beats of thousands of tiny birds. This fluttering filled Gautama's ears as he tried to fathom the meaning of the universe.

After six days and six nights he achieved his goal and attained enlightenment. He had found an explanation for human suffering and a way to end it. He had become the Buddha. Some stories say he was so grateful to the fig tree that he gazed at it with motionless eyes for a full week. He stared at forest royalty.

Ficus religiosa is one of the strangler figs. It does best when it grows from a seed that has landed, not on the ground, but in a hollow on a tall tree. When its aerial roots reach the ground, they thicken into strong scaffolds. When its figs are red and ripe they won't last long before colourful birds fly in to feed. Rufous treepies and golden orioles, rosy starlings and yellow-footed green pigeons are among the species that love these figs. Monkeys might swing along too but at night large fruit bats called flying foxes often take over. Chital deer and nilgai antelopes will forage on any figs that fall to the ground. Some of these creatures depend on such fig feasts when other fruits are scarce, and most of them can disperse the fig tree's seeds. They help ensure the species they feed upon survives.

Unlike other strangler figs, which use their hosts only for support, a *Ficus religiosa* can carve its way into its host's wood, splitting it apart. These fig trees can live for hundreds of years, long after all trace of their host has gone. By now they stand free. Their robust roots have merged to form a stout trunk in whose deep-fluted hollows a wanderer can sit to shelter and contemplate the world. Siddhārtha Gautama is said to have done just that. His purported choice of tree would shift the fortunes of the entire species. But it was not the first time the fate of *Ficus religiosa* had entwined with that of the people who walked beneath it. This species had insinuated itself into human affairs thousands of years earlier.

Ficus religiosa had long played the game of life in forests where no human trod. Its struggle for existence was marked by conflict with seed-destroying animals and partnerships with pollinators and seed dispersers. Its life was a balancing act. Then, tens of thousands of year ago, along came a new player who tipped the scales. It was our species. We were few in number at first, but would leave deep footprints. We had developed a way to loosen the shackles of evolution. We had culture. Our ideas and technologies could spread faster than our genes.

With our big brains and grasping hands, our axes and our fire, we would have a disproportionate impact on the species that surrounded us. Against the forests and *Ficus religiosa*, the dice were now loaded. Unlike most forest species though, *Ficus religiosa* was able to gain by becoming part of that which sets humans apart: our culture.

It began early. Those first people found in *Ficus religiosa* giants among trees. Unstoppable, they grow into hulking forms. Yet each has its own distinct shape and character. They would have been landmarks to the wandering bands of forest people. They were also sources of food. Each periodic outburst of fruiting drew dozens of wild animal species. Those first people to encounter *Ficus religiosa* would have joined the feast but also hunted the animals they dined alongside. Over thousands of years, as the human population grew and began to settle and farm the land, new cultures developed. The value of *Ficus religiosa* would shift from the material to the symbolic and the sacred.

By 3300 BCE the Harappan people of the Indus and Saraswati valleys of what are now Pakistan and India were laying the foundations of a great civilisation. They cleared forest to plant crops and build houses. Their cities were the most advanced settlements of the time, with the world's first sanitation systems. The Harappan people had transformed a wild landscape into the pinnacle of urban planning. *Ficus religiosa* rode out these great changes. The tree was special to these people.

The earliest depictions of any tree in South Asian art or literature are the images of *Ficus religiosa* the Harappan people left more than four thousand years ago on small soapstone seals. These are stone stamps that a merchant or administrator might have used to mark clay tags on documents or packages. Some seals show a human figure beneath an arch of *Ficus religiosa* leaves. Others depict a person with a leafy branch from the tree on their head. One intriguing seal shows a man kneeling before a *Ficus religiosa* tree. Within the tree stands a figure, their arms bedecked with bangles, their hair in a single long plait. Alongside the kneeling man is what appears to be a severed human head. Some scholars think the scene represents a ritual sacrifice to a spirit or deity who resides in the fig tree.

The image offers a tantalising glimpse into a mysterious people whose writing remains undeciphered and whose civilisation fell into decline when calamity struck. Around 3,500 years ago, the rivers this culture depended on changed course and the people abandoned their cities. For their favourite trees, the future was uncertain. But there were strangers on the horizon, new minds to seduce. The changes began around 1500–1400 BCE, when nomadic herders moved into the Indus Valley. The migrants would come to dominate the landscape, in time settling and farming the land. They brought their own gods and stories, but as they mixed with the people already there, something new was born: the Vedic culture.

The surviving Vedic hymns reveal just how well this new force valued *Ficus religiosa*. They tell how the people used the tree's wood in important rituals to ignite fire and prepare a hallucinogenic drink. *Ficus religiosa* was central to these

Mike Shanahan

A FIGURE IN A FIG TREE:
An ancient Indus seal depicts what may be a sacrifice to a deity in a fig tree

34

rituals that helped bind the new culture together. The trees were also early pharmacies. People in India today use medicines made from this tree's bark, leaves or roots to treat dozens of conditions. Some of these remedies date back thousands of years to the Vedic culture.

The Vedic people called *Ficus religiosa* an 'abode of the gods' and home of the 'universe's mighty keeper'. They adopted the species as a symbol of strength, a destroyer of enemies. A Vedic prayer directed to the fig tree includes this vivid couplet: 'As you climb up the trees and render them subordinate, so split in two the head of my enemy and overcome him!' *Ficus religiosa* had once again become cemented into the dominant culture. Greater roles were to come.

As the Vedic culture spread east into the dense forests of the Indo-Gangetic Plain, it encountered local cults who believed spirits dwelt in *Ficus religiosa* trees. The Vedic culture assimilated these people along with their stories. The blend of cultures gave rise to Hinduism, which elevated *Ficus religiosa* to new heights. The species symbolises three core Hindu deities – the roots representing Brahma the Creator, the leaves Shiva the Destroyer and the trunk Vishnu the Preserver. The many other Hindu gods associated with this kind of fig tree include Krishna, Shani, Hanuman and Lakshmi.

Ficus religiosa has been described as both a tree of knowledge and tree of life, a place people can go to pray for fertility and longevity. This species would become sacred to every Hindu caste, a tree to both protect and worship. To harm one became a deadly sin, so these trees were free to grow into giant forms. Where better for Siddhārtha Gautama to seek enlightenment? The species had survived thousands of years in the company of humans. It had thrived, but thanks to the Buddha's decision to meditate beneath one, its fate took a new turn.

After the Buddha died in c.483 BCE his followers began to flock to the fig tree, which they treated as a living embodiment of the Buddha himself. The tree became known as the bodhi tree, or tree of enlightenment, from the Sanskrit word *bodhi*, which means awakened or knowing. It would become the most famous tree in the world. Few of the pilgrims would have such an impact on the future of Buddhism – or on the fig tree – as a man called Ashoka who lived from 304–232 BCE and, as Emperor Ashoka the Great, became the third in his line to rule the vast Mauryan Empire.

Accounts of Ashoka's early life paint him as a monster. He is said to have murdered 99 half-brothers, burnt alive 500 women he kept in a harem, and executed 500 of his ministers. He ruled over much of what is now India, as well as parts of Afghanistan, Bangladesh and Pakistan. But something was missing: the Kalinga Kingdom, which neither his father nor grandfather had conquered. In 261 BCE, Ashoka poured in 400,000 soldiers. They outnumbered those defending Kalinga by more than six to one.

For days sounds of violence filled the air and at the end of it all the Daya River ran red with blood. More than 100,000 civilians lay dead. Ashoka captured and deported thousands more who survived. Kalinga was broken. Ashoka had achieved what none of his ancestors had. But he had won like a tiger against a cat. A more difficult conquest was soon to come – the conquest of himself. The turning point came when Ashoka surveyed the carnage he had wreaked.

Corpses buzzed with flies. Vultures circled overhead. The stink of burnt and rotting flesh filled Ashoka's nostrils. The wails of orphaned children and widowed women assailed his ears. The weight of responsibility was crushing. Ashoka renounced violence and said in future he would conquer by kindness. Ashoka the Wicked had become Ashoka the Righteous. He embraced Buddhism and made it the official faith of his empire. For *Ficus religiosa* this would mean a passport to world travel.

The change of fortune began in about 250 BCE when Ashoka visited the fig tree where the Buddha had attained enlightenment nearly three centuries earlier. Ashoka consecrated the site, built a shrine there and held a festival every year in honour of the tree. For hundreds of years before any image of the Buddha appeared, it was the fig tree surrounded by adoring devotees that sculptors portrayed at Buddhist temples.

In time, the original bodhi tree died but Buddhists say it lives on elsewhere because of how Ashoka spread his message of peace to another recent convert, the Sri Lankan King Devanampiya Tissa. And what better way than by sending him a branch of the bodhi tree itself? Never before nor since has a plant travelled in such style. Its journey has

TREE OF ENLIGHTENMENT:
Winged spirits and earth-bound devotees at the Buddha's *Ficus religiosa*,
from a first century BCE sculpture at Sanchi, India

become steeped in legend as described in the *Mahavamsa*, or 'Great Chronicle', an epic Pali-language poem that recounts 900 years of Sri Lankan history.

The *Mahavamsa* says Ashoka had the branch planted in a vase of solid gold that was eight-fingers thick and had a rim the size of a young elephant's trunk. Ashoka bestowed kingship upon the plant and appointed a diverse retinue, dozens strong, to accompany him on the branch's journey to the sea. They included nobles and cowherds, potters and weavers. Royal maidens watered the branch in public ceremonies at key stages of the journey. The branch and its entourage first voyaged by ship down the River Ganges to the Bay of Bengal. Here, Ashoka's daughter, Saṅghamittā, and his son, Mahinda, took the bodhi tree's branch aboard a seafaring ship. As the ship sailed away, Ashoka – once the hard man of the subcontinent – stood on the shore and shed tears.

When the ship arrived in northern Sri Lanka, Devanampiya Tissa was there to meet it. Sixteen nobles strode out into the warm sea with the King. They walked on until the water lapped around their necks so they could collect the golden vase and carry it ashore. After a long journey inland, Devanampiya Tissa planted the branch in his capital Anuradhapura. He employed archers to protect the tree from foraging monkeys, relatives of the fig-loving monkeys I saw in the Udawattakele forest that day in 1994.

Visit Anuradhapura today and you will see a giant *Ficus religiosa* that Buddhists say is the same one Devanampiya Tissa planted, making it the world's oldest living tree with a known year of planting. Sceptics say it is more likely that today's tree is a descendant of the original. What's certain is that the fig tree began life a long time ago. It is vast now, its branches thick and strong. They reach for the sky and support a wide crown of leaves, which pilgrims treasure as souvenirs when they fall to the ground. Buddhists come from all over the world to see the tree and make offerings of rice and lotus flowers. The air is perfumed with incense and coconut oil. Colourful prayer flags festoon the golden rails that surround the tree and protect it from the thousands of visitors who flock to see it each year.

This tree, the Sri Maha Bodhi, has itself helped spread the Buddha's philosophy. Saplings that sprang up near it were sent to various parts of Sri Lanka. Someone humped one up and down many hills to Kandy where a monk planted it in the Udawattakele forest in which I walked centuries later. Today clones grown from cuttings of the Sri Maha Bodhi tree can be found at Buddhist temples throughout Sri Lanka and in Buddhist communities the world over.

In March 2011, some of the pomp and ceremony that surrounded the tree's arrival in Sri Lanka burst out again. Monks took a cutting – little more than a slender branch with around 20 leaves – from the Sri Maha Bodhi and placed it in a gilded casket so it could journey back to Bodh Gaya, the site of Buddha's enlightenment in India. The circle was complete – a round trip of 3,600 kilometres.

When the original branch left India for Sri Lanka, it left a land of thick forests and bullock carts. The branch that returned now grows in a country with skyscrapers and a space programme. Much has changed but much has stayed the same. Today millions of Hindus, Buddhists and Jains there consider *Ficus religiosa* to be not just a tree, but an embodiment of divine power that can bring benefits to those who worship it. The species features in an array of rituals that include prayers for fertility, marital bliss, health, wealth and good luck.

Among the most famous of people reported to have had a close encounter with this tree species in modern times is Aishwarya Rai, the Bollywood superstar and former Miss World. According to Hindu astrology, she was born a 'manglik'. This means the positions of the planets at the time of her birth carried an omen, a prophecy of misfortune. This could manifest through marital woes, such as fighting, or even the untimely death of a partner. When Rai and actor Abhishek Bachchan decided to marry, this put him and their relationship in the firing line. So, according to media reports, Rai followed an ancient tradition and first married a fig tree, a *Ficus religiosa*, which would absorb all of the bad luck and leave her free to then marry her human love. Her creative solution was part of a chain of events that has tied humanity to this special fig tree for more than five thousand years, since the time of the Indus Valley Civilisation and long before that. It is a chain upon which the Buddha's enlightenment beneath a *Ficus religiosa* is just one link.

When I looked at that painting of the Buddha beneath the tree in that forest cave in 1994, I still had no idea about the secret to the fig trees' success. But I can draw a direct line between that encounter and my journey into the story of *Ficus*. In that moment of golden peace and the company of monkeys and a high canopy of tall trees, something inside me clicked. The forest had touched me. If this was awe, I wanted more. Fig trees would be my gateway.

Ficus religiosa is not alone. It is one of more than 750 fig species, each with its own story, and its own role in our story. The journey to understand this great diversity of species began more than 2,300 years ago in Greece. While fig trees played many important roles in the development of Eastern philosophy, the early Western philosophers had figs of their own to ponder. And as the first followers of Buddhism began to spread the faith, far to the west these other fig trees were present at the birth of biology, the science that would reveal why *Ficus religiosa* ever mattered enough to make people revere it in the first place.

FOUR

Banyans and the Birth of Botany

Sykeus was big. Sykeus was strong. But Sykeus needed his mummy. He was on the wrong side of a one-sided war and it was all her fault. His mother was Gaia, the Earth goddess of ancient Greece. She had compelled Sykeus and his siblings to rise up and overthrow the gods on Mount Olympus. But her offspring were hopelessly outmatched.

Gaia watched helpless as Zeus and his fellow Olympians slew them one by one. They were clubbed to death, crushed by rocks, torched or flayed alive. Sykeus was next. Zeus pursued him, flinging bolts of lightning at him as he fled. Just when Sykeus could run no more Gaia opened up her chest, took him inside and transformed him into the first fig tree. And that is why there are fig trees in the world.

Oh no, argues another ancient Greek account, it is the fertility goddess Demeter we should thank. She gave figs to humanity to repay the hospitality of King Phytalus after he gave her shelter when she sought her lost daughter,

Persephone. But no, insists a third story, that's simply not true. It was Dionysus, the Greek god of wine, who found the first fig tree. Tasty as these tales were, they could not sate the intellectual hunger of a philosopher called Theophrastus who lived from c.371–287 BCE. Theophrastus hankered for truth.

Theophrastus is little known today, though his impact was immense and when he died Athens mourned en masse. He studied and wrote about history and philosophy, poetry and grammar, politics and religion. But his greatest legacy comes from his scientific enquiries into the lives of plants. Not for nothing is he considered the founder of botany. For more than 1,500 years after his death, nobody made a greater contribution to the field. He was the first in a long line of men and women who, by peering at figs, have peeled away layers of mystery and exposed reality to the light of their reason. But nearly 2,400 years after Theophrastus began to name and describe the world's fig species, the task is not yet complete.

The fig species Theophrastus knew best was *Ficus carica*, a tree with pale grey bark, unmistakeable lobed leaves and plump perfumed figs that ripen purple, green or black. This species, the 'edible fig', had been an important source of food in Greece for thousands of years. By the time of Theophrastus, the citizens of Athens were known as *philosykos* – literally 'fig lovers'. His contemporary, the poet Alexis, wrote of 'that god-given inheritance of our mother country, darling of my heart, a dried fig'. These figs were like treasures. Theophrastus noted how the climate and soil and strange little insects combined to decide the quality of fig crops. But he was just scratching the surface of one of biology's most fascinating stories.

As Theophrastus focused on the *Ficus carica* trees all around him, he was unaware of hundreds of other fig species, each with its own way of solving life's challenges. He didn't know the interiors of figs are scenes where great dramas play out daily, with consequences for thousands of off-stage actors from the plant and animal worlds. Patchy though his knowledge was, Theophrastus still came to learn about the most astounding fig species of them all. It was thanks to the unrelenting drive of one of the most powerful people to have lived: Alexander the Great.

In 326 BCE, after conquering swathes of what are now Greece, Turkey, Syria, Lebanon, Israel, Egypt, Iraq, Iran, Afghanistan, Uzbekistan, Tajikistan and Pakistan, Alexander and his army reached India. Alexander valued knowledge about the nature of the lands he occupied, so had brought along naturalists to collect specimens and report on the fauna and flora. For these explorers, everything was new. They met monkeys, massive snakes and beautiful birds such as parrots and peacocks, none of which they had ever before seen. The plant life was no less exotic, but one species seized their imaginations like no other. West had met East and found the giant among fig trees, the banyan (*Ficus benghalensis*).

At first, it must have seemed like a forest. Hundreds of trees held aloft a vast green canopy that cast deep cool shade. When a group of Alexander's men stepped under that leafy umbrella, they realised it was in fact a single tree, though one with hundreds of 'trunks' that propped up its biggest branches. Alexander's admiral, Nearchus, said ten thousand people could have sheltered under that banyan.

The tree was old. Many years earlier another tree had occupied that spot. Its fate shifted when a bird, or perhaps a bat or monkey, passed by having fed earlier on ripe *Ficus benghalensis* figs. The animal pooped on the tree and condemned it to a slow death by smothering. The animal's droppings had delivered a banyan seed to a moist nook. Within weeks, the fig seed had split open. It sent up a firm stalk with a collar of two tiny green leaves. It sent down tiny roots that hugged the host tree as they stretched earthwards in search of soil. In time these roots would expand and enlace. They would encase the host tree and erase all trace of it.

As the banyan grew, its branches also sent out roots. They dangled like strands of unkempt hair. When they reached the ground these roots grew thick and woody and merged to form what looked like new tree trunks. The massive branches reached ever outwards, sending down yet more and more prop roots. These false trunks increasingly wide circles around the banyan's core, enclosing it in nested cloisters.

There is little to stop a banyan expanding. The biggest one on record is said to have begun life in 1434 at the spot where a woman called Thimmamma died when she threw herself onto her husband's funeral pyre. That tree, in Andhra

BENEATH A BANYAN:
A single *Ficus benghalensis* can resemble a small forest thanks to the
false trunks its pillar roots form

Pradesh, now covers two hectares. Twenty thousand people can shelter beneath its crown.

All this from a seed that is just a couple of millimetres in length. Crack one open with your thumbnail and you won't find much inside, yet the genetic material within has the power to create a tree vast enough to resemble a small forest. Long before Alexander arrived in India, Hindu sages employed this paradox in a parable, which used the imperceptible power within a banyan seed as a parallel of Atman, the invisible essence Hindus say permeates and sustains the universe and all it contains.

The sheer size and weird form of India's banyans amazed Alexander and his men, but local people saw them as much more than impressive trees. The banyans had been part of the cultural fabric for thousands of years. Settlements had grown up around these trees. To bodies, they provided shelter, food and medicines. To minds, these awesome structures formed bridges to the supernatural. Gods and spirits moved among the banyan's leaves and pillar roots. By 500 BCE, Hindu texts described a cosmic 'world tree', a banyan that grew upside down with its roots in the heavens, and its trunk and branches extending to earth to bring blessings to humankind.

The banyan became a potent symbol of fertility, life and resurrection. It features in stories of the Maha Pralaya, a periodic death and rebirth of the universe, when everything that exists dissolves into a ceaseless sea. One version of the story says an 'undying' banyan is the only thing to survive the deluge. Another says that to ride the sea's currents, the god Vishnu assumes the form of a baby, lying on his back on a raft formed of a banyan leaf. With one breath the baby swallows all that surrounds it, taking the turbulent universe into the safety of his stomach before exhaling it into fresh existence.

Another Hindu story from more than 2,500 years ago tells how a woman called Savriti convinced Yama, the god of death, to resurrect her husband who had died beneath a banyan tree. Today, married women in north India emulate Savitri's devotion in an annual ceremony in which they tie coloured thread around a banyan tree while praying for the wellbeing of their husbands.

These symbols of love and life became agents of death after the British arrived in India and began to subjugate the local population. They defiled many sacred banyans by using them as gallows to execute rebels who resisted their rule. By the 1850s, there had been multiple occasions when they hanged over a hundred men to death from a single banyan tree.

Alexander's army were more respectful of these trees. They had come from a land where people revered figs, thought them to be divine, used them as food and medicine and symbols of fertility, and said spirits dwelt among them. Thousands of kilometres away, they found people who held remarkably similar beliefs about utterly different fig trees. The parallels are a testament to the depth *Ficus* species have implanted themselves into human culture.

In time, the Greek explorers' tales of banyan trees reached Theophrastus, who wrote: 'The Indian land has its

A BANYAN'S BLESSINGS:
In an ancient Hindu tradition married women tie threads around a banyan tree
and pray for their husbands' wellbeing

so-called "fig tree", which drops its roots from its branches every year . . . the fruit is very small, only as large as a chickpea, and it resembles a fig.' With these words he joined two distant dots, which his intellectual heirs would reveal to be part of a glittering constellation of hundreds of fig species. And so began the long journey to identify them all. It's a journey whose end biologists say seems near but, more than two thousand years later, is still somewhere around the next corner.

Theophrastus's words echoed through time to influence the eighteenth-century Swedish botanist Carl Linnaeus who developed the system scientists use to name species and gather them into related groups. It was Linnaeus who gave fig trees the formal scientific name *Ficus*. He was using a ready-made word in Latin, the language of Rome, a city whose origin story happens to feature a fig tree. The legend says Rome was founded by Romulus and Remus, twins rescued from drowning in the River Tiber by the fig tree's roots. Under the convention Linnaeus developed, each species receives a two-part name: a noun followed by an adjective. The first part is shared by each member of a genus (e.g. *Ficus*) of closely related species. The second part is unique to each individual species.

Linnaeus gave the name *Ficus carica* to the common domesticated fig species after Caria – a region of ancient Anatolia in what is now Turkey. The scientific name he gave the other fig of my childhood, *Ficus benjamina*, has a more convoluted origin. Cut the tree and white latex will bleed out. Various other species also produce this particular kind of sticky fluid, which people have used for centuries to make perfumes, incense, medicines and other products. This substance is known as gum benzoin, from an Italian interpretation of a Javan word that is Arabic in origin. English tongues mangled the word some more to form 'gum benjamin'. So over time, the benzoin trees ended up being called benjamin trees, hence the benjamin fig (*Ficus benjamina*). I prefer its better-known name – the weeping fig – which it got because, when it sheds its leaves, they fall like green tears to the ground.

Linnaeus mentioned just seven species of *Ficus*. While that is more than double the number Theophrastus wrote about two millennia earlier, it is still less than one per cent of the world's fig species. Since Linnaeus, scientists have identified about 750 *Ficus* species and are still finding new ones. We know about much of this diversity because figs captured the imagination of a man called Edred John Henry Corner, a titan of tropical botany who was as flawed as he was brilliant. What Corner learned over decades studying figs shows just how wrong the Greek myths were. The fig tree wasn't a gift from Demeter or Dionysus. Gaia didn't form the first *Ficus* from Sykeus, her son. No, the fig trees came from forests far away, and they arose long before the first people gave voice to the first gods.

FIVE

Botanical Monkeys

It's 1937 and in a dense rainforest in what is now Malaysia, a tall Englishman with a short temper is shouting at a giant of a tree. It is E. J. H. Corner, his white shirt tucked into khaki shorts, his white socks reaching near to his knees. He looks like an overgrown boy scout except a smoking pipe hangs from the corner of his mouth, angled like a shotgun waiting to be loaded. '*Ambil itu*,' he shouts upwards. '. . . *Ambil itu!*'

More than forty metres above him, the rainforest canopy abounds with life. A monkey scampers along one of the tree's uppermost limbs, its eyes and mind alert for something tasty to eat. Large figs adorn a creeper that hugs the branch, but the figs are green and unripe: no good to the monkey yet. Perhaps it will find a lizard to catch, or a juicy cicada to stuff into a cheek pouch. Then something clicks in the monkey's mind. It remembers what '*ambil itu*' means.

The monkey tears loose one of the hard figs and hurls it at Corner. And then another. And another. The monkey is now a flash of brown fur, grabbing more figs and sending them hurtling down. Corner runs for cover from what he will later liken to a barrage of hand grenades. When the violence ends, he returns to the scene. Scattered in the leaf litter are about fifty figs of a kind he has never before seen. He has struck botanical gold.

Corner had left England eight years earlier, aged just 23, to become assistant director of the Singapore Botanic Garden. It was a plum job, but Corner despised the colonial social scene, with its golf games, drinks and vacuous chatter. Whenever he could he escaped across the causeway linking Singapore to Malaya, where he seized: '. . . the unparalleled opportunity to explore primeval forest at every step.' The forests were tall, dense and rich. They were also under threat from logging and the rapid spread of rubber and oil palm plantations. Corner vowed to study them before they fell.

'To be in the jungle is a biological consummation,' he wrote in 1930. 'To stumble among the riot of enormous trees and to cut a path through the tangle of creepers which knit the life of the rainforest into one gigantic web, is like a dream.' And in that dream grew the strange plants that would occupy Corner's mind for the rest of his days: the *Ficus.*

They were everywhere. Corner encountered giant strangler figs whose sinuous aerial roots resembled masses of snakes. He found trees that dangled ropes of figs from their trunks. He found climbing species of *Ficus* that hauled themselves up big forest trees and epiphytic *Ficus* species that lived high in the canopy and never needed to send down roots.

Just as these plants grew in different ways, so did their figs vary. Some were smaller than a pea, others as big as a tennis ball. They ripened red, orange or green, purple, brown or black. Some figs were smooth, others hairy. Among the strangest species was a tree called *Ficus treubii*. Its figs are the off-white of a smoker's teeth. They grow not on leafy branches but on ground level runners, which scramble over and under the soil. This species buries its figs like dirty secrets.

'By themselves the figs could build a forest,' Corner wrote. It was a comment on the large numbers of very different *Ficus* species that can coexist in one place. As biologist Rhett Harrison has shown, many tropical forests around the world have more *Ficus* species than species of any other genus of plants. For Corner, this meant plenty of opportunities to encounter fig species he had never before seen. As he tramped through the forests around him, he discovered and named dozens of new *Ficus* species. In their great variety he saw an opportunity to understand how the world's plants had evolved to display such diverse forms as tall trees, climbers and epiphytes.

But Corner had a problem. Evolution had run wild. Whichever way he glanced his eyes met hundreds of different tree species. To tell species apart, Corner needed to examine their leaves and flowers, their fruits and seeds,

ALL SHAPES AND SIZES:
Figs of ten *Ficus* species collected by the author on a single day in Borneo

often for microscopic differences. But the trees soared to 50, 60 or even 80 metres in height and kept their botanical clues far beyond his reach. Until, that is, he hit upon his idea of 'a little hand in the canopy'.

Corner had seen trained monkeys called pig-tailed macaques climbing tall palms to harvest coconuts. He reasoned that if they could do that, they could collect other things too. So he bought a monkey and began to train it to follow new commands. Soon he had four of what he called his 'botanical monkeys'. He joked that they were the first primates to become civil servants, as the then Straits Government paid an annual allowance to provide each with a collar and lead and a supply of rice, bananas and raw eggs. Merah, the monkey that bombarded Corner with unripe figs, managed to pluck samples from more than 350 plant species in just six months. Another monkey Corner called Puteh was the star, able to understand 24 Malay words. But as Puteh matured, he reminded Corner that he was a sentient being with a mind of his own.

One day Corner was in his garden when Puteh charged at him with 'open jaws and slobbering fangs'. Corner raised his right arm to protect his face and neck just in time for Puteh to sink his teeth into the arm and clamp his jaws shut. Only by tearing his arm from the monkey's mouth could Corner escape. The bite was severe. It severed a nerve. A long slab of flesh hung down from its bone. After surgery and a week in hospital Corner returned home with his arm in sling, and advice not to use it for four months. He banished Puteh to a cage. The monkey would botanise no more.

The injury was the least of Corner's problems. It was 1941 – the world was at war. Singapore was Britain's strategic jewel in South-east Asia and Japan wanted it. Its forces were advancing fast. Corner reckoned that if the fighting reached Singapore, Japanese soldiers or local looters would destroy the botanical garden's biological collections and the cultural treasures in the Raffles Museum.

In February 1942 the attack began. For a few days Japan bombarded Singapore's defences, then came the ground assault. Corner knew which way the wind was blowing. He liberated the last of his botanical monkeys, but could not free Puteh for fear he would attack somebody. With deep regret, Corner shot Puteh dead. 'I did not then know,' he later wrote, 'that I killed the one who in all probability saved my life.'

Five days later Britain surrendered. What followed was three and a half years of brutal occupation. Japan summarily executed many ethnic Chinese civilians and imprisoned the British, Indian and Australian military men, working many to their deaths in forced labour camps. Had Puteh the monkey not put Corner's arm out of use, Corner would have remained conscripted into the Singapore Volunteer Force. Instead he was invalided out and so avoided becoming a prisoner of war.

Corner should still have been interned in a civilian camp, but he avoided this grim fate too. Instead, he and two of his colleagues were placed under house arrest at the botanical gardens, where they continued to work. As Japan committed atrocities all about him, Corner spent days staring down a microscope at fig seeds. Many of those languishing in the camps branded him a collaborator, a label he didn't shake off before he died more than 50 years later. In truth, it was a strange act of scientific diplomacy that left Corner free while his compatriots languished in the camps. It was driven by Corner's ability to see the bigger picture and his belief that science was all that mattered.

Before Britain surrendered, Corner had implored the British Governor of Singapore to write to the invading Japanese commander and urge him to ensure the safety of Singapore's scientific and cultural wealth. His pleas succeeded. Corner hand-delivered the note. It was Japan's Emperor Hirohito – a marine biologist and amateur botanist – who gave the order that Corner and his two colleagues should remain at work, under the watch of two Japanese botanists. Together they protected the garden's valuable resources in the name of science, not nations. Corner went further. He gave secret support to those interned in the camps and smuggled to safety large collections of books from private libraries, and artefacts from the Raffles Museum.

Even back in 1945, Corner's efforts were recognised, but not publicly. A report sent that year to the British Colonial Office stated: 'The action of these officers in remaining at their scientific posts despite the adverse view of this which inevitably arose among those who were interned, has had results of the utmost value and scientific importance, and is to be highly commended.' No commendation was forthcoming. The facts only came to light in 2001, five years after Corner's death. Only then was he exonerated.

After the war, Corner worked for a while in Brazil before returning in 1948 to England, where he became a lecturer in botany and later professor of tropical botany, at Cambridge University. It was from there that Corner's work on *Ficus* could take off. He led expeditions to explore forests in Borneo and the Solomon Islands, where he found a fig species whose leaves were as long as he was tall. On Bougainville Island, east of New Guinea, Corner collected specimens from 40 species of *Ficus* in one small valley, where one tree in five was a fig. He more than doubled that tally on Borneo's tallest mountain, Mount Kinabalu, where he found 82 *Ficus* species.

In all, Corner had seen more than 300 fig species in nature. He combined his forest knowledge with studies of more than twenty thousand *Ficus* specimens in botanical repositories called herbaria, where he stared through microscopes for hours at leaves and twigs and figs, looking for tiny differences between species. He was thwarted in the 1950s, however, when he visited the herbarium at Utrecht University. Corner had wanted to look at the original *Ficus sumatrana* specimen the Dutch botanist Friedrich Miquel used when he named the species in 1867. When Corner opened the envelope that should have contained the preserved figs, he found only the stale remains of a cheese sandwich.

But Corner's bread and butter was botany, and it would take more than some missing figs to slow him down. By 1965, his knowledge of figs had coalesced into a landmark paper. It listed and explained how to distinguish 480 *Ficus* species that live in the arc stretching from India to Australia. To achieve this, Corner cut down a virtual forest of more than 2,000 false *Ficus* species – names botanists had created for fig species that other botanists had already named. Corner's document would guide generations of later biologists, myself included. It is just part of his immense legacy. He was also a pioneer of conservation, who lobbied successfully to protect large areas of tropical rainforest. And his exquisite writing for non-scientific audiences engaged thousands of readers with nature. But Corner's brilliance had an evil twin. A fault line cut the rock of his character in two.

Even Corner's friends would say he was spiky, imperious, unforgiving. He could flip. Many suffered as a result. And when it came to work/life balance, Corner placed all of his weights on the work side of the scales. His family suffered and his marriage disintegrated. His children bore the burden of it all, and especially his son John, whom Corner refused to see or speak to for decades. Yet it is thanks to this estranged son and his extraordinary book – *My Father in His Suitcase* – that much of the truth about this complex man is known.

Corner's personality spilled over into the story of *Ficus*, when he fell out with botanist C. J. J. G. van Steenis, the editor of what Corner intended to be his masterpiece, the most comprehensive publication on fig species ever. The rift between the two men was so great that 35 years and Corner's last breath would pass before the text appeared, in

2005. This great tome, completed after Corner's death by Dutch botanist C. C. Berg, runs to 750 pages. It is a direct descendent of those sparse notes Theophrastus, the father of botany, had written about fig trees nearly 2,400 years before.

It is fitting then that Theophrastus is recognised among the fig species whose names Corner retained. In 1868, a German botanist called Berthold Carl Seemann had named a fig species from the Solomon Islands after him: *Ficus theophrastoides*, a tree that grows just five metres tall and has such a slender trunk that you could encircle it with your hands. It is a far cry from the banyan, the species Theophrastus never saw but knew to be a fig.

Theophrastus had noted the thing that binds *Ficus* species together, their defining trait: the fig itself. But he never realised that the fig is in truth not a fruit. That fact, which helps explain the power of the fig trees, would elude science for hundreds of years. What Theophrastus didn't realise is that these magnificent trees have a biological secret.

It is a secret that solves the riddle of the *udumbara*, a species of Asian fig tree (*Ficus racemosa*) that Buddhist scriptures say flowers only once every 3,000 years. In fact, an adult *udumbara* flowers at least once a year, but like all fig species it keeps its flowers hidden from human eyes. These flowers are for fig-wasps, tiny insects whose story is surely one of the most astounding in all of biology. It is one of the most important as well, for without these tiny creatures and their interactions with fig trees, the world would be very different.

SIX

Sex and Violence in the Hanging Gardens

On a moonlit night in southern Africa a reproductive race is about to begin. The stakes are high but so are the risks. Most of the competitors will be dead or doomed by dawn. The starting line is a solitary fig tree whose gnarled form towers over a small stream. Figs hang in clumps from its branches like a plague of green boils. Tonight they erupt with life.

An insect emerges from a hole in one of the figs. She's so small you could swallow her and not notice. She's a fig-wasp with an urgent mission and her time is running out. All around her, thousands of her kind are crawling out of figs. Each one is a female with the same quest and each faces immediate danger. Ants patrol the figs and they show no mercy. Their huge jaws will crush and dismember any fig-wasp that delays her maiden flight.

Our fig-wasp avoids this fate with a flap of her wings that

lifts her clear of the carnage. She carries inside her body a precious cargo, hundreds of fertilised eggs that she can only lay in a fig on another tree. But she is fussy. The fig she seeks must be from the right species of *Ficus* and it must be at the right stage of development. If it is ripe, she will be too late. If it is too small, the fig will not let her enter. The nearest fig that fits the bill could be tens of kilometres away.

The wasp does not have time on her side. With every minute that passes her energy stores deplete and can never rise again, for in her short adult life she never once eats. She has less than 48 hours to complete her mission and although she has left the ants behind, the air brings fresh danger. Out of the dark night swoop bats, their mouths agape, their stomachs empty and expectant. The bats fly looping sorties through the clouds of dispersing wasps, condemning those they swallow to an early death. Our wasp escapes only when a gust of wind blows her high into the sky. She has eluded the predators. Now she must face the elements.

The fig-wasp is less than two millimetres long and her wings are thinner than a human hair. But relative to her body they act as huge sails. With them she rides the wild winds in search of a fig. She relinquishes control. Her fate is random now. Some of her cohort will be lucky and find their target within the hour. Many more will drop out of the sky, dead from exhaustion. The wind buffets her this way and that. All the while she awaits a signal from below, for the fig-wasp has allies in the trees she seeks. The trees need the wasps just as much as the wasps need their figs. Fortunately for both, fig trees are great chemists, and this makes them great communicators. At just the right time, they pump into the air a cocktail of chemicals that is unique to each species of *Ficus*. These compounds act in concert, like a choir of distinct voices that calls out 'welcome' in a language only certain kinds of wasps can understand.

There it is – a whiff of the perfume she seeks. As soon as she recognises it, she seizes control of her destiny and drops down out of the sky. She has found a patch of forest. Somewhere within it is a fig tree whose figs emit the signal scent. Away from the wind, she must now rely on her weak wings to carry her to the odour's source. The tree's figs are just right – smaller and harder than the one she departed. The fig-wasp has found her target but she has no time to rest. The final centimetre of her immense journey is among the hardest.

At the tip of the fig is a tiny hole. The fig-wasp squeczes her head into the hole and, with a resolute push from her slender legs, she forces herself forward into darkness. The narrow tunnel in which she finds herself is tight. As she struggles forward its walls snap her antennae and wrench the wings from her back. It does not matter. This is a one-way journey and she will not need them again. She has come to give life but also to die, deep in the hollow heart of this special kind of fig.

The fig-wasp has other anatomical adaptations to help her reach her goal. Her head is shaped like a flattened wedge, ideal for forcing her way into the fig. Her jaws bear tooth-like ridges that dig into the tunnel walls. By opening and closing her mouth, the wasp ratchets herself forward. At last she reaches the fig's hollow centre. She can complete her mission. And though the darkness blinds her she knows exactly what she must do, in these, the last hours of her life. If her genes are to have a chance to survive she must start to lay eggs, for the cavity at the centre of the fig will be both her tomb and her offspring's nursery.

Our wasp belongs to a species scientists call *Ceratosolen arabicus* and her partner is the sycamore fig (*Ficus sycomorus*). This tree reaches up to 25 metres in height, with a dense crown of leaves that can spread twice as wide to form a canopy the sun's rays struggle to breach. The sycamore fig grows wild across a great swathe of Africa. Wherever it grows it has become embedded in local cultures, often as a symbol of peace and unity – a place elders go to settle disputes. It is an ironic choice of icon, for figs are violent places. Within these 'fruit' you can find parasites that feed on living flesh and assassins that can only survive by killing babies. Figs are arenas of deadly gladiatorial battles and hasty incestuous sex. As biologist Bill Hamilton noted, in just one day as many as a million insects can die violent deaths inside the figs of a single tree.

Our fig-wasp's quest to reproduce does not end when she finds a fig where she can lay eggs. She has enemies ahead. She is deep inside the fig now. Flowers line its entire inner surface. They are packed together, their heads forming a carpet on which the wasp walks. As she does, she deposits pollen she has brought with her from the fig of her birth.

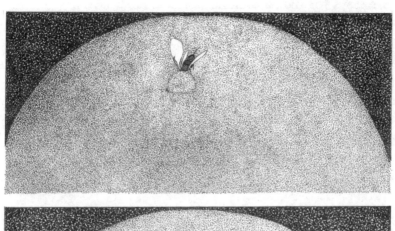

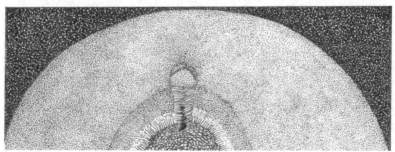

JOURNEY'S END:
A fig-wasp enters a fig through a tiny hole, then forces her way to the fig's
hollow, flower-lined centre

Each flower she pollinates can develop into a miniscule fruit with a single seed, an embryonic *Ficus sycomorus* that has the potential to grow into a giant tree. But not every flower shares this fate. Some of the fig's flowers will produce a new wasp instead of a seed. This is the price the fig tree pays for such a reliable pollination service.

To take her payment, the mother wasp gets down to the urgent business of laying eggs. One by one she penetrates the fig's female flowers with a flexible, needle-like structure at the end of her body. Through this hollow tube, she injects an egg into the part of the flower that would normally produce a seed. Each time she lays an egg she also injects a drop of fluid. This induces the flower to develop a growth called a gall that will enclose and sustain her offspring. The larvae that hatch from her eggs will feed on the plant tissue in their galls until they are ready to metamorphose into adults.

The mother wasp must work fast. Her energy reserves are running low and she has competition. Others of her kind have arrived and they too covet the limited supply of flowers. If she is fast our wasp can lay more than 200 eggs. Finally, exhausted, she dies. Her final act will help ensure the fig species survives. And, because of this, the tiny wasp will affect the fates of thousands of other species, all bound up in an intricate web of interactions that connects plants and fungi, microscopic mites and parasitic worms, birds and bats, monkeys and apes – and even you and me.

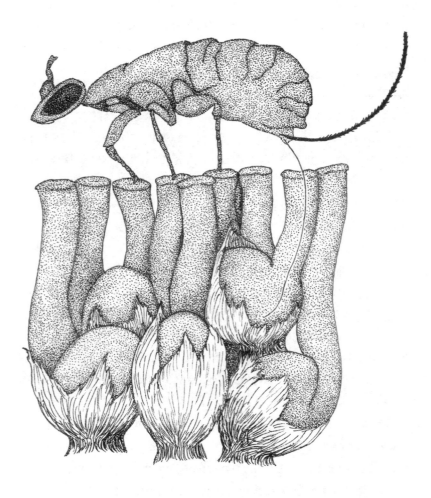

LIFE IN A DEAD-END:
Now wingless, a female fig-wasp pollinates fig flowers and lays eggs in some
of them through a tube at the end of her body

Fig-wasps have occupied enquiring minds since ancient times. Nearly 2,500 years ago the Greek historian Herodotus wrote about 'gallflies' he found inside figs. A little later, in 350 BCE, his compatriot Aristotle described fig-wasps that emerged from figs and penetrated unripe ones. Another fifty years on, and Theophrastus was making notes on the insects he observed on figs. But it would then take eighteen centuries and the invention of magnifying glasses before anyone described fig flowers, which German botanist Valerius Cordus was the first to do, in 1544. That news did not spread. More than 200 years later, botanists still believed figs to be flowerless plants that reproduced with spores – as mosses and mushrooms do.

Only in the twentieth century, did the quest to understand figs and their wasps really take off. A small but industrious band of biologists has spent decades examining the relationship in ever closer detail. The mathematical beauty they found in the way figs and their wasps interact matters to us, because while everything in nature is ultimately connected, the fig trees and their wasps appear to be disproportionately important cogs in the clockwork of life.

These biologists have shown that each of the 750 plus *Ficus* species depends on specific wasps to pollinate its flowers. For many *Ficus* species just a single species of wasp performs this service. Less commonly, two or more wasp species do the job. This relationship liberates *Ficus* species from a constraint that limits other plants. It enables them to persist even at low densities yet maintain high genetic diversity, because their partner wasps can carry pollen for as far as 160 kilometres – ten times further than the insect pollinators of any other plants. The relationship also has a critical side effect, ensuring a year-round supply of figs for hungry animals.

But the partnership between figs and their pollinators is under constant pressure from other tiny wasp species that are parasites of the relationship. Some sneak into a fig and lay eggs in its flowers but bring no pollen in return for the nursery the fig provides. These interlopers deprive the pollinators of places to lay their own eggs, whilst preventing fig seeds from developing in each flower they exploit.

Other wasps disturb the relationship between figs and their pollinators in more wicked ways. These parasitic wasps do not even need to enter a fig to cause trouble. They inject their eggs from outside – through delivery tubes that are several times longer than their bodies – and their offspring feed on the living flesh of the pollinator wasp larvae. Each *Ficus* species hosts up to 35 species of non-pollinating wasps. Overall hundreds of wasps of various species of pollinators and seed-parasites and pollinator-parasites can develop in each fig. The outcomes of their interactions have impacts that ripple across entire ecosystems.

After a few weeks, the surviving offspring of the pollinator wasps are ready to emerge from their galls as adults. The males come out first. Their time on earth is short conducted almost entirely in darkness inside the fig of their birth. They have adapted to this lifestyle so much over millions of years that they are barely recognisable as members of the same species as the delicate females. A male fig-wasp's eyes are tiny or even absent. The males also lack wings. Another big difference between the sexes is in their mouthparts. The female never feeds as an adult, relying instead on energy she has stored after eating plant tissue as a larva. This will serve her well on the long journey ahead. It also means she has been able to evolve a slim head that makes it easier for her to enter a new fig.

The males, in contrast, need strong jaws. When they reach adulthood, they chew their way out of their galls then use their stout legs to dig through the dense thicket of fig flowers to find a gall with a female wasp inside. The males gnaw holes in those galls then curl their telescopic abdomens under their bodies to penetrate the galls and deliver sperm to the females trapped within. The males then move on, mating as quickly as they can and with as many females as possible, even if this includes their sisters.

The female wasps are soon ready to fly off in search of a fig in which to lay their fertilised eggs, but before they leave they take receipt of the pollen they must deliver to their destination fig. In some fig-wasp species this is a passive process. The fig's male flowers shed clouds of pollen grains that rain down and adhere to bodies of the wasps. But our *Ceratosolen arabicus* belongs in the other class of pollinators, the active ones. What these wasps have evolved to do is extraordinary.

After mating inside the *Ficus sycomorus* fig, the male *Ceratosolen arabicus* wasps use their massive jaws to chop down the pollen-bearing parts of the fig's male flowers. The female wasps then harvest the pollen with their forelegs, which are bedecked with stiff bristles like those on a broom. They sweep the pollen into cavities on the undersides of their chests called pollen pockets, which yawn open as they flex their bodies.

The female wasps are now laden with both eggs and pollen, but they are trapped inside their figs. To release them, the males, in their last act, do something otherwise unheard of in the insect world. They cooperate even when there is no direct benefit to themselves. These little males team up to chew a hole in the wall of the fig through which the females can escape. The males crawl out and die when they tumble from the fig or find themselves in the jaws of a predatory ant. In some fig-wasp species, the males appear to protect the departing females by sacrificing themselves to the ants. Off the females fly in search of the special scent that only their kind of fig emits.

The fig tree's pollen disperses into the night sky, bound to the bodies of its courier wasps. Thanks to these winged mediators the *Ficus sycomorus* tree may mix its genes with hundreds of other individuals. But this is only one side of the tree's reproductive effort. While some *Ficus* species have separate male and female trees, in others like *Ficus sycomorus* each tree performs both sexual roles. Long before our tree's male pollen departed, its female ovules combined with the pollen its wasp partners brought from other trees. And so seeds formed alongside the new generation of fig-wasps, and soon they too are ready to disperse.

The tree's figs change in function, from incubators of wasps into attractants aimed at far bigger animals. They swell until they are three centimetres across and change in colour from buff-green to yellow or red. The plant withdraws its sticky latex from the figs and pumps in sugars instead. Birds, bats, monkeys and other animals come to feed on them. They will disperse the tiny *Ficus sycomorus* seeds that create a new generation of giant trees. Those trees will harbour future generations of fig-wasps and will feed future generations of seed-dispersing birds and mammals.

Without figs and their fig-wasps many of these animals would starve. That's because most plant species produce their fruit at a specific time of year – often when many other species fruit too. This means fruit-eating animals experience periods of feast and famine as the amount of fruit in an area peaks in just a short period. But if all members of a *Ficus* species produced their figs at the same time, the short-lived female wasps that emerge from the figs would have no new immature figs in which to lay their eggs. It would mean no more pollination. This would doom both wasp and tree species to extinction.

Instead many *Ficus* species produce figs all year round, never all at the same time, and individual trees can produce two or more crops each year. Each day, the figs and their wasps introduce new beats to a rolling rhythm of fig production. It is one of nature's coolest tunes. It offers a lifeline to wild animals and so places *Ficus* species at the centre of vast ecological webs. The birds and mammals that eat figs will also disperse the seeds of many other plants whose fruit they eat. It is because of this that ecologists have described figs as keystone resources in tropical forests.

A keystone on a bridge or an archway locks all of the other stones into position. Remove it and the structure will come tumbling down. Remove keystone figs from a tropical rainforest, the analogy suggests, and this could trigger a cascade of local extinctions as birds, monkeys and fruit bats starve and are no longer around to disperse the seeds of thousands of other plant species.

In 1986, John Terborgh, then a biology professor at Princeton University, suggested that if figs disappeared from Peru's Amazon basin, the entire ecosystem could collapse. Later studies have identified a keystone role for figs in other forests, from Panama to South Africa to Malaysia and Indonesia. Biologist Daniel Kissling showed that across all of sub-Saharan Africa, the number of *Ficus* species in an area was the main factor affecting how many fruit-eating bird species lived there. Kissling concludes that figs are keystone resources on a continent-wide scale.

Right now, as you read these words, fresh dramas are playing out at fig trees across the tropics and subtropics, just as they have done every day for tens of millions of years. At some trees, fig-wasps are emerging from their figs and setting out on their bizarre and fatal journeys. At other trees, fig-wasps are arriving, bearing pollen and eggs. Without these ancient odysseys, the world would be utterly different.

For from the wings of tiny fig-wasps hang the fates of hundreds of bird and mammal species, and perhaps even entire rainforests.

SEVEN

Struggles for Existence

A mother-to-be is alone, hungry and helpless, jailed in a dark cell of her own design. She is a rhinoceros hornbill, the most striking of all Borneo's wildlife. This swan-sized bird wears a cloak of coal-black plumage from which bursts a figment of fire. It is the bird's casque, a curious horny ornament that curves skyward from the base of her huge bill and burns a flaming blend of red, orange and yellow. When the sun is behind it, her hollow casque can seem to glow like a hot ember. It sits atop a long bill that arcs down from its deep base to its sharp tip, fading from yellow to ivory-white as it goes. She is rainforest royalty. But for now her majesty must reign inside and unseen.

Days earlier, she forced herself into a dark cavity in the trunk of a tall rainforest tree. Her mate flew up to the hole and clung to its edge with his toes, fanning his white tail feathers against the tree for support. The pair then used their beaks like trowels to seal up the hole. For cement, they mixed a grim slurry of mud, regurgitated figs and fresh faeces. They ceased only when nothing but a small vertical slit remained unfilled. In the darkness, the female heard a tell-tale *whoosh . . . whoosh . . . whoosh*. It was air rushing through her mate's wing feathers with each beat of his departure.

When Tim Laman first heard that sound, in 1987, his life tilted in a new direction. The previous year he had been far away in the United States, a postgraduate student of neuroscience and animal behaviour at Harvard University. Laman was itching to escape lab work when he saw a curious poster in the biology building. The black-and-white illustration showed an orangutan in an urgent tussle with a spear-toting man. Laman didn't yet know the image came from a book by the co-founder of evolution Alfred Russel Wallace, his future hero. What caught Laman's eye next was the text: 'Wanted: Field Assistants for Rain Forest Research in Borneo. Contact Prof. Mark Leighton.'

Mark Leighton had spent several years studying the rainforests of Indonesian Borneo. He had shown that fig trees were important food sources for hornbills, orangutans and many other wildlife species. Once, he watched as a rhinoceros hornbill plucked, tossed, caught and swallowed 27 *Ficus binnendykii* figs in a minute. Now he wanted help at a research camp he had established deep inside Gunung Palung National Park, a vast area of rainforest. Leighton needed someone to manage the camp, carry out censuses of fruit-eating animals and track patterns of fig and other fruit availability. Laman got the one-year job and put his doctorate on hold.

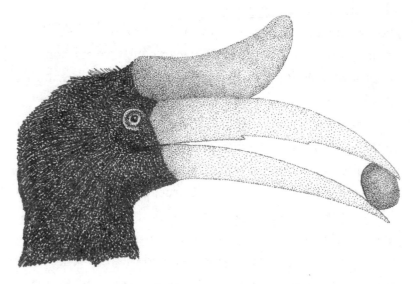

ANCIENT ALLIES:
Rhinoceros hornbills depend on figs to survive; in return for their food they
sow *Ficus* seeds as they fly

The forest was pristine. The nearest people were several hours away and the wildlife was abundant. It was on Laman's first day there that he heard that whooshing noise. He looked up and caught a glimpse of a massive black bird flying far above him at the roof of the forest. A flash of red told him it was a rhinoceros hornbill. Laman was an avid photographer but had no chance of taking a picture from the ground. From that day on it became his 'overwhelming obsession' to find a way to get up into the canopy with his camera.

Laman's year off became permanent. He fell in love with the forest, switched departments at Harvard and became a fig biologist. He attempted to answer a question that had vexed E. J. H. Corner. In 1940, Corner had noted that strangler figs grew on only a small proportion of rainforest trees, yet in parks and fields they grew 'on every tree that is a roosting place for birds'. Laman wanted to know what challenges these stupendous plants must overcome to reach adulthood.

The National Park had 28 species of strangler figs. Laman focused on five of them and showed that each prefers host trees of a certain size and type, and has an ideal height at which to colonise its host. Some preferred to start out in life on big trees, high in the canopy. Others grew on smaller tree species and did best when they established in the gloomier sub-canopy. These differences limit competition among the *Ficus* species and mean more of them can coexist. But they also impose big limits on the strangler figs, by draining the pool of potential host trees for each species.

And as Laman would show, it is not even enough for a fig seed to land at the right height on the right kind of tree. Of the 134 strangler figs he studied, most had colonised their host in one of three places: the crotch between a branch and the host tree's trunk; a bulge on the trunk; or in a knothole that formed when a branch fell off. To learn what else limits these species, Laman had to emulate the birds and mammals that disperse their seeds. He focused on *Ficus stupenda*.

Unlike the strangler figs that can outlive their support trees and become free-standing, *Ficus stupenda* remains forever dependent on its host. Rather than encasing its host in cascading roots, this fig species tends to send a single root down the host's trunk and into the soil of the forest floor. As this pillar root thickens it produces smaller side roots, which wrap around the support tree creating a bond between plant species that only death can break. As Laman found out, *Ficus stupenda* prefers to grow on the 60-metre-tall trees in a family called the dipterocarps. So these giants were the trees he had to climb.

Laman used a compound bow, fibreglass arrows and a reel of monofilament fishing line to send a climbing rope up and over big branches on such trees. Once his rope was secure and he had attached himself to it with a harness, he could pull himself up with a set of mechanical ascenders. Before he started he donned thick gloves and went through his mental checklist. The tree was safe and his equipment well-maintained. The main danger now was human error.

Laman inch-wormed his way up to about 30 metres, the height he had found *Ficus stupenda* most often established itself and thrived. He took his time. He didn't want to aggravate the snakes, wasps or aggressive ants he was likely to meet. Once he fell foul of a bellicose bee that stung him right between the eyes as he hung from his rope. It was hot, sweaty and tiring work, but it was always worth it. From his vantage point he could survey the roof of the rainforest. At last, the rhinoceros hornbill was in reach of his camera's lens. Laman began developing the skills that would make him one of the world's foremost wildlife photographers.

In all Laman hauled himself up 45 big trees and planted nearly 7,000 *Ficus stupenda* seeds on their branches, crotches, knot-holes and trunks. He climbed up again 18 days later to check on his seeds, then again after seven months and once more after a year had passed. Laman had blessed those seeds with the right sites at the right height on the right trees, but their struggles had only just started. Eleven of the trees were already home to a species of ant for which Laman's seeds were the perfect takeaway meal. They carried many of the seeds off to their nests. Of the remainder that germinated where Laman had laid them, many then dried out and shrivelled and died. Others succumbed to insects that came to munch at their leaves. Only 1.3 per cent of the seeds survived a full year, and fewer than one in a thousand showed vigorous growth.

The seeds that fared best were those Laman planted on wood that was rotting. Soil and moss were the next best substrates. Leaf litter and bark were the worst. This all suggested that moisture, and not light, was the most vital factor. Laman confirmed this with a neat parallel experiment. He hoisted into the canopy ten lengths of plastic roof gutter and lashed them to his study trees. Each gutter contained moist soil and a pair of three-week-old *Ficus stupenda* plants, which Laman had grown from seed. His gutter figs, with their water-retaining soil, fared far better than the seedlings he grew on the host tree.

Laman confirmed that Alfred Russel Wallace had been right about the benefits strangler figs gain from germinating high in the forest canopy. Light helps them to grow faster. But what matters most is the presence of a substrate that can retain water, such as soil, rotting wood or moss. *Ficus stupenda* faces a challenge to ensure its seeds reach the rare knotholes and other crevices where moisture can accumulate. To deliver its seeds to these specific sites, a parent tree must employ couriers. It pays them with its figs.

Until now, its figs have been incubating a new generation of pollinator wasps. When those wasps have departed and her seeds are ready to disperse, the figs undergo a remarkable transformation. An influx of sugars sweetens their flesh. The sticky protective latex that had rendered them unpalatable retreats. A chemical blush turns the green figs first orange then red. She's letting the animal world know a feast is imminent.

While each fig species can rely on its pollinator wasps to

be faithful partners, it engages with less trustworthy animals to disperse its seeds. And while *Ficus* species pay their pollinator wasps only after they have done their work, they must pay potential seed dispersers up front, so risk being exploited. A *Ficus stupenda* has no way of telling if it will attract paying diners, thieves that eat and run, or worse, killers with appetites for destruction. It's a lottery, but each *Ficus stupenda* invests in hundreds of thousands of tickets. If its pollinators have done their work well, each of its tens of thousands of figs will hold 160 or more seeds.

The first challenge these seeds face is to be eaten and survive the experience. It's a crazy way to start out in life. The fig flesh is there to entice animals to swallow the seeds. It helps that the seeds are tiny, just a couple of millimetres long. Even the smallest of fruit eaters can swallow them and not choke. But many of the animals that arrive are piratical. Green pigeons will gobble plenty of figs but the grit in their gizzards grinds each seed into dust. Parrots destroy fig seeds too, their horny tongues crushing them against their hard bills. More seeds fall prey to fig-eating squirrels. In each case, these animals are predators of *Ficus stupenda* seeds.

The seeds will survive a journey through the gut of most other fig-eating animals, but the smaller of these species – birds such as flowerpeckers and bulbuls – cannot open their gapes wide enough to swallow a *Ficus stupenda* fig. Instead they peck at the flesh, leaving most of the seeds untouched. These species are good dispersers of other fig species but aren't much help to *Ficus stupenda*. Nor are the animals that swallow fig seeds but live at lower levels of the forest and return there from the canopy soon after their feast. Any seeds dropped there will be too low. These creatures exploit the generosity of *Ficus stupenda* and provide little or nothing in return.

Another group of birds offers more. The barbets and the leafbirds, the fairy bluebird and the green broadbill are all fig specialists. They spend their days in and around strangler figs and swallow plenty of seeds, but they don't travel very far. What *Ficus stupenda* really needs are animals that eat a lot of its figs, move long distances, pass fig seeds intact and rarely travel below the forest canopy. Among the mammals, these seed dispersers include gibbons, orangutans and bats called flying foxes. Among birds, it is the hornbills, and especially the most impressive bird in Borneo, the rhinoceros hornbill. Here it comes . . .

Whoosh . . . whoosh . . . whoosh. The powerful wingbeats announce the arrival of the sky king. The male rhinoceros hornbill in flight is a vision of sharp angles and exquisite curves. His long wing feathers splay like gloved fingers. His neck stretches out to support that huge beak and its fiery casque. Smaller birds scatter as he flaps up to the giant *Ficus stupenda*, spreading his white tail into a fan as he lands on a stout branch. He has flown three kilometres to find this tree and he is hungry.

The oblong figs are on slender branches that would bend and snap if the three kilogram hornbill tried to walk on them. His beak, though, is long enough to reach them from a sturdier perch. Its serrated edges help him grip and mani-

ALL HAIL THE SKY KING:
A rhinoceros hornbill arrives at a fig tree to feast

pulate each fig. With a quick backward jerk of his head he flings the fig from bill-tip to gullet. He shuffles and side-hops about until he has eaten all he can reach then he flies on to another branch and starts again: pluck, toss, catch and swallow. But the figs are not only for him.

For 40 days now, after sating his appetite, he has returned from this and other fig trees to feed his partner in her hollow. She has laid two eggs. Soon there will be three hungry hornbills for him to feed. The male will bring liz-ards, mice and whatever fruit he can find. But it is ripe figs more than anything that he can count on. They are available year round, thanks to the partnership between fig trees and their tiny short-lived pollinating wasps. The rhinoceros hornbills take full advantage. Studies have shown that figs can make up between 50 and 93 per cent of everything a female rhinoceros hornbill eats during her time at the nest. These birds eat figs from at least 24 *Ficus* species, fitting in other fare around this, their staple food.

Each day, the male bird delivers fresh rations of figs, poking his bill through the slit in the nest cover and cough-ing them into his mate's mouth. She is naked now, having shed all her feathers. If anything happens to him she will become a skeleton entombed in the tree. For now at least, she is dry and safe from storms and snakes. From her secure cell she may find solace in the periodic calls he makes to claim his piece of sky. It is a kind of nasal cough that can carry over hundreds of metres, a deep and reedy '*Hok! Hwok! Hok! Hok!*'

The male bird is helping more than his family. The figs

stand to gain too. Laman calculated that half of all *Ficus stupenda* seeds fall beneath their parent tree's crown. For a species as picky as this about where its seeds germinate, that is just not good enough. It may seem improbable that a *Ficus stupenda* could ever reproduce, given its needs, but these are patient plants with ancient partnerships. The rhinoceros hornbill is an important ally that helps improve the odds of seeds reaching the right sites on the right kinds of host tree.

Adult hornbills can fly 10 kilometres in a day but must rest often on tall trees. For the hundreds or even thousands of fig seeds they excrete daily, these are perfect perches. A *Ficus stupenda* seed that falls from here has a better chance than most of reaching a moist crotch or knothole further down the tree. Once in a while, such a seed will survive long enough to germinate. Within days it will have sent forth roots to begin anchoring itself to its host. One root will begin its long journey down the tree's trunk to the forest floor. The fig's first pair of leaves will bask in the sun and power further growth. In time strong branches will spread wide, holding up a vast crown of leaves and fresh crops of ripe figs. They will provide food for future hornbills, birds that acquire a taste for figs before they even see the sky.

For after rhinoceros hornbill chicks hatch they must remain in their tree hole. The adult male will continue to feed them and their mother for three months. Having regrown her feathers, she will then escape from her hollow, reseal the hole and together the parents will devote another three months to feeding figs to their chicks. It is rare for both chicks to survive, but the one that does will be strong. If all goes well, this bird will live for nearly three decades. In the years ahead, it will feed from fig trees that grew from seeds its grandparents dispersed. In turn, it will spread seeds that grow into giant stranglers that feed its own grandchildren. At least, that is what has happened for millions of years. But the future of the partnership between *Ficus stupenda* and the rhinoceros hornbill is far from certain.

In the past century, loggers have carved up and cut down large areas of Borneo's forests. There are fewer tall trees for hornbills to nest in or for *Ficus stupenda* to colonise. The distances between fig trees and the hornbill seed dispersers they nourish has grown. The strain on their relationship is just one symptom of the disruptive effects of deforestation. When Tim Laman saw the threats habitat loss and hunting posed to Indonesia's forests and their wildlife, he felt compelled to do something about them. Writing scientific papers about a landscape that was so threatened frustrated him. He instead turned to another string in his bow. He reasoned that photos and stories could convince people to protect rainforests better than dry academic papers in science journals few people read. And he had the skills and the opportunities to take pictures nobody else could.

By 1992, Laman had climbed giant dipterocarp trees more than 500 times, but he wasn't only studying seedling strangler figs up there. He had found the trees rhinoceros hornbills would regularly visit to feed or display. Laman devised a way to build a hide from camouflage cloth, netting and leafy branches as he dangled from his rope high up a dipterocarp tree. Day after day he would spend hours behind his hide while he waited for rhinoceros hornbills to feed on a nearby *Ficus*. His patience has yielded stunning portraits of these majestic birds.

By 1999 photography would be Laman's full-time job. He would go on to win numerous awards, but his big break had come in April 1997 when *National Geographic* published some of those hornbill photos in his first feature article: on Borneo's strangling figs. When I saw the magazine on sale in the Students Union at the University of Leeds it felt like an omen. I had recently bought airline tickets – within a month I would be in Borneo, studying strangler figs, hoping to see a rhinoceros hornbill.

Three years had passed since I encountered the monk and his monkeys in Sri Lanka. I had completed my degree, worked for nine months in a bird garden, spent all my savings on a trip to the Amazon, then returned to university to study for a master's degree in biodiversity and conservation. My project supervisor was Steve Compton, the lecturer who had taught me the story of the fig-wasps. Steve arranged for me to visit fig biologist Rhett Harrison who was based in Lambir Hills National Park in Sarawak, one of two Malaysian states on Borneo. My mission was to study scores of wild *Ficus* species and the animals that eat their figs and disperse their seeds.

At just 70 square kilometres in area, Lambir Hills

National Park secures only a small remnant of forest but it is botanically rich. In just one 52-hectare patch, researchers have identified 1,178 tree species. That's more than in any other equal area of forest on the planet and more species than in all of the temperate forests of the northern hemisphere combined. In Britain there are just 36 native tree species. By contrast, in parts of Lambir Hills, if you enclosed an area of just 100 metres by 100 metres and identified every tree within it, you would find more than 600 tree species. Rhett had found more than 70 *Ficus* species in the forest. This diversity daunted me.

Few people alive know more than Rhett about Borneo's fig trees, and this book would not exist without all that he taught me about them. He was a great host. He's one of the most humane, humorous, and humble men I have met. Though he was still in his 20s, his hair was grey and this struck a contrast with his youthful appearance and propensity for cracking up in gales of laughter.

Rhett was born in Scotland but soon fell in love with the tropics. As an undergraduate zoology student he led an expedition to a rainforest in Peru, and ended up working just over the border in Bolivia for a spell to study mercury pollution. So he learned Spanish. His wanderlust led him next to Japan where he studied for a masters degree. So he learned Japanese. This degree and his later doctorate took him to Malaysian Borneo to study figs and their wasps. So he learned Malay and a lot of Iban too. While living in the National Park he had thrown himself into local life. As well as making his own rice wine, he attempted Iban weaving and performed the *ngajat*, a dramatic solo dance to the tune of gongs and drumbeats.

On my first night, over a dinner of barbecued fish, Rhett filled me in on the set-up there and his work in the forest. As the sun set and the forest's frogs began to belch and bark, we drank his rice wine and gorged on durian, the stinking fruit that is a favourite food for orangutans. But as we chatted about his research I started to feel out of my depth. It was complex talk that I did not fully understand. I started to wonder what I was doing in Borneo and whether I would be able to get a project out of my stay there. My doubts only grew the next morning when – after Rhett drove off to a wedding in a longhouse several hours away – his assistant Siba anak Aji arrived on his noisy motorbike and with him I entered the forest for the first time.

EIGHT

Goodbye to the Gardeners, Hello to the Heat

'If you drop, you are dead,' said Siba anak Aji. I had met him just an hour earlier and already I liked his sense of humour. But he was right about the drop. A fall would provide plenty of opportunities to snap my neck. We were 30 metres high, dangling on a walkway that blazed an aerial trail through the rainforest canopy in Lambir Hills National Park in northern Borneo. The walkway was little more than a series of planks suspended in mid-air by a mesh of plastic coated cables anchored around big trees. With every step I took, the structure jolted, slid and creaked.

I tasted fear that first day. A safety harness tethered me to the walkway but I did not trust it yet. Nor the insects. Little black bees hauled their bodies over my bare arms, thirsty for my sweat. Giant ants scuttled across my hands and boots. My skin crawled. What vanquished my nerves was the view. It was a vision of a distant past. Thick forests had dominated this landscape for a hundred million years. From the walkway we could see the crowns of thousands of trees of hundreds of species. The tallest had burst through the canopy and reached 80 metres into the sky.

Colourful sunbirds and spiderhunters, barbets and flower-peckers accompanied us as we traversed the 300-metre walkway. Squirrels crashed from tree to tree, their fur a blur of russet and cream. They sought what I sought – a pulse of life from the forest's beating heart. Siba found it first, a strangler fig whose branches bore thousands of orange figs. Within days they would be red and ripe. I would be shackled to the walkway, alone before dawn, waiting to discover what ate them.

In recent years biologists had been saying big fig trees were the most important fruiting plants in the rainforest and should be conserved wherever possible. Siba had another reason these plants were special and must not be cut down. 'Spirits live there,' he told me. These two ways of thinking are linked. Taboos on felling figs have deep ecological roots – people who protect *Ficus* species benefit from the vast webs of nature these trees sustain. But as biologist Daniel Janzen wrote in 1979: 'A **fig** is not a *fig* is not a FIG', and Borneo's 160 *Ficus* species are more diverse than those anywhere else on Earth. I wanted to know what their variety meant, for both the *Ficus* species and for the animals that ate them.

Were all fig species important, or were some critical and

others expendable? Such questions matter as we decide which aspects of wild nature to conserve and to which we wave goodbye. My short project grew into a doctorate, through which I would spend 18 months in the National Park over the next three years. To find out what ate the figs of each of 34 *Ficus* species – a diverse mix of trees, climbers and giant stranglers – I watched them for hours on end, starting before dawn broke, then returning late afternoon and again at night.

Each time I stepped into that forest I entered another world. It was hot and humid and full of mosquitoes. The forest's palette of greens and browns flooded my vision. Countless trees crowded in on me. Vines crept and corkscrewed their way skywards at every possible angle. Some were as thick as a thigh. Strange sounds tricked my ears. Strange shapes moved then vanished. There were musty scents whose sources I never found.

Most of the trees were just a few centimetres thick but were so numerous I could only take a couple of steps off a trail before hitting one. Others were giants, as broad as a small car. And none was as spookily beautiful as the first free-standing strangler fig I saw there. Its host tree had long since died and rotted away and the strangler's roots now formed a scaffold with a hollow core. I stepped inside and looked up. Shafts of light shone down at me from far above. This *Ficus kerkhovenii* became my favourite landmark in the forest.

It soon grew clear that figs were ecological linchpins.

Mike Shanahan

STRANGLER'S HEART:
When a strangler fig's host dies a hollow core remains

In time I would record 49 of the park's bird species and 20 of its mammals eating figs. For each *Ficus* species the size, colour and height of the figs determined which animals came to feed. While all figs were equal, some were more equal than others. I watched as rats gnawed on the tough brown figs that grew like huge warts at the base of *Ficus cereicarpa* trees. I stared through a night-vision scope at small *Ficus schwarzii* trees that thrust green chestnut-sized figs out of their trunks on short leafless stalks. Nothing but bats would dine on those scented figs. *Ficus punctata* meanwhile could count only on monkeys eating its red tennis-ball-sized figs, which were too big for most other animals to tackle. Another group of *Ficus* species, made up of slim trees and climbers with orange-red figs, attracted small birds and mammals that dwelt in the forest's lower storey.

The strangler figs were the pop-up restaurants of the rainforest. Their red, orange or purple figs attracted as many as 30 species of birds and mammals. The bigger the strangler's figs, the bigger the animals it attracted. These *Ficus* species operated on a boom-and-bust basis. They ripened as many as a million figs in just a few days and triggered a feeding frenzy that fell quiet as quickly as it began. Other *Ficus* species that grew as creepers or small trees drip-fed their seed dispersers, ripening just a small proportion of their figs each day for weeks or months on end. Some *Ficus* produced two or even three crops in a year. And thanks to the pollinator wasps, there were ripe figs every day somewhere in the forest. The daily pulses of fig production ensured that many animal species always had something to eat. Until, that is, the forest's heart stopped beating.

From January to April 1998 a severe drought parched all of northern Borneo. These months are normally among the region's wettest but only seven per cent of the average amount of rain fell. The drought wreaked havoc. The rain-fed rice fields of Siba's longhouse community needed daily downpours but the soil there was now cracked and dry and thirsty. Across a large area of the National Park, trees died at three times the pre-drought rate. For some species, the mortality rate shot up to between 12 and 30 times greater than normal.

Many of Lambir's fig trees died. The drought forced the survivors to make drastic changes to their biological business. To conserve water, they stopped producing figs. This deprived their fig-wasp partners of a place to lay eggs, and drove many of the wasp species locally extinct. As if the drought were not enough for the trees to contend with, fires broke out. They tore through the parched forest. The flames reduced part of my research area to a bleak landscape of charred lifeless trees. All but one of the 43 *Ficus* plants in that area died. Lambir was not alone. Fires raged all across Borneo. Plantation developers on the Indonesian side of the island had started fires to clear the wild forest. The numbers of strangler figs, the *Ficus* species most important to wildlife, fell by 95 per cent in some areas of forest that burned there.

There is a fine line between resilience and vulnerability to such shocks. In Lambir, the drought receded as the rains returned. The *Ficus* trees that had survived began to produce figs again but there were no wasps to pollinate their flowers. With no seeds to disperse, the figs didn't develop and dropped dead to the ground. Even six months later most *Ficus* species were still without their pollinators. In time the wasps returned, aided by their prodigious ability to disperse over tens of kilometres. For many birds and mammals though, they came too late. The period without ripe figs had been deadly.

The drought was a relatively short shock, but the number and severity of these events has increased since 1970. If the trend continues, Borneo's forests and wildlife will face repeated tests. Another kind of change is already guaranteed. Our greenhouse gas emissions are set to increase the global average temperature by 1.5–4°C by the end of this century. In 2013 Nanthinee Jevanandam and colleagues at the National University of Singapore provided a chilling insight into what a warmer world could mean for fig-wasps.

In a laboratory, they exposed the pollinators of four *Ficus* species to rising temperatures and watched as the lifespan of all four fig-wasp species fell steadily. Jevanandam and colleagues studied wasp species from distinct branches of the fig-wasp family tree, so they think their results will be relevant to most other fig-wasps – many hundreds of species. They say global warming will reduce wasp lifespans and so limit the time the wasps have to find a fig of the right species and at the right stage of development in which to lay their eggs. If so, both the fig-wasps and the *Ficus* species they pollinate would suffer – with knock-on effects for the many bird and mammal species that rely on their bond.

Raise the temperature in a lab and you can affect the chemistry within animals like these wasps. To increase the temperature globally makes all the world an experiment. Yet that is what is happening as a result of humanity burning fossil fuels and clearing forests. Will climate change spell the end of a relationship that has lasted 80 million years and forced thousands of species to dance to its rhythm? Fig-wasps may surprise us yet. After all, they have survived periods much warmer than today.

Steve Compton points out that the figs themselves may offer safe havens to heat-prone wasps. His doctoral student Areej al-Khalaf showed this with an experiment in Leeds, where Compton maintains a captive population of *Ficus montana* shrubs and their pollinator wasps in a huge greenhouse. Al-Khalaf waited until adult female wasps had entered figs to lay eggs in them, then she altered the temperature. Even a 10°C increase had no effect on the wasps' ability to reproduce and pollinate fig flowers.

Figs, it seems, provide their wasps with a relatively cool refuge. As these insects spend most of their lives inside figs, the real danger global warming poses will be to the short-lived adult females during their flights between figs. Steve told me he thinks fig-wasps could adapt to a rise in temperature, either in their physiology or their behaviour – by flying at a cooler time of day, for instance.

Right now, many *Ficus* species face more pressing challenges than rising temperatures. Unbroken forest once cloaked all of Borneo but today only patches remain. Logging has heavily impacted 80 per cent of Sarawak's lowland forests. The habitat of fig species and the wild creatures they sustain has shrunk. Across the South China Sea in Peninsular Malaysia, biologist Andrew Johns found that the density of strangler figs fell by 74 per cent after supposedly low-impact 'selective' logging. Protected areas are meant to help, but in Lambir Hills, the tapestry I studied unravelled before my eyes. Science should be replicable, but if someone went there now the forest would tell them a different story, a drama with fewer actors.

By the time I arrived in 1997 the bigger fig-eating animals were already hard to find. I saw few hornbills despite spending thousands of hours in the forest, often watching crops of the figs these birds crave most. I saw only tiny gangs of green pigeons, a species that once flocked in their hundreds. I rarely saw monkeys. Gibbons, I heard only once and never saw. Where were all the barking deer and flying foxes, the sun bears and bearded pigs?

One answer became clear as I sat in the forest one day with Siba. On breaks he would offer me some rice wine from his flask and teach me the Iban and Malay names for the species pictured in my battered *Field Guide to the Mammals of Borneo*. This day the lesson was different. 'Boleh makan . . . Boleh . . . Boleh,' said Siba as he turned the pages. 'Can eat . . . Can . . . Can.' The list was long. The only animal categorically off the menu was the moonrat, a weird white-furred creature that stinks of ammonia. Everything else, said Siba, was fit for the pot.

Hunting was banned in Lambir Hills National Park and for Siba and many other members of his community the park was a source of jobs, not meat. But for other people the forest was an unlocked larder. At night on the road that ran through the park I often saw hunting parties from the nearby town of Miri. With powerful torches or spotlights mounted on trucks they caught the eyes of deer and other creatures to shoot. I heard shotguns at night in the forest and found snares or camps that poachers had used.

The experience of two Malaysian scientists is telling. In 2004, Jayasilan Mohd-Azlan and Engkamat Lading set camera traps throughout the National Park for a total of 1,127 camera-days. In that time they photographed only one bearded pig, once one of the commonest large mammals in Borneo. But the cameras caught four separate images of poachers, some toting shotguns. Three of the cameras were sabotaged – smashed or thrown away.

Two years earlier, Igor Debski and I had published a paper on the wildlife recorded in the National Park, some 237 bird species and 64 mammals. While we added plenty of species to the list ourselves, many of those that people had seen before remained elusive. And since the 1980s nobody had recorded three large and conspicuous species – a monkey called a banded langur, and two birds, the helmeted hornbill and great slaty woodpecker. This led us to conclude they might have gone locally extinct.

A decade later, in 2012, Rhett published research that painted a far worse picture. It described how surveys from 2003–2007 failed to find one in five of the park's bird and mammal species. The losses include half of the park's primate species and six out of seven hornbill species. If Lambir loses these animals it will lose much more besides, for they are supreme seed dispersers not only of figs, but also of many more species. Across Asia, hornbills disperse the seeds of more than 500 plant species. But it is the *Ficus* species they disperse that affect the most other species, most immediately. Between them, Borneo's eight hornbill species disperse the seeds of at least 45 different *Ficus* species, whose figs feed more than a hundred species of birds and mammals, which in turn disperse the seeds of thousands more plant species.

Early in 2012, two weeks before I heard about Rhett's new paper, I bumped into someone who used to work for the Sarawak National Parks and Wildlife Office. I told him 10 years had passed since I had been in Sarawak and I asked him how the state's hornbills were doing. 'Who cares?' he said with a smile and shook his head. He cared of course, and he knew I did too. He meant it was already too late to care because no one with any power did.

In under 20 years, hunting has stripped Lambir Hills National Park of its bigger animals. When I worked there in the late 1990s, I could still find 25 to 30 species of birds and mammals feeding on the figs of a single *Ficus* tree over the course of three days. A decade later Rhett reported that the same *Ficus* species could only attract half as many animal species. Many of their figs fall uneaten. Their seeds are not spread. It's a pattern repeated across the tropics and it has a name: 'empty forest syndrome'.

It doesn't need to be this way. Rhett points out that Lambir's missing species seem to be doing okay in Sungai Wain, a similarly sized but far more degraded forest in the Indonesian part of Borneo where local hunting has been regulated. But in Lambir, the decline in numbers of large fruit-eating animals – the gibbons, monkeys, flying foxes and hornbills – spells trouble for the species whose seeds they disperse. And that includes the fig trees upon which so much else depends.

The irony is that the fig trees helped sow the seeds of this situation. Indeed, we can trace its origin back millions of years to a time when figs nourished our pre-human ancestors. These trees shaped the world in which we evolved and then fed our bellies and fuelled our imaginations for thousands of years through important episodes of human history. With the rise of humanity and our hands, hunger and hubris, it was only a matter of time before we took control. Our success has changed the rules of the game.

NINE

From Dependence to Domination

Dear Reader: You and I are related, both in blood and through figs. We share ancestors that survived and thrived because they dwelt among *Ficus* trees and ate often from their ripe crops. Figs helped make us. If we had a time machine I could show you. The story begins 80 million years ago, when giant dinosaurs still roamed the world. The alliance between fig trees and their wasps had taken root. Our ancestors were small, furry creatures. Their prospects changed 66 million years ago, when the universe propelled an asteroid into the planet. It blasted a new future into being.

The asteroid was at least 10 kilometres wide and travelling 20 kilometres a second when it smashed into the Earth at the edge of what is now Mexico's Yucatan Peninsula. Shockwaves ripped around the world, sparking volcanoes and earthquakes and tsunamis that rose hundreds of metres into the air before crashing across coastlines with devastating force. A pall of dust and ash lingered in the atmosphere for years, blocking out sunlight and cooling the planet. Three-quarters of the planet's animal and plant species went extinct. The giant dinosaurs could not cope with the change. They fell like stones and exist now only as fossils.

For the fig trees, though, it was just the start of a new chapter in an already long story. They and their partner wasps survived the apocalypse. So did the mammals. They diversified into new forms and thousands of species. Figs would feed many of the newcomers, from rats and bats to antelopes and elephants. They became particularly import-ant to the primates: the group whose modern members include monkeys, apes, and you and me.

Figs matter so much and to so many primates today that it seems likely they have been feeding our family for tens of millions of years. Our close relatives, the gorillas, chim-panzees and orangutans, all love a meal of figs. So do lemurs and gibbons and dozens of monkey species in Africa, Asia and South America. As our ancestors scam-pered along branches, then grew bigger and brainier and ultimately descended to walk upright, figs were rarely beyond their reach.

Evidence that figs sustained the ancestors from which humans evolved has emerged from a site called Aramis in the Afar desert, a bleak landscape in Ethiopia's Middle Awash region. It's an unforgiving place: hot, dry and largely barren. Any urbanite stranded there today would struggle to survive. But 4.4 million years ago this sandscape was a grassy woodland, green and moist and full of life.

The raucous calls of parrots and peacocks rang out from the woods each day. Porcupines and spiral-horned antelopes foraged in the undergrowth. Monkeys rollicked around in the treetops high above. Fossil evidence shows that fig trees grew in that woodland. Among the species they likely fed was *Ardipithecus ramidus*, a 1.2-metre-tall primate that may be the ancestor of us all.

Ardipithecus ramidus was not an ape, but a member of the human side of the family tree. It had a small head, long arms and very long fingers. It could walk upright better than a chimp and climb trees better than any human. Its big toes splayed out to the side of its feet, enabling it to grasp branches as it clambered about on all fours when up trees.

This species was unknown until 1992, when palaeontologists Tim White, Berhane Asfaw and colleagues began to crawl across Aramis, their eyes alert for tiny fragments of bone. First they found a single tooth and an arm bone. These finds were distinct enough from anything else known for the researchers to declare a new species, but not enough for them to conclude much about how *Ardipithecus ramidus* lived. In 1994 though the team struck fossil gold. They had unearthed the first of more than a hundred bones from a single *Ardipithecus ramidus*, a female they would call Ardi.

The fragile, off-white bone fragments were so soft they would crumble when touched. The researchers used dental picks, bamboo strips and even porcupine quills to expose the bones, then used plaster and aluminium foil to extract them from the sediment. It would take the team 15 years to clean, assemble, measure and analyse their finds. Not until October 2009 could they publish their detailed description of Ardi and the landscape she inhabited. It was one of the greatest fossil discoveries of all time, a window into our evolutionary past. The researchers say that if *Ardipithecus ramidus* is not our direct ancestor, she must have been closely related to it, and would have been similar in appearance and adaptation.

The shape, size and structure of Ardi's teeth suggest she ate fruit, leaves and small mammals. On some days she and her family would have woken with rocks of hunger rolling in their bellies. The fig trees Ardi lived among would have offered a lifeline. Just how important figs were to our ancestors that long ago we can only guess, but a sidelong glance at another relative may help. Ardi's brain was about the size of a chimpanzee's. While chimps are very different animals than Ardi was, they also live among trees and divide their time between the forest floor and the branches above. Chimps, then, may give us insights into how our pre-human ancestors interacted with fig trees.

Chimpanzees love figs. They pluck them from at least 30 *Ficus* species and eat them whenever they can. Richard Wrangham and colleagues at Harvard University got a sense of how important figs are to these animals during research in a forest in Uganda. Wrangham's team collected nearly two thousand piles of chimp faeces over a four year period. For most of that time, from every single sample, fig seeds shone like little nuggets of gold.

Figs are a chimp's perfect source of energy. But in their

FIGS IN THE FAMILY:
High in an African fig tree more than four million years ago, an *Ardipithecus ramidus* reaches for a fig

daily quest to find ripe figs, chimps face challenges that would have dogged our pre-human ancestors too. Big fig trees are rare, scattered throughout forests and other landscapes at low density. Ripe crops appear randomly in time and space. The terrain is tough. Nor are chimps alone in their love of figs. Monkeys, hornbills and dozens of other animals all desire them too, just as they did in Ardi's time. Competition can be intense.

Chimpanzees overcome these challenges with brainpower. Biologist Emmanuelle Normand has shown that chimps are smart enough to remember where various fruit trees stand in a patch of forest. This means they can efficiently patrol their territory and never miss a ripe crop. In research published in 2014, Karline Janmaat and colleagues showed that chimps even plan where to sleep at night so they can beat other foragers to a breakfast of ripe figs. They set off earlier the more distant the figs are. This ability to weigh up information about when and where figs are available helps chimps beat their competitors to food supplies that are here today, gone tomorrow. It means they can secure a steady supply of the high-energy figs they need to fuel their large brains.

Research published in 2016 by Nathaniel Dominy and colleagues shows how chimps gain another important advantage over their competitors. Unlike other animals, chimps can use their fingers and thumbs to squeeze figs before deciding whether to eat them. Even monkeys cannot do this. The chimps are assessing softness which is a good proxy for how much sugar the figs contain, and therefore how much energy the chimp can gain from eating them. It means chimps don't waste time and effort biting into unripe figs. Ardi would have been able to do this even more precisely than a chimp. Dominy says dependence on figs may have played a key role in the evolution of manual dexterity in our pre-human ancestors, a trait that reached its pinnacle in the fully opposable thumb that sets our species apart from other primates and enables us to make and use tools.

Chimps may even use fig trees as pharmacies, according to Shelly Masi of the National Museum of Natural History in Paris. Working in a forest in Uganda, Masi and colleagues observed wild chimpanzees eating unusual foods, including the leaves and bark of five *Ficus* species. Although these foods were common, the chimps ate them only rarely. Masi's team thinks that this could be because the chimps ate these foods for their medical benefits, rather than for nutrition. The fig leaves and bark contain compounds that have shown effects in laboratory tests against bacteria, the malaria parasite, tumours and parasitic worms. Masi's study raises the tantalising possibility that our pre-human ancestors also visited their favourite fig trees for drugs as well as food.

I wonder what Ardi would have thought about those giant fig trees whose bark was smooth to her touch, whose soft nourishing figs she could so often count on finding. We don't know how important figs were to her kind but I cannot imagine she didn't relish the sight of them. A creature like that was the ancestor of us all. She could hunger just like we do.

After Ardi died, more than four million years would pass before the first anatomically modern humans took their first steps. Throughout that time figs would have continued to feed our ancestral line, even as our branch of the family tree bent down to the ground. Our ancestors walked away from a life in the trees but the trees of life, those beneficent figs, had taken root in their consciousness.

When the first people spread across Africa, they found figs almost everywhere they went – more than a hundred *Ficus* species inhabit the continent's forests, savannahs, swamps and drylands. The figs appeared year-round, a bounty they could count on. But fig trees also had other gifts. They provided medicines and shade and good hunting. Just as today hunters in forests across the tropics will stake out *Ficus* trees, the early humans would have realised these trees are meat magnets. A canny hunter with a rock or a spear could have taken out a monkey or a large bird for a double win, a mixed meal of figs and flesh.

In serving several basic human needs, fig trees began to cement themselves into culture. Over time and across the entire African continent, this would translate into myths, rituals and taboos. New links formed when people stepped out of Africa for the first time. As the wanderers reached the Mediterranean and the Middle East, then Asia and Australasia, and even in time the Americas, they found fig trees waiting with gifts to share. They created new stories in which these trees starred.

A turning point came around 12,000 years ago as people started to do something they had not done before. They stopped moving and settled the land. One of the first places they did this was in the lower Jordan Valley. Fig trees helped tether people there, says Mordechai Kislev of Israel's Bar-Ilan University. In 2006, Kislev and colleagues reported that they had discovered the part-fossilised remains of figs people had stored in a building around 11,400 years ago, alongside wild barley, wild oats and acorns. The figs were seedless. Kislev's team concluded they were from a sterile form of *Ficus* trees that could only increase in number if people planted branches in the soil. Kislev argues that people did this with intent, to create a local food supply, thousands of years before anyone in the region domesticated wheat or millet. He says they subsisted by foraging for wild seeds, nuts and meat, and harvesting figs from the trees they had cultivated.

It was a controversial claim. Other biologists have argued there is not enough evidence that the figs were indeed sterile. Even if Kislev is wrong, figs were still among the first plants that people domesticated. Other researchers have found evidence of fig cultivation dating back to the early Bronze Age, five thousand years ago. It was only a matter of time before farmed figs were feeding the great civilisations of the Sumerians, Egyptians, Minoans, Greeks, Babylonians and Romans.

Humankind was making a critical switch. We had long danced to nature's rhythm, now we tried to set the beat. The twin forces of agriculture and urbanisation would alter us and our planet for ever. Back in Africa, fig trees would play key roles in the foundation of ancient Egypt. They provided timber for construction and boat-building. Their figs fed slave and pharaoh alike.

The species that sustained ancient Egypt was the sycamore fig (*Ficus sycomorus*). This huge tree can grow even at the edge of the desert, far from the Nile, thanks to extensive roots that seek out water deep underground. Yet a death sentence hung over these trees. In Egypt, the species was doomed. Its pollinator wasp was nowhere to be found. Each year the trees pushed out expectant figs, whose hundreds of tiny flowers never felt the feet of a pollen-bearing wasp. Without its wasp a *Ficus* plant produces figs in vain. Without pollen, there can be no seeds, no need for dispersers. So the figs stay small, hard and green then drop to the ground where they rot. More than five thousand years ago though, someone made a discovery that would subvert nature and change history. They had found a way to trick the figs with just a flick of the wrist.

Pierce an unripe *Ficus sycomorus* fig with a sharp blade and the fig seems to think it has been pollinated and has seeds to disperse. In just a few days it will swell and grow sweet. This ancient innovation gave Egypt's dead-end figs a new lease of life. Farmers could grow new trees by planting branches in the soil. Some farmers trained baboons to harvest the ripe figs, pre-dating E. J. H. Corner's botanical monkeys by thousands of years. The trees would produce two, three or even more crops of figs a year. After being tricked into ripening, the figs could be eaten fresh or dried for later use. They provided a year-round food supply.

HEAVEN'S GATE:
The Egyptian goddess Hathor emerges from her sacred fig tree to meet souls
bound for the afterlife

The sycamore fig tree came to embody various goddesses, including Nut, Isis and Hathor. Each has been called
'Lady of the Sycamore' but it was with Hathor that the
connection was strongest. She and the mythic fig tree she
inhabited were milestones on the journey to heaven. Pharaohs were buried in coffins of *Ficus sycomorus* wood to
speed their return to the womb of this mother tree goddess.
They took to their graves figs from the same species to
sustain them on their journey into the afterlife. The pharaohs believed that after death their soul would encounter
Hathor in a fig tree that grew on the eastern horizon.
Beyond it was the underworld. Hieroglyphs inscribed inside
pyramids at Saqqara in about 2400 BCE describe how
Hathor would emerge from her tree to offer the dead pharaoh's soul figs, bread and water. By accepting these gifts
his soul would become her guest and feed for eternity on
the figs of paradise.

By the time of the Middle Kingdom (2040–1640 BCE),
this route into heaven was open not only to the pharaohs.
Egyptian commoners also believed that if they lived correctly, their souls could join Hathor in her fig tree. Beyond
the tree was a hellish swamp populated by dangerous
snakes and crocodiles. Fearsome giant baboons trawled the
murky waters with nets in search of food, including lost
souls. Every day the rising sun reminded the Egyptians that
the underworld lay beyond the fig tree. For it was Hathor
who made the day possible by giving birth each morning to
Horus, the sun-child who then rose to the fig tree's crown

before transforming into the sun god Ra and entering the sky.

For all that *Ficus sycomorus* meant though, it was a tastier cousin that would become the queen of figs. While the Egyptian figs were powering the arms that built the pyramids, farmers in what is now Greece were mastering *Ficus carica*, a species now grown for its energy-packed figs in more than 70 countries. Those figs are more than just a sweet treat. They are the original superfood. They are rich in vitamins and minerals such as calcium, iron and potassium. They also have more fibre than any other commonly grown fruit.

Around 2,500 years ago, the Greek figs had become so highly prized that the Athenian statesman Solon made it illegal to export them. Bans of course create criminals. In doing so, this ban also changed the Greek language and created a word we use in English today: sycophant. The word originally referred to the people who showed that figs were ripe and ready to eat. It later came to describe people who snitched to the authorities about anyone exporting figs illegally.

It wasn't long before people started to see figs as more than mere food. They noted that people who ate them fared well. Roman author Pliny the Elder wrote that: 'Figs are restorative . . . the best food that can be taken by those who are brought low by long sickness . . . They increase the strength of young people, preserve the elderly in better health and make them look younger with fewer wrinkles.' The Prophet Muhammad later declared figs to have been heaven-sent. According to Islam's Hadith literature, he distributed figs to his followers and told them: 'Eat it as it cures various diseases.'

Meanwhile across Africa, Asia, the Pacific and South America, people made medicines from their own wild fig species. In India, there is a written record. Nearly 2,000 years ago, scribes there began to document the Ayurveda system of traditional medicine. Its remedies use extracts from several fig species to treat diarrhoea and constipation, mumps and jaundice, boils and haemorrhoids, diabetes and dysentery, open wounds and tooth decay. Today in Nepal, people use the leaves, bark and roots of just one fig species, *Ficus benghalensis*, to treat more than twenty disorders.

Among indigenous peoples who live in the forests of Guyana, French Guiana, Colombia and Brazil, there are more remedies. Some use the sticky latex that flows from the cut stem of a fig tree to treat swelling, cuts, sprains, fracture, abscesses and worm infections. Others use powdered ash of burnt *Ficus* stems to treat children with diarrhoea. Many of these traditional medicines are still in use today. Meanwhile, every week scientists publish new research assessing figs as potential sources of drugs for cancer and other diseases. It's a fusion of modern science with knowledge so ancient that it may well date back to before we descended from the trees.

For millions of years, then, our ancestors gained much from fig trees. They took from them food and shelter, medicines and materials – gifts that must on some days have seemed divine. Add to this the awesome appearance of many fig trees, their power to crush and conquer other trees, and their seemingly endless fertility. It's not hard to imagine why people would protect and even worship these trees – nor why so many cultures planted them in their soil and their stories.

Fig trees often also provide less direct benefits, as centrepieces of intricate natural webs. They support the seed dispersers of other plants that provide us with fruit, medicine and timber, and plants whose flowers feed the bees that pollinate our food crops. Nature would reward any community that protected fig trees, and many chose to thank their gods for those blessings. Others went as far as saying that these gods, or the ghosts of their ancestors, inhabited the trees. Often there is a clear ecological basis to such thinking.

In the Congo basin, Bakongo people founding a new village traditionally planted *Ficus thonningii* fig trees to assess whether a site had adequate water. If the fig tree thrived this meant the water spirits were content, and that other trees which supplied fruit or shade could follow. On the island of Pohnpei in Micronesia, the local name for a large *Ficus prolixa* fig tree means 'that which holds the land', a reference to the tree's deep roots, which limit erosion. These trees are also known as the home of spirits. In Guatemala, Maya communities believe that felling a *Ficus cotinifolia* will cause the rain to stop, as the tree is the source of water. Stories there tell how angels and ancestral spirits rested on a giant fig tree, and woe befell anyone who tried to harm it. One man who tried to cut the tree had a stroke and was part-paralysed for life. Another tried to climb the tree and was turned into a monkey.

The traditions are dying. But go to the highlands of central Madagascar and you'll find the beliefs are still strong. Taboos are intact. The Betsileo people there are farmers whose villages dot a landscape of hills and valleys. In many a field a giant fig tree stands tall. Some of these are trees the Betsileo left standing when they cleared the surrounding vegetation. Others, they planted in religious ceremonies. When biologist Emily Martin and colleagues went to study the value of these trees they found that they enhanced the diversity of birds. Without the fig trees, they said, forest birds would not enter open farmland. The trees serve as stepping stones across which genes – not only of the birds, but also of the seeds they disperse – can travel between distant patches of forest.

These isolated fig trees provide the Betsileo with shade, fruit, medicines and fibres, which people weave into baskets. The hungry birds and bats the fig trees lure are sure in turn to attract Betsileo hunters. The fig trees are clearly worth more alive than dead and so the Betsileo spare them. Over many generations they have woven these figs trees into their rituals and taboos. Some fig trees represent ancestors. Others serve as markers of land boundaries, memorials to ancient villages or sacred posts for rituals. Anyone who chooses to cut one down risks misfortune. In the case of *Ficus tiliifolia*, this could mean blindness in a family member or a new mother failing to lactate.

'Don't cut down fig trees' – it's a message people across

the planet have repeated over millennia. This gem of wisdom pre-dates the dawns of agriculture and civilisation. From before the first humans left Africa, people would have known that a fig tree alive is a lifeline. In return for the gifts the fig trees offered, our ancestors provided protection and – for many of the *Ficus* species – a fine seed dispersal service too. Over millions of years, our family was a partner to the *Ficus* species. Today we destroy them with casual indifference. It's a reversal epitomised by the fortunes of fig trees in Kenya. These trees have played many curious roles there, from wartime lookout post to clandestine post office, from conduit of divine power to symbol of society. In this particular story, they star alongside a queen and a seer, a Nobel Prize winner and the most wanted man in the British Empire.

TEN

The War of the Trees

In the mid-1940s, a little girl called Wangari played beneath a giant fig tree near her home in the highlands of Kenya. 'That is a tree of God,' her mother told her. 'We don't cut it. We don't burn it. We don't use it. They live for as long as they can, and they fall on their own when they are too old.' At the time Wangari did not know why the fig tree was so special. She just knew the stream that flowed beneath it was a good place to hunt for tadpoles.

Six decades later, after battling corrupt politicians, enduring police brutality and winning the Nobel Peace Prize, Wangari Maathai would speak often of that giant *Ficus*. In the intervening years she had learned why her ancestors had let fig trees stand tall. She had seen too what happens when these trees fall. And this had helped bring forth from her mind a 'little big idea'.

The fig tree was a *Ficus natalensis*, a species Maathai's Kikuyu people called 'mugumo'. These elephant grey trees are wonderful things. They can tower to more than 20 metres in height with an evergreen crown of leaves that reaches 30 metres across. As they grow their branches drop aerial roots which can smother other trees. Their thick trunks have supplied a local metaphor for the ineffectual: 'Like cutting a mugumo with a razor blade.'

A mugumo's small round figs ripen a warm orange tone, luring in hungry monkeys, fruit bats and birds including tinkerbirds and turacos. Elsewhere in Africa *Ficus natalensis* figs feed our close relatives, the chimpanzees and gorillas. It's one of the species whose figs likely fed some of the first humans too. For Maathai's mother, though, a mugumo meant faith not food.

In the traditions of her Kikuyu culture both the mugumo and another fig species, the mukuyu (*Ficus sycomorus*) could become sacred places. Her people are, in a literal sense, children of the fig tree. They trace their origin back to a founding couple, a woman called Mūmbi and a man called Gīkūyū, whose name means 'giant *Ficus sycomorus* tree'. Their god Ngai had told Gīkūyū to settle in an area rich in fig trees close to Mount Kenya, Ngai's abode on Earth. Ngai said Gīkūyū could commune with him in times of crisis by making offerings at the fig trees.

The couple soon started to produce children – all girls, one after another. By the time their ninth daughter had reached marrying age there was still no sign of a man to wed any of the sisters. So Gīkūyū and Mūmbi went beneath a fig tree, sacrificed a lamb and prayed to their god. When they returned to the tree the next morning they found nine men who, upon marrying the first of the couple's daughters, gave rise to the first nine of the ten Kikuyu clans.

Over centuries, the wild fig trees insinuated themselves into the culture, religion and identity of the Kikuyu people. The mugumo trees provided fodder for livestock and medicines for people. With their milky latex and abundant figs, they were symbols of female fertility. 'May you be blessed by Ngai,' goes one Kikuyu saying. 'May you be as fruitful as the mugumo tree.'

With their massive size and power to dominate landscapes and other life forms, the mugumo trees became the people's prime symbol. Once consecrated as a holy tree, a mugumo was protected from felling. It became a site of sacrifices and ceremonies, from circumcisions to transitions of power and prayers for rain. The sacred tree was the meeting place that gathered people from their dispersed homesteads. For all of these reasons, the Kikuyu protected the wild fig trees. Everything changed when the Europeans arrived.

By the mid-1800s missionaries were active in Kenya. Many of the Kikuyu converted to Christianity. Churches replaced mugumo trees as places of prayer, sometimes springing up alongside the sacred trees. One group of missionaries sent the wood of a fallen mugumo tree all the way to Scotland, where it was carved into a cross and returned for display in their church. Many of the converts retained some of their traditional beliefs, blending them into their new faith.

While the missionaries thought they were liberating local

people, other Europeans came with brazen intent to exploit them. In 1884-5, when the European powers carved up Africa, Britain's slices included Kenya, which it claimed as a protectorate and made a colony ten years later. Over the decades preceding Maathai's birth in 1940, Kenya's colonial government had seized vast areas of land and allocated it to white settlers. Plantations replaced forests. Shabby little tea bushes usurped mighty ancient fig trees. The colonial administration forced the people it evicted into overcrowded reserves and enacted policies of forced labour, conscription and taxation that further alienated and impoverished the African majority.

By 1952, when Wangari Maathai was 12 years old, an armed uprising against colonial rule had begun. Most of the rebels were poor and landless Kikuyu. They named themselves the Kenya Land and Freedom Army, but became known as the Mau Mau. The violent episode that was unfolding would set the stage for Kenyan independence. Historian John Lonsdale has called it a 'symbolic war of the trees'. For the Kikuyu especially, control over ancestral forests was at stake. Fig trees played many curious roles in the conflict. And few among the Mau Mau took their fig trees more seriously than their commander-in-chief, Dedan Kimathi.

Kimathi dubbed himself Field Marshal, and later Prime Minister of the Southern Hemisphere and Knight Commander of the East African Empire. In reality, he had worked at several dairies, a timber company and at a Shell oil depot. In 1940 he had enlisted in the British Army but was kicked out for violent conduct. Now though he could call himself what he wanted. He commanded fighters in the Aberdare and Nyandarua forests with magnetic oratory and threats of violence. They did his bidding with flinching loyalty.

Before long Kimathi had a price on his head. The bounty was £500, a small fortune. Yet, even as he fled through Kenya's forested highlands from soldiers with orders to shoot to kill, Kimathi still took time to connect with the fig trees. One of his favourites had a thick trunk and massive weighty branches that hung down almost to the ground. Taking refuge from the moonlight beneath this tree, Kimathi raised his arms into the air and pressed his dreadlocked head against its cool bark. He smeared an offering of sticky honey at the tree's base and prayed to his god Ngai to come and save him. His prayers over, he slipped away into the forest and the night, knowing that only death or victory lay ahead.

Nearby, and on the opposite side of the conflict, lived Eric Sherbrooke Walker, a retired British Army Major. Walker also knew a thing or two about being on the run, and he too had a soft spot for fig trees. He had served in both World Wars and when captured by the German forces in the first, he had tried to escape 36 times. After World War I, Walker became a smuggler, trafficking rum from Canada to the United States of America during Prohibition. This funded his move to Kenya, where a giant fig tree would soon seize his imagination.

In 1932, Walker built a two-room tree-house in a huge

The War of the Trees

CROWNING GLORY:
Treetops Hotel, Kenya in 1952, when a princess climbed the fig tree and
returned to earth the next day a queen

mugumo tree in what is now Kenya's Aberdare National Park. It was an ideal spot for viewing the elephants, hippos and other wildlife that visited a nearby watering hole. In time Walker developed this modest shelter into a luxury lodge called Treetops Hotel. On the night of February 5th, 1952 the life of its most famous guest – a 25-year-old English woman called Elizabeth – was transformed.

Back at home in England, the young woman's father, King George VI, had died in the night. Before she had descended from the tree she had ascended to the throne as Queen Elizabeth II. Along with the crown, she inherited the vast British Empire, whose subjects ached for independence. Nowhere was this truer than in Kenya.

Within months, conflict gripped the colony. The uprising had taken root. The rebels fought a guerrilla war, hiding out in the forested highlands, including the Aberdare range where Walker's hotel perched amid the fig leaves. Britain took to the air and bombed the forests to flush out the fighters. More than six million bombs fell from British planes in less than two years. As the uprising intensified, Walker lent his hotel to the British army to use as a lookout point. It was a costly decision. In May 1954, rebel fighters torched the giant fig tree and destroyed the hotel. A bull elephant later pushed what remained of the charred tree to the ground.

Another mugumo a few kilometres away served Dedan Kimathi. This giant's aerial roots had coalesced into three great pillars whose surfaces bore the scars of their birth, myriad cracks and crevices where the roots had not fully merged. Kimathi saw potential in those hollows. The tree's false trunks stretched skyward like a trio of sinewy limbs that had come together to hold aloft the vast crown of leaves.

This landmark would become a Mau Mau communications hub. Its nooks and crannies served as post office boxes for different Mau Mau groups and sympathetic villagers. They used charcoal or even their own blood to write coded messages on strips of animal hide, which they tucked into their intended recipient's specific recess on the tree. Through the tree, the Mau Mau coordinated their troops, shared military intelligence and requested food supplies from villages. The Kimathi Post Office, as it came to be known, is now a national monument in recognition of the role it played in the struggle for independence.

It was a dirty war. The Mau Mau staged some sickening acts of violence against civilian targets. For their part, the British committed massacres and extra-judicial killings. They forced hundreds of thousands of Kikuyu men and women into concentration camps, and subjected many of them to extreme violence and torture. By 1956 the British forces had killed, captured or converted to their cause nearly all of the Mau Mau fighters. Some now worked for the British, hunting down their former comrades.

There was no bigger prize than Dedan Kimathi. A colonial policeman called Ian Henderson led the chase. He remains a controversial figure. In 2013, Kenya's Truth, Justice and Reconciliation Commission would state: 'The historical record suggests that Henderson committed or aided in the commission of extra-judicial killings of Kenyan freedom fighters, as well as contributed to the construction of a system for repressing democratic opposition through illegal killings and enforced disappearances.'

Henderson's breakthrough in the hunt for Kimathi came when his team found a letter the latter had written to his brother. The letter described a dream in which Kimathi's god Ngai had taken him by the hand and walked him through a 'beautiful forest where there were many red and yellow flowers and big birds with green wings'. Ngai took Kimathi to the biggest fig tree in the forest, a mugumo 'that was like a father of all trees'. Ngai told him, 'This is my house in this forest, and here I will guard you.' Then the fig tree rose out of the ground and disappeared into the clouds. When Kimathi woke he could no longer recall where he had seen the tree but knew he must find it. In recounting this dream, Kimathi invited a nightmare.

Henderson's team later caught and interrogated one of Kimathi's lieutenants who revealed that Kimathi made weekly pilgrimages to pray at giant fig trees in the forest. Kimathi believed that if he did this, his god would never let him die. Henderson said he jumped for joy when he learned this. 'We would watch the mugumo trees like hungry vultures and take him by surprise when he came to pray,' he later wrote. 'It would certainly be easier to watch the trees than work almost blindly in those hundreds of square miles of forest.'

'Operation Wild Fig' was underway. Kimathi's lieutenant told Henderson there were at least 40 mugumo trees in the forest where Kimathi hid. Henderson's team found only

18, but could rule out 10 of them in places Kimathi would never feel safe enough to visit. Eight teams of men – a mix of British soldiers, Kenyan Home Guard and Mau Mau insurgents-turned-collaborators – staked out the eight remaining fig trees. They had to avoid leaving a footprint or making any noise, even as horseflies bit at their flesh while they lay in wait. The ambushers watched as butterflies flocked to the bases of two of the trees. They had come to feed on the honey that Kimathi had offered as a libation to Ngai just days earlier. The plan was working.

After three days and three nights, a figure appeared near one of the trees. It was one of Kimathi's men. He had come to see if the tree was safe for his leader to approach. Henderson's team followed his tracks back through the forest for more than 13 miles when Kimathi's voice called out. Within seconds gunfire blazed and a grenade exploded. In the chaos Kimathi escaped. The mission had failed, but it had left Kimathi trapped in a small area of forest. Within weeks he was caught and in custody. On November 19th, 1956, he was convicted of carrying a firearm without a permit and sentenced to death by hanging.

Legend has it that when Kimathi was executed, on February 18th, 1957, his favourite mugumo prayer tree crashed to the ground. His death marked the end of the uprising. Thirty-two European civilians and 200 members of the security forces had lost their lives. This toll was dwarfed by that of insurgents, thousands of whom were dead. Many Kenyan civilians were caught in the conflict; both side's bullets drew their blood. Britain had quashed the uprising but its grip over the Kenya colony had become untenable. Within a few years, the British had handed power to African hands and an old prophecy about another famous fig tree had come true.

In the late 1800s, a Kikuyu seer called Cege wa Kibiru foresaw the arrival of pale-skinned people who would carry 'fire sticks', their guns. He saw an iron snake that would eat people and vomit them out – the train. He also predicted that when a huge fig tree in Thika fell, his people would be free. When representatives of the British Colonial Government heard this story, they reinforced the tree with a fence. It did not help. Part of the tree fell in May 1963 and a month later Kenya had gained internal self-rule. The remainder of the tree fell six months later. Within a month – on December 12th, 1963 – Kenya became an independent country, and Jomo Kenyatta its first Prime Minister.

One of Kenyatta's first acts was to plant a mugumo fig tree at the spot in central Nairobi where for years a tall pole had held aloft the British flag. It was a potent statement. Across the world, other colonies that gained their independence adopted fig trees as symbols of their societies. Independent Indonesia had put a fig tree on its coat of arms, as would Barbados. India chose as its national tree the banyan *Ficus benghalensis*, and Sri Lanka would put four *Ficus religiosa* leaves on its national flag. Attempts to reconnect formally colonised cultures with key features of their local ecology were not always matched by policies.

In Kenya, one of the first people to notice and try to correct this was Wangari Maathai, the woman who had played beneath a sacred fig tree as a child.

Three years before independence, Maathai had left to study in the United States, where she picked up bachelor's and master's degrees in biology. Back in Kenya she would become the first East African woman to be awarded a doctorate. She was not content to be a quiet scientist. When she returned to an independent Kenya in 1966, she found that the giant fig tree she had played beneath as a child had been felled. The stream that ran beneath it had dried up. Maathai was starting to understand why fig trees had become embedded in her culture in the first place. She would prove visionary in her realisation of what it meant for the traditions and the trees to disappear.

As the plantations spread in the 1960s and 1970s, yet more fig trees fell. The forests shrank. Women there told Maathai they could no longer find firewood to cook with, that their soil was eroded and their springs had run dry. When Maathai heard this she had what she called a 'simple and big idea . . . It just came to me. Why not plant trees?' In 1977, working through the National Council of Women of Kenya, she set up the Green Belt Movement. Her simple idea was to empower women to plant seedlings of native trees and re-green the denuded land. She made powerful enemies as a result. Politicians and businessmen saw the women as a challenge to their control of the land and of the women themselves.

Maathai's husband divorced her, stating that she was 'too educated, too strong, too successful, too stubborn and too hard to control'. Her biggest challenges were yet to come. She would endure death threats, police harassment, imprisonment and beatings. One left her in a coma. President Daniel arap Moi called her a 'madwoman'. Maathai did not bend. She and her colleagues dug in to score spectacular victories.

In 1989, they blocked a major development President Moi had planned in Nairobi's Uhuru Park. Ten years later their protests prevented the government from privatising parts of a forest and handing it to cronies. By December 2002, Moi's time was over. Voters kicked out his party, which had enjoyed nearly 40 years of power. Maathai was elected to parliament with 98 per cent of her constituency's vote. She noted that the police who had jailed her the previous year were now her escorts.

For all she endured and all she achieved, Maathai would win the 2004 Nobel Peace Prize. In 30 years her movement planted tens of millions of trees in Kenya and has expanded to other countries. She showed that something as simple as a tree could provide security, prosperity and hope. Through media interviews and speeches, in books and documentaries, Maathai told millions of people how she traced the roots of her environmental consciousness back to the giant fig tree she played beneath as a child.

Maathai concluded that her people's protection of certain *Ficus* species had more than a religious basis, that it drew also on an ancient appreciation of the benefits these trees provide. Those benefits are many, varied and free. A mugumo's dense canopy provides shade and slows the flow of

rainwater onto the ground, limiting soil erosion. Its figs
sustain a myriad of birds and mammals, which disperse the
seeds of many other species. Its roots are strong. They help
stabilise soil and prevent landslides. These roots are also
long. When they reach underground water, the liquid can
rise up through the channels the roots have carved and
break through to the open air to form springs of clean water,
even in arid lands. That, said Maathai, is why the figs
became trees of God.

Not everyone agreed. This became clear in 1996, when
Kenya's parliament debated whether to protect three
mugumo fig trees that had long been sacred to Kikuyu
people. 'All that we are asking the Assistant Minister to do,'
said Stephen Ndicho, the MP for Juja, 'is to allocate about
an acre of land for a mugumo tree and declare it a national
shrine, so that if we fail to get our prayers answered in the
churches we can go back to ask our Ngai to give us rain.'
'This is devil worship!' replied Dr Lwali Oyondi, MP for
Nakuru. When the Speaker of the House ordered Oyondi to
withdraw his comment and apologise, he did only the
former.

After centuries of being central to Kenyan cultures and
histories, the fig trees are being shuffled off stage. There is
a chance, however, that they could return to the limelight.
Because in Kenya, as in many other places, fig trees can be
vital allies in our efforts to restore damaged forests and
protect wild species. For, as violent volcanoes have taught
us, these trees can help restore life to even apocalyptic landscapes.

ELEVEN

The Testimony of Volcanoes

The Time of Darkness was a time of terror. For three days thick ash choked the sky. Red-hot rocks rained down. They crushed houses and sparked fires where they fell. The debris that plummeted from the air killed many people. Yet more starved to death because the ash fell like hot snow, smothering crops and ruining them. People tell this tale across a vast area of Papua New Guinea, from the Pacific coast to the highlands over 400 kilometres away. Dozens of versions of the story exist in more than 30 local languages. These stories have passed from generation to generation by word of mouth and although they vary from place to place, on most of the details above they agree.

When geologist Russell J. Blong first heard these tales in the late 1970s he set out to identify the cause of the catastrophe. Clues sprang from the versions of the story that say the darkness followed explosions and earthquakes and immense waves that tore into the shore. To Blong, these were tell-tale signs of a massive volcanic eruption. His research showed the stories originated when Long Island, a volcano 55 kilometres off Papua New Guinea's north-east coast, erupted with titanic fury sometime around 1660.

Long Island is a misnomer. Seen from the air, the island is a roughly hexagonal ring of land surrounding a 13-kilometre-wide lake, which formed in the crater the eruption created. The island got its name in 1700 when British navigator Captain William Dampier sailed past on his way to Australia and saw 'a long island with a high hill at each end; this I named Long Island'. Had Dampier visited a few decades earlier he would have seen a very different silhouette on the horizon. The huge eruption had decapitated the island.

Dampier wrote that the island 'appeared very pleasant, having spots of green savannahs mixed among the woodland: the trees appeared very green and flourishing, and some of them looked white and full of blossoms'. What he saw was a landscape in recovery from a destructive past. Had he gone ashore he would have found an abundance of fig trees, the vanguard of nature's relentless drive to reclaim and restart.

In the past 10,000 years there have only been 64 eruptions as big as Long Island's. The Smithsonian Institution's global volcanism programme ranks the eruption as 'colossal' on its 'volcanic explosivity index'. It shot enough material into the sky to fill 12,000 Olympic-sized swimming pools. Some of this matter reached 25 kilometres into the atmosphere. The debris that rained down covered 87,000

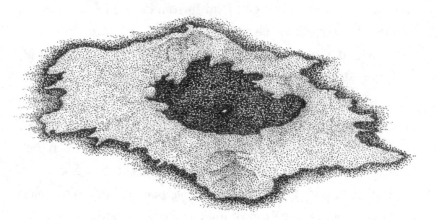

VOLCANO IN RECOVERY:
Fig trees are dominant forces on Papua New Guinea's Long Island and, near
the centre of its crater lake, the tiny island of Motmot

square kilometres of New Guinea to a depth of 1.5 centimetres. But on what was left of Long Island itself the blanket of ash was thirty metres thick.

The volcanic had sterilised itself. The sole survivor, according to some accounts of the Time of Darkness, was a woman who fled the carnage on a raft and washed up on the mainland. By purging the island of all life, the eruption created a natural experiment that scientists would study centuries later. My call to join that endeavour came in 1999 when, during my research in Borneo, I was invited on an expedition to check on Long Island's recovery. The plan was to spend two weeks camped in the forest there while we identified every plant and animal we could find.

And so, on a June day that year I stood at the epicentre of the cataclysm, on an outcrop of lava called Motmot in the crater lake of Long Island's still active volcano. It was a fierce, bleak landscape. There was no shelter from the intense sun; the sharp black lava tore shreds from my shoes. This island within an island was 200–300 metres wide and rose 50 metres above the lake's surface. It was mostly barren, for Motmot was young. It had formed in 1968 when a small eruption forced material above the lake's surface. Further eruptions on Motmot in 1973 and 1974 included lava flows that ensured the island's permanence but also wiped out what little life there was there.

By the time I visited Motmot a quarter of a century later, the animal life was dominated by just two species of spider and one kind of ant. But standing there in that hostile environment was a two-metre-tall *Ficus benjamina* fig tree, the same species whose leaves I had dusted as a child. Other figs were there too. Motmot had just 45 plant species and most were small weedy ferns, sedges and grasses, but among them were eight species of fig trees. Their presence was a testament to the power of these plants to colonise near-lifeless landscapes.

I had gone to Long Island on an expedition led by Ian Thornton, a 72-year-old Yorkshireman who was a professor of biology at La Trobe University in Melbourne, Australia. Thornton was a no-nonsense straight talker with an untamed rebel streak, a wicked sense of humour, and an even stronger sense of justice. When Professor John Zachary Young of University College London criticised the work of one of Thornton's students, Thornton challenged him to a duel. The pair faced off on a table top with toy swords in their hands, and did battle until they both fell from the table. When our team met for the first time on mainland Papua New Guinea, Thornton told us he had been hospitalised for a 'slight heart attack' just two days earlier. He said he would be 'taking it easy'. He then took a glug of cold beer and dragged on a Spear – a six-inch-long local cigarette. We were in for an adventure.

Within 48 hours Thornton and another professor, John Edwards of the University of Washington, would be stranded on Motmot, their inflatable boat having slipped its mooring and scudded away across the lake. Two other colleagues were missing, adrift somewhere in the water having tried in vain to swim after the boat. Thanks to some quick thinking, clear protocols and a dose of good luck, everyone was safe by sundown. The following night the malaria pills I was taking induced me to leap up and charge into the forest where I collapsed, hallucinating and convinced I could not breathe. On later nights men from the nearest village snuck into our camp on the shore of the crater lake to steal clothes, shoes and food. We ran out of supplies and were stranded on the island when our return boat failed to appear. We eventually made our way back to the mainland on a small fishing boat. Dolphins escorted us, riding the boat's bow wave as we filled our hungry bellies with pan-fried tuna that had been swimming in the sea just moments earlier.

In between these episodes the biology kept us busy. We found that at least 50 species of land birds had colonised the island since it exploded, as well as thirteen species of mammals, fourteen reptiles and two amphibians. More than half of the bird and mammal species were fig-eaters. Their home was a forest in which fig trees were a dominant force. We found 31 species of *Ficus* there. That's more than one in ten of all of Long Island's plant species. Some of the *Ficus* species may have arrived when people resettled Long Island and brought seeds and plants they could grow for food. Most though would have arrived as seeds carried by fruit bats and pigeons that had fed on figs on the mainland before flying over 45 kilometres of open sea to Long Island.

What's more remarkable is that in just two weeks we found 16 of these *Ficus* species with figs on their branches. For each of them, the pollinator wasps had successfully colonised Long Island too. Our snapshot survey revealed the power of fig trees to sustain the island's fruit-eating animals. Some of the *Ficus* species had large green figs, which would attract bats but fail to arouse any interest among the birds. Others had small red figs that would turn the tree's crown into a carnival of colour as yellow-billed fruit doves, rainbow lorikeets and metallic starlings flocked to feed.

These animals and many others would struggle to survive on Long Island without its year-round supply of figs. For such species to establish themselves after the island's eruption, the fig trees must have been there first. That's why the fig trees on Motmot were so interesting. They showed that *Ficus* species would have been able to colonise Long Island itself fairly soon after it erupted, their seeds germinating in little more than bare lava having been dispersed by birds and bats roaming in search of food.

Ficus species are better colonists than most trees because they have small seeds that fig-eating animals can carry long distances in their guts before they excrete them. Fig trees produce these seeds in great numbers, more than once a year, and this raises the odds of some of them reaching new land. Once there, the seeds that germinate produce roots that grow fast and strong, even in the toughest of ground, and can keep growing through or over several metres of earth until they reach water.

Of course, for a population of any *Ficus* species to thrive it needs its pollinator wasps, but they too can travel tens of kilometres in just the day or two they live. Fig-wasps have

NIGHT GARDENERS:
Fruit bats have been important dispersers of fig seeds for tens of
millions of years

been caught in traps on ships up to 50 kilometres offshore. Research in Namibia has revealed that fig-wasps can carry pollen more than three times that distance.

Colonisation is only the start of a fig tree's power. When pioneer *Ficus* trees are big enough to produce figs and their wasp partners pollinate the flowers within, the resulting crops of ripe figs attract fruit-eating animals, which carry the seeds of other plant species in their guts. It is likely that on Long Island, fig trees played a critical role in giving seed-dispersing animals a reason to visit. As the pioneer figs grow they provide important shade for other species. The fig trees herald the arrival of many more plant species, and so a forest forms.

Researchers have measured this effect in a region of central Mexico called Los Tuxtlas where big *Ficus* trees stand isolated in fields – lone remnants of former rainforest. When Sergio Guevara and colleagues collected all the seeds that fell beneath five of these isolated fig trees, they identified 149 different plant species, mostly those dispersed by fruit-eating birds and bats. The researchers also recorded 47 species of fruit-eating birds visiting the trees. They erected fences around the trees to keep cattle out and after three years a dense layer of new trees of dozens of species, some four to five metres tall, had established themselves there. Guevara's team showed that even a single fig tree can have a profound effect on the land that surrounds it. Taken together, such research suggests that when Long Island hit the road to recovery, fig trees were in the driving seat.

Long Island is not alone. Two centuries after it erupted,

another natural experiment began with a bang that people felt all around the world. On August 27th, 1883, Krakatoa, a volcanic island west of Java, Indonesia erupted with such spectacular force that it triggered a tsunami that killed people 3,000 kilometres away in Sri Lanka.

Early in 1884, the French government sent investigators to report on the aftermath of the eruption. They said that, in Bantam, on the Javan mainland 50 kilometres away from Krakatoa, some fig trees were all that remained of the forest: 'The wave which rushed with such force upon this coast destroyed the forest for a distance of three hundred or four hundred metres inland, leaving nothing standing except the great *Ficus religiosa*, which stretched their dry and bark less stems toward the heavens.' On Sebesi, an island 22 kilometres from Krakatoa, 'the destruction was complete – hardly a bit of herbage, hardly a trace of life remained'. Sebesi was buried to a depth of 10 metres in cinders and ash. A large portion of Krakatoa itself had vaporised. On what was left of the island, the ashes were 60–80 metres deep. Everything on Krakatoa and the two islands nearby was dead.

Visit today and you will see a very different picture. In little more than a century since the volcano erupted, more than 200 plant species arrived. Thick forest covers what remains of Krakatoa– from the coast to its 800-metre peak. The animals that have colonised include 30 species of birds, 17 species of bats and thousands of insects and other invertebrates. The wings of more than 50 kinds of butterflies bring flashes of colour to the once lifeless island. Each of these species had to cross at least 44 kilometres of sea to reach the island then establish themselves there for the long term.

As on Long Island, fig trees appear to have been instrumental in establishing nature's toehold on the land and attracting other species to follow suit. In fact several of the same *Ficus* species are present on both of these islands, despite them being more than 4,500 kilometres apart. These volcanoes highlight the ways in which different kinds of fig trees have different biological powers. Whilst it is the giant trees and strangler figs that offer most fruit to animals in mature forests, it is often the smaller species of fig trees that are best at colonising bare land and kick-starting rainforest regeneration.

Long Island and Krakatoa show that if left alone for long enough rainforests can recover from even catastrophic damage. But they also show that there is an order to all things in nature, and that before big rainforest trees must come smaller pioneers that attract animals that disperse the seeds of other species. The rebirth of life on these tropical volcanoes suggests that fig trees could help forests to recover elsewhere in the tropics, where logging and mining have taken their toll. Nature, though, may be too slow to withstand what we throw at it. It may need a helping hand.

Around the world, scientists are using fig trees to provide that help. One project in Indonesia is looking at establishing strangler figs to boost seed disperser populations in a protected area in the hope they will fly out over degraded forests and spread seeds there. In another project, in Rwanda, researchers have planted 400 branches from mature *Ficus* species to assess whether these trees can help restore forest rapidly. In Costa Rica, biologist Rakan Zahawi scaled up this approach, lopping off huge branches, more than four metres long, from *Ficus pertusa* trees and planting the stakes as 'instant trees'.

In each of these projects, the aim is to increase the availability of figs and so attract and sustain populations of animals that disperse seeds of other forest trees. Birds, primates, fruit bats and other animals do indeed provide a free dispersal service. But as the recent history of forests worldwide shows, when the bigger birds and mammals disappear, so do the services they provide. When biologist Steve Elliott got to thinking about how to overcome this challenge, he found an answer, or rather a question: can robots restore rainforests?

TWELVE

Once Destroyed, Forever Lost?

'We were viewed as crackpots even by conservationists. They thought we were mad. We got opposition from just about everyone.' It's 2013 and Thailand-based biologist Steve Elliott is telling me a remarkable story, in which fig trees are the heroes. Today the doubters are converts. Elliott wants them to follow him into a future where technology and ecology combine to restore degraded rainforests.

Elliott ended up working in Thailand by accident. He went there on holiday on his way back to his native Britain after completing his PhD research on medicinal plants in Indonesia in 1986. Before long, three Thai universities had offered him jobs. He chose Chiang Mai University in the north of the country, where a one-year contract to teach wildlife conservation would grow into a career. It was an ecologist's dream – the university sits right on the border of Doi Suthep-Pui National Park.

'You could finish a lecture at 11.30,' he says, 'and by

12.30 be sitting on a log, eating sandwiches for lunch, in a fairly pristine natural forest.' The park covers steep mountain slopes and is home to more than 300 species of birds. But despite the high biodiversity, large areas of the park were treeless. Local Hmong villagers had converted nearly a fifth of it to farmland. Cabbages, carrots and corn now grew where tall trees once stood. The villagers had abandoned some of their fields and the weeds that now choked them prevented the forest's return.

One community that lived in the National Park's Mae Sa valley learned the hard way what the loss of trees can mean. In the 1960s the villagers felled most of the surrounding forest for timber to build houses and fuelwood to cook food. But with the trees gone, the spring the villagers depended upon dwindled to a trickle then died. Without water, the people abandoned their homes and moved downhill to start again, but they did not forget the lesson nature had taught them. Three springs flowed in the forest that surrounded their new village of Baan Mae Sa Mai. The villagers protected this area as a community forest, and with it the water that bathed their babies and fed their fields downstream. In the mid-1980s they set up a conservation group and began to plant trees in the upper watershed. But their good intentions were not matched by results.

The Royal Forest Department of Thailand had given the villagers seedlings of exotic trees such as eucalyptus to plant, but villagers did not like them. They burnt easily, and were good neither for local wildlife nor to protect the watershed. 'When we said we wanted to test native trees, they welcomed us with open arms,' says Elliott. He had no idea he would be working in the village for 20 years. That was in 1996. Two years earlier, Elliott and one of his university colleagues, Vilaiwan Anusarnsunthorn had founded the Forest Restoration Research Unit (FORRU) to work out how to restore forest on land that had been logged, farmed and abandoned.

FORRU convinced the Doi Suthep-Pui National Park authorities to support their plan to learn how to grow native trees. The FORRU team gathered any seeds they could find in the forest. They picked them up from the ground. They climbed trees to get them. They used 10-metre-long poles to knock down fruit. Corner's botanical monkeys would have come in handy. The plan was to germinate the seeds in a nursery, let the seedlings grow for a year then plant the young trees in a deforested area of the National Park. But the first experiments failed. 'We started planting out trees from the nursery,' says Elliott, 'and then pretty much monitored them as they died.'

It became clear that very few species would survive without considerable and costly help in the form of manual weeding and fertiliser. FORRU was floundering, but everything changed when, later in 1996, Elliott went to a conference in Washington D.C. It was one of the first big international gatherings of experts in the art of tropical forest restoration. The conclave covered a wide spectrum of approaches, from eucalyptus plantations to agroforestry and the restoration of natural forest ecosystems, but the speaker who had the greatest impact on Elliott was an Australian called Nigel Tucker.

Tucker had grown up in the vast outdoors of north Queensland where, aged just 15, he discovered a species of legless lizard that was new to science. The wilderness was both his playground and his teacher. It would become his workplace. As an adult he worked to restore the degraded forests there, to reconnect patches of habitat and heal damaged land. Along the way he developed what would become known as the framework species approach. This involves planting species that can shade out weeds and produce fleshy fruit that attract seed-dispersing animals from nearby patches of intact forest. These animals bring in their bellies the seeds of other plant species and then deposit them when they defecate. The seeds are better able to germinate and thrive in the weed-free shade that the planted trees provide. From the ground up, the forest's physical structure and species composition return.

Tucker, in turn, recalls Elliott's talk about his challenges in Thailand well. 'His presentation in Washington took me back 10 years,' he told me. 'Obviously, you don't want to see people repeat the painful lessons you've already learned, so over pizza one night I suggested he and his co-researcher, Kate Hardwick, come to north Queensland and have a look at our techniques.' Elliott's visit to see Tucker's framework species demonstration plots in early 1997 would knock 10 years off FORRU's struggling research programme. That's when Elliott learned the power of the fig trees. 'What we had been doing was reinventing the wheel, going through the same processes Nigel had struggled with years earlier,' says Elliott. 'One of the first things he told us was that nearly all *Ficus* species can act as framework species. Provided you select species that grow naturally in the type of forest ecosystem you are trying to restore, then you can plant them and they will boost ecosystem recovery.'

Back in Thailand the FORRU team ploughed through their data and identified local trees, including several kinds of *Ficus*, with the same characteristics as Tucker's framework species. By June 1997 they were ready to take their new tools into the forest, and the village of Baan Mae Sa Mai. In just a year the results were clear. 'The villagers were scratching their heads,' says Elliott. 'These trees were waist high. Normally the eucalyptus would be dying, and the pines covered in weeds. We went from watching trees die slowly to watching them grow fast and close canopy in two years.' But it was just a start. Within eight years of FORRU planting their framework species, more than 70 other tree species had recolonised the experimental plots.

The *Ficus* species played a critical role thanks to a set of traits that make them so suited to the framework-species method. First, they have phenomenal roots, which grow fast and can even tear rocks apart. 'They can find water in the dry season when other tree species can't,' says Elliott. 'At the end of the rainy season there are three to four months without rain. Fig trees find so much water with their fantastic roots that they are evergreen when all around them in lowland areas of the park, trees have shed their leaves.' Second, *Ficus* species have fantastic growth rates and their thick green leaves cast a dense shadow and shade out grasses and climbers. Third, fig trees are magnets for biodiversity, attracting animals that disperse the seeds of many other species – including of course more fig trees. Within just three years, several of the *Ficus* species FORRU planted produced figs that attracted birds and mammals such as monkeys, civets and barking deer. Other planted fig trees served as nest sites for seed-dispersing birds. The number of bird species rose from 30, before planting, to at least 87.

Tucker says at least one in every five seedlings planted should be a fig species. The FORRU team followed this advice and used experiment after experiment to refine the knowledge they needed to ensure that seeds become trees, and that trees grown in the nursery survive when someone takes them into the forest and plants them in the ground. They worked out which containers and potting medium worked best, as well as how and when to water and fertilise the seedlings in the nursery. Their forest grew. By 2008 they would write that FORRU 'rejects the adage, adopted by many conservation organisations, that "tropical forests, once destroyed, are lost forever". The unit bases its work on the more optimistic view that it is possible to transform largely deforested landscapes into lush tropical forests, in a few years.'

They are mimicking what happened on the volcanoes of Krakatoa, Indonesia and Papua New Guinea's Long Island, where fig trees helped forests return to what was once black lava. But they are doing it much faster, at a cost of about one dollar for each tree established from seed. The villagers have benefited too, and from more than just the jobs the project created. More trees means more biodiversity, more secure water supplies, and less risk of flooding or landslides or soil erosion. And by showing themselves to be effective custodians of the natural resources that surround them, the villagers stake a claim to continue living in the National Park.

The FORRU project has inspired several international organisations to implement similar framework-species schemes elsewhere in Asia and in Africa. Buoyed by their success, the FORRU team now wants to set fig trees a tougher test – to restore landscapes that seem to be beyond repair: the rocky churned-up scars left behind by open cast mining. It comes from the observation that fig seeds germinate just about anywhere. 'All over the university campus we see fig seeds germinating in cracks in walls and walkways and as the roots of the trees expand, the cracks get wider,' says Elliott. 'If they can do that to university infrastructure, they will have no trouble opening up mine substrates, but the trick is to encourage them to germinate under such harsh conditions.'

The hope is that fig tree roots will break open the rocks, create drainage channels and allow oxygen to enter the substrate. As soil begins to form, these conditions will enable other, less hardy, tree species to colonise the site. Local wildlife would disperse seeds from these other species when they come to eat figs.

Today, says Elliott, FORRU is overwhelmed with interest. The turning point came at the UN climate change negotiations in 2007. That's when nearly 200 governments began to work out how to compensate nations that protect forests, locking away carbon that would otherwise contribute to climate change. The original proposal focused on avoiding deforestation to prevent carbon entering the atmosphere, but after years of intergovernmental negotiations, it now includes 'enhancement of carbon stocks' – in other words, forest restoration – and aims also to preserve biodiversity and benefit local communities.

It just so happens that FORRU has developed a way to do all three. But the challenge is scale, as fig biologist Rhett Harrison points out. 'Planting out large numbers of seedlings, even with the relatively efficient framework approach, is expensive and not really an option if you are faced with hundreds of thousands or even millions of hectares to restore.'

Elliott recognises this. He says while the framework-species approach seems to work and villagers are keen to use it, it is a big job to collect seeds year-round, grow trees for two years in a nursery and then carry them to distant and often steep areas to plant them. The villagers would have to put the trees in baskets and haul them up on foot, often walking for hours with 20–30 kilograms on their backs. As Elliott says: 'People don't want to lug seedlings down 45-degree slopes.' His plan is to fly unmanned aerial vehicles – drones – over remote sites and drop fig seeds in containers of hydrating gel. Tests are already underway.

Ultimately, Elliott sees a role for robots in seed collection too.

In stage one of his vision, people would use smartphones to control small flying robots with rotor blades at each of their four upper corners. These highly manoeuvrable drones could fly deep into a forest. A camera mounted upon them would transmit video back to the smartphone and allow the controller to locate fruiting trees. The robots would also transmit the GPS coordinates of such trees, making it simple for people to find them to collect the seeds.

In stage two, says Elliott, the robots would take over. They would use image-recognition software to identify tree species and electronic tools to harvest and carry their fruit. They would return each day to their base, a bamboo hut mounted with solar panels, to recharge their batteries by landing on electromagnetic induction pads. 'After recharging overnight,' says Elliott, 'our little flying robots are ready to continue their mission – to seek out new fruiting trees – to boldly go where no one has collected seeds before.' Elliott says the only human intervention needed would be for someone to pick up the fruits collected by the flying robots and perhaps clean off the solar panels and repair any mechanical failures.

'Parts of the vision are already possible,' says Lian Pin Koh, professor of applied ecology and conservation at the University of Adelaide's Environment Institute. 'For example, sending a drone on an autonomous mission to take images of the forest canopy to detect flowering or fruiting trees. Currently, the technology still doesn't allow us to

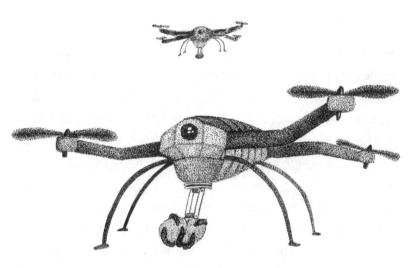

ROBOTS IN THE RAINFOREST:
Aerial drones on a mission to gather rare fig seeds for other drones to
disperse

send drones under the canopy, although that might change pretty soon. The other parts of the vision, on induction charging and image recognition, are probably five to ten years away.' By the time you read this, drones may already hover over forests, doing the work of wildlife that has vanished.

With or without robots, Elliott recommends replicating, over many communities, the small-scale work FORRU has pioneered rather than planning large-scale restoration programmes, which has often been the approach government agencies have adopted so far. He says many small-scale projects, continuing over many years, would be more effective than a single, large-scale project implemented over a few years. At the heart of Elliott's vision is a simple message, one that was among the first our species ever learned: Look after fig trees and they will look after you. It's a lesson we have all but forgotten, but one we could learn again.

EPILOGUE:

A Wedding Invitation

The bride and groom were as silent as stones throughout the wedding that took place on June 10th, 2008 in Jimiti, a village in the Indian state of Odisha. This was no ordinary marriage for they were both fig trees, he a banyan (*Ficus benghalensis*) and she a pipal (*Ficus religiosa*). The villagers spoke for the trees, the men representing the groom and the women the bride.

The practice of marrying trees is ancient and widespread in India; it has various meanings, but this time the purpose was to raise awareness of the need to protect trees. 'Our village was covered with hundreds of trees four decades ago,' said local man Nabin Rout, in an interview with *The Times of India*. 'But the green areas have been shrinking year by year and if we do not protect them they will disappear in a few years.'

Jimiti village is by no means unique. Across the world, forests fall faster than they grow. Deforestation drives climate change by destroying trees that suck heat-trapping carbon out of the atmosphere. Populations of forest creatures shrink in number and range, and so are less able to provide services such as seed dispersal and pollination. Extinction claims species before we can even name them. These trends, born of our own success, threaten to diminish our children's futures.

Forests are where we came from and forests retain a strong grip on our species today. But there's a paradox at play. The more forests there are in the world, the more liberated humanity can be. By contrast, the more forests we fell, the more we play dice with the climate, with water supplies, with complex ecological webs that provide us with vital goods and services. What should concern us is not the resilience of nature, but our own resilience to the new nature we are bringing into being.

It will take more than a marriage of fig trees to solve our problems. But other kinds of weddings that involve fig trees could help. I'm thinking of marriages of world views – those of scientists and religious people, of environmentalists and economists, of poets and politicians – because stories of fig trees and what they offer may resonate with these groups in different, yet complementary, ways.

Fig trees are great connecters. Whatever our political or philosophical differences, we are all descended from some fig-eating ancestors. It is a good starting point. Fig trees stood tall long before the first human footprint graced the Earth. They helped to make us and the world we inhabit. The gifts they offer are ancient but remain relevant today.

We can use these trees not only to strengthen our standing forests but also to restore those that have fallen. On logged land *Ficus* species can kick-start regrowth of rich forests whose trees and soils lock away carbon and so limit global warming. They can provide materials and medicines that turn poor farmers into entrepreneurs. Their figs can sustain the wild birds and mammals whose daily defecations will plant the forests of the future.

To take these gifts we will need to protect both the trees and the animals with which they are bound by contracts of co-dependence. We will need to do this in ways that are rooted in science but also owned by, and beneficial to, local communities. In this respect fig trees also have great potential. They already have prominent roles in many cultures, in some cases forgotten but waiting to be remembered. They are symbols of what we all share, and their success and longevity as a group puts humanity's short stint on earth into humbling perspective.

Fig trees have watched in silence as civilisations have climbed high only to crumble. From the lost city of Gedi in Kenya and the abandoned town of Kayaköy in Turkey, to the slopes of Mohenjo-daro in Pakistan, fig trees have reclaimed landscapes no longer in the grip of human hands. The people who lived in Mohenjo-daro adopted fig trees as symbols more than 4,000 years ago. Life was good until it wasn't. By the time Charles Masson walked there in 1827, there was little to see other than some mysterious mounds from which ruins poked like broken teeth. Masson said the whole area was populated by giant *Ficus religiosa* trees 'some of them in the last stage of lingering existence; bespeaking a great antiquity, when we remember their longevity.' They were living links to a long-dead civilisation.

Local people told Masson there had once been a vast urban centre there but that it 'was destroyed by a particular visitation of Providence, brought down by the lust and crimes of the sovereign'. In fact, it was local climate change and a brutal long-term drought that forced the people to abandon their city. The course of the Indus River, upon which they depended, had shifted and sentenced their civilisation to oblivion.

Far away in present-day Guatemala and Cambodia, droughts hundreds of years ago forced the Maya and Khmer people to abandon fabulous cities that were destined to share something curious in common, something at once beautiful and profound. The surrounding forests swiftly reclaimed the abandoned buildings. In each case awesome strangler figs accelerated the return of nature. Their seeds germinated in cracks in the stonework and grew into giant plants that in time disguised or demolished the stone structures. Their ripe figs attracted hungry animals that brought in their bellies the seeds of many other rainforest species.

Centuries later, the ruins have since been unearthed and protected as tourist attractions, but the stranglers remain, their sinuous aerial roots festooned over ruined temples and palaces. Inch by inch these elephant-grey roots tighten their grip on the ancient buildings. They are living reminders that the good times don't last forever, that despite humanity's perceived dominion over all creatures great and small, we remain part of nature, not apart from it.

Fig trees have been on Earth for about 80 million years longer than humans. They have seen off asteroid impacts and climate change that wiped out millions of other species. Their story reminds us that we are just new here and that between our kisses, our fights, our struggles and our smiles, we tend to break things before we realise how much we need them. It's a story that tells us much about where we have come from and where we might go from here.

Mike Shanahan

NATURE VERSUS STRUCTURE:
A giant strangler fig dominates a ruined temple in Cambodia

ACKNOWLEDGEMENTS

I am grateful to the many, many people whose generosity and good ways have enabled me to bring this book into the world. First, I owe huge thanks to everyone who supported the book by pledging through Unbound. Without you it would simply not exist. I hope you enjoy reading it as much as I have enjoyed writing it.

Thanks, too, to everyone at Unbound and especially Phil Connor, who saw potential in my idea, gave me the green light to pursue my dream and guided me through the process. Thanks also to Unbounders Emily Shipp, Jimmy Leach, Isobel Frankish, DeAndra Lupu, Mathew Clayton and Georgia Odd for your invaluable advice and support.

I thank Kris McManus for producing such a great pitch video, Paul Fulton for some incisive copyedits, and Mark Ecob for letting me get involved in designing the book's cover. That was a great experience.

I am indebted to the community of fig biologists – too

many to name here – whose work has inspired much of this book. I have had the great pleasure of meeting and working with many of these scientists. What they have discovered is way more mind-boggling than anything I have written here. Interested readers can find references to their key works in the list of sources at the end of the book.

I owe special thanks to the four men who were my guides through my years as a fig biologist: Steve Compton, Rhett Harrison, Siba anak Aji and the late Ian Thornton. Your knowledge and ideas have informed and inspired me. Without you I would not have found myself so often in ancient forests, awestruck. I can't thank you enough.

It was Thornton who led the expedition to Long Island described in Chapter 11. That trip was one of my life's best experiences, thanks in large part to the great team Prof assembled: Ruby Yamuna; Rose Singadan; William Boen; Ross Clark; Clint Schipper; Simon Cook; Rhett Harrison and the late John Edwards. I'm grateful for all the wit and the wisdom you shared during that special fortnight.

Many people sent me their research papers, answered my questions, reviewed drafts of my text or otherwise encouraged me to write this book. I thank you all: Alex Kirby; Alfonso Peter Castro; Allen Herre; Asko Parpola; Barbara Kiser; Bas Verschuuren; Ben Knighton; Beverly Natividad; Bruce Beehler; Caspar Henderson; Catherine Brahic; Charles Smith; Charlotte Forfieh; Cornelis Berg; Craig Stanford; David Wilson; Eden Cottee-Jones; Edward Lempinen; Elisabeth Kalko; Emmanuelle Normand; Emily Martin; Finn Kjellberg; Fred Pearce; Henry Howe; James

Fahn; Jay Matternes; John K. Corner; John Lonsdale; John Rashford; John Terborgh; Jonathan S. Walker; Joyce Tyldesley; June Rubis; Karline Janmaat; Kathy Willis; Katrin Böhning-Gaese; Keith Summerville; Kenneth Sayers; Kent Redford; Kimani Chege; Laurie Godfrey; Lian Pin Koh; M. Amirthalingam; M.G. Chandrakanth; Madeleine Nyiratuza; Matthew Muriuki Karangi; Mauricio Anton; Michael Renner; Nanditha Krishna; Nathaniel Dominy; Nigel Tucker; Oliver Heintz; Paul Sillitoe; Perpetua Ipulet; Peter Ashton; Peter Schmidt; Rakan (Zak) Zahawi; Rhett Harrison; Robert Hodgkison; Rosie Sharpe; Russell Blong; Shardul S. Bajikar; Shonil Bhagwat; Siew Te Wong; Silvia Lomascolo; Song Qishi; Stéphanie M. Carrière; Steve Compton; Steve Elliot; Ted Fleming; Tim Denhan; Tim Laman; Tim White; TV Padma; W. Daniel Kissling; Wanjira Mathai and William Murphy.

Thank you to my parents, John and Jennifer Shanahan, for nurturing my curiosity and my desire to travel and learn about the world around us. Finally, I want to thank my wonderful partner, Charlotte, who has inspired and encouraged me throughout the process of bringing this book to life, and who more than once talked me out of giving up. This book is for you and our beautiful boy, Noah.

Sources

SOURCES USED IN CHAPTER ONE

Arita, HT & Wilson, DE (1987). Long-nosed bats and agaves: The tequila connection. *BATS Magazine*, Winter 1987.

Austin, DF (2004). *Florida Ethnobotany*. CRC Press.

Bauer, G et al. (2013). Investigating the rheological properties of native plant latex. *Journal of the Royal Society Interface* 11, 20130847

Berg, CC & Corner, EJH (2005). *Ficus* – Moraceae. *Flora Malesiana*, Series I, 17, 1–730.

Berg, CC (1989). Classification and distribution of *Ficus*. *Experientia* 45, 605–611.

Datwyler, SL & Weiblen, GD (2004). On the origin of the fig: phylogenetic relationships of Moraceae from ndhF sequences. *American Journal of Botany* 91, 767–777.

Gandhi, M (2009). Fresh figs subzi. Kitchen Tantra — tease your palate. A food blog for Indian recipes, 19 February 2009.

Homer, *The Iliad*, trans. I Johnston (2006). Richer Resources Publications.

Homer, *The Odyssey*, trans. I Johnston (2006). Richer Resources Publications.

Sources

Shanahan, M et al. (2001). Fig-eating by vertebrate frugivores: a global review. *Biological Reviews* 76, 529–572.

Simoons, FJ (1998). *Plants of Life, Plants of Death*. Diane Publishing Co.

Wilson, D & Wilson, A (2013). Figs as a global spiritual and material resource for humans. *Human Ecology* 41, 459–464.

SOURCES USED IN CHAPTER TWO

'JM' (1905). A man of the time: Dr Alfred Russel Wallace and his coming autobiography. *The Book Monthly*, May 1905.

Anon. (1911). We are guarded by spirits, declares Dr A. R. Wallace. *New York Times Magazine*, 8 October 2011.

Beccaloni, G & Smith, C (2015). Biography of Wallace [online article]. www.wallacefund.info

Berry, A (2013). Alfred Russel Wallace – natural selection, socialism, and spiritualism. *Current Biology* 23, R1066–R1069.

Bhikkhu Bodhi (2000). *The Connected Discourses of the Buddha: A New Translation of the Samyutta Nikaya*. Wisdom Publications.

Chen, A. (2005). Weight of expectations proves too much for the 'jinxed' Wishing Tree. *South China Morning Post*, 13 February 2005.

Coder, KD (1996). Trees and Humankind: Cultural and Psychological Bindings. University of Georgia Cooperative Extension Service Forest Resources Unit Publication FOR96–46, 10.

Cumont, FVM (2008). *Mysteries of Mithra*. Cosimo Inc.

Gandhi, M & Singh, Y (1990). *Brahma's Hair: The Mythology of Indian Plants*. Rupa & Co.

Grenand, F (1982). Et l'homme devint jaguar: Univers imaginaire et quotidien des indiens wayapi de Guyane. *Collection Ams indiens*. l'Harmattan.

Harding, L (2006). *Holy Bingo, the Lingo of Eden, Jumpin' Jehosophat and the Land of Nod: A Dictionary of the Names, Expressions and Folklore of Christianity.* McFarland.

Hooper, R (2015). When nature evolves to be awesome. *The Japan Times*, 14 March 2015.

Keltner, D & Haidt, J (2003). Approaching awe, a moral, spiritual, and aesthetic emotion. *Cognition and Emotion* 17, 297–314.

Lam, A. (2005). Offerings ban on Tai Po Wishing Tree to stay. *South China Morning Post*, 23 February 2005.

Lurker, M (2004). *The Routledge Dictionary of Gods and Goddesses, Devils and Demons.* Routledge.

Martratt, JI (2008). What is taotaomona tree? *Pacific Edge*, 17 October 2008.

Mwakikagile, G (2007). *Kenya: Identity of a Nation.* New Africa Press.

Peters, S (2011). *Material Revolution: Sustainable and Multi-Purpose Materials for Design and Architecture.* Walter de Gruyter.

Piff, P & Keltner, D (2015). Why do we experience awe? *New York Times*, 24 May 2015.

Ramirez, BW (1977). Evolution of the strangling habit in *Ficus* L. subgenus *Urostigma* (Moraceae). *Brenesia* 12/13, 11–19.

Rashford, JA (2013). Candomblé's cosmic tree and Brazil's *Ficus* species, in R Voeks & J Rashford (eds.) *African Ethnobotany in the Americas.* Springer, 311–333.

Simoons, FJ (1998). *Plants of Life, Plants of Death.* Diane Publishing Co.

Slenes, RW (2007). L'arbre Nsanda replanté: Cultures d'affliction Kongo et identité des esclaves de plantation dans le Brésil du Sud-Est (1810–1888). *Cahiers du Brésil comtemporain* 67-68, 217–313.

Smith, WR (1932). *Myths and Legends of the Australian Aboriginals.* Farrar & Rinehart.

Stoeltje, BJ (1995). Asante queenmothers: a study in identity and continuity, in M Reh & G Ludwar-Ene (eds.) *Gender and Identity in Africa.* LIT Verlag, 15-32.

Sources

Tai, E (2000). The Wishing Tree. *Varsity* magazine (Chinese University of Hong Kong), March 2000.

van Wyhe, J & Rookmaaker, K (2013). *Alfred Russel Wallace: Letters from the Malay Archipelago*. Oxford University Press.

Wallace, AR (1858). On the tendency of varieties to depart indefinitely from the original type. *Proceedings of the Linnean Society of London* 3, 53–62.

Wallace, AR (1869). *The Malay Archipelago: The Land of the Orang-Utan, and the Bird of Paradise*. Macmillan.

Wallace, AR (1878). Tropical vegetation. *Tropical Nature and Other Essays*. Macmillan and Co., 27–68.

Wallace, AR (1885). Are the phenomena of spiritualism in harmony with science? *The Sunday Herald* (Boston), 26 April 1885.

Wallace, AR (1889). *A Narrative of Travels on the Amazon and Rio Negro*. Reeve and Co.

Wood, J (2013). Wallace as a writer. *Current Biology* 23, R1072–R1073.

SOURCES USED IN CHAPTER THREE

Cunningham, A (1875). Harappa. *Archaeological Survey of India Report for the Year 1872–3* Vol. 5, 105–108.

Farmer, S (2004). Mythological functions of Indus inscriptions. Sixth Harvard Indology Roundtable, 8–10 May 2004.

Forlong, JGR (1883). *Rivers of Life. Or Sources and Streams of the Faiths of Man in all Lands*. Vols 1 and 2. Bernard Quaritch.

Foster, P (2007). Film star faces lawsuits after marrying a tree. *Daily Telegraph*, 1 February 2007.

Frazer, JG (1890). *The Golden Bough: A Study in Comparative Religion*. Macmillan.

Galil, J (2008). *Ficus religiosa* L. – the tree-splitter. *Botanical Journal of the Linnean Society* 88, 185–203.

Geiger, W (1912). *The Mahavamsa. The Great Chronicle of Lanka.* (Translated from Pali). Ceylon Government Information Department.

Griffith, RTH (trans.) (1896). *Hymns of the Atharva Veda.* E. J. Lazarus & Co.

Griffith, RTH (trans.) (1896). *Hymns of the Rig Veda.* E. J. Lazarus & Co.

Haberman, D (2013). *People Trees: Worship of Trees in Northern India.* Oxford University Press.

Krishna, N & Amirthalingam, M (2014). *Sacred Plants of India.* Penguin.

Mansberger, J (1987). In search of the tree spirit: evolution of the sacred tree (*Ficus religiosa*). MA thesis. University of Hawaii.

Parpola, A (1988). Religion reflected in the iconic signs of the Indus script: penetrating into long-forgotten picto+graphic messages. *Visible Religion* 6, 114–133.

Parpola, A (2005). Study of the Indus script. *Transactions of the International Conference of Eastern Studies* 50, 28–66.

Parpola, A (2009). 'Hind Leg' + 'Fish': towards further understanding of the Indus Script. *Scripta* 1, 37–76.

Parpola, A (2010). A Dravidian solution to the Indus script problem. Kalaignar M Karunanidhi Classical Tamil Research Endowment Lecture. World Classical Tamil Conference, Coimbatore (25 June 2010).

Parpola, A (2015). *The Roots of Hinduism: The Early Aryans and the Indus Civilization.* Oxford University Press.

Sargeant, W (trans.) (2009). *The Bhagavad Gita: Twenty-fifth Anniversary Edition.* Excelsior editions, State University of New York Press.

Seneviratna, A (1994). *King Asoka and Buddhism: Historical and Literary Studies.* Buddhist Publication Society.

Shanahan, M et al. (2001). Fig-eating by vertebrate frugivores: a global review. *Biological Reviews* 76, 529–572.

Strong, JS. *The Legend of King Aśoka: A Study and Translation of the Aśokāvadāna.* Motilal Banarsidass.

Sources

Tewary, A (2013). Poor Indian children make a living from 'holy leaves' [online article]. BBC Online, 9 March 2013.

SOURCES USED IN CHAPTER FOUR

Agarwal, P (2015). Municipal Corporation to light up memorial of 257 freedom fighters. *The Times of India*, 16 February 2015.

Arrian. *Indica*, trans. PA Brunt (1983). Loeb Classical Library.

Bodson, L (1991). Alexander the Great and the scientific exploration of the oriental part of his empire. An overview of the background, trends and results. *Ancient Society* 22, 127–138.

Chopra, PN (1969). *Who's Who of Indian Martyrs*. Ministry of Education and Youth Services, Government of India.

Noehden, GH (1824). Account of the banyan-tree, or *Ficus indica*, as found in the Ancient Greek and Roman authors. *Transactions of the Royal Asiatic Society of Great Britain and Ireland* 1, 119–132.

Sayeed, VA (2012). Arboreal wonder. *Frontline Magazine*, June 2012.

Strabo, *Geography*, trans. HL Jones (1932). Vol 7. Loeb Classical Library.

Thanos CA (1994). Aristotle and Theophrastus on plant–animal interactions, in M Arianoutsou & RH Groves (eds.), *Plant–Animal Interactions in Mediterranean-type Ecosystems*, 3–11. Kluwer Academic Publishers.

Thanos CA (2005). The geography of Theophrastus' life and of his botanical writings (Περι Φυτων). In: AJ Karamanos & CA Thanos (eds.), *Biodiversity and Natural Heritage in the Aegean*, Proceedings of the Conference 'Theophrastus 2000', Eressos-Sigri, Lesbos. (6–8 July 2000), Frangoudis, 113–131.

Theophrastus, *Enquiry into Plants*, trans. A Hort (1916). W. Heinemann.

Theophrastus, *De Causis Plantarum*, trans. B Einarson & GKK Link (1990). Harvard University Press.

SOURCES USED IN CHAPTER FIVE

Barlow, HS (1993). Botanical Monkeys by E. J. H. Corner (book review). *Journal of Southeast Asian Studies* 24, 182–184.

Berg, CC & Corner, EJH (2005). *Ficus* – Moraceae. *Flora Malesiana*, Series I, 17, 1–730.

Burkhill, HM (1977). Introduction. *Gardens' Bulletin Singapore* 29, 1–2.

Colonial Office: Straits Settlements. (1945). Miscellaneous reports – British Military Administration, Malaya. British National Archives Reference No: CO 273/675/6.

Corner, EJH (1940). *Wayside Trees of Malaya*. Government Printing Office, Singapore.

Corner, EJH (1956). Merah the berok: A little hand among the trees. *The Straits Times*, 1 January 1956, 13.

Corner, EJH (1960). Taxonomic notes on *Ficus* L., Asia and Australasia. Sections 1-4 *Gardens' Bulletin Singapore* 17, 368–485.

Corner, EJH (1964). Royal Society Expedition to North Borneo 1961: Special Reports: 3. *Ficus* on Mt. Kinabalu. *Proceedings of the Linnean Society of London* 175, 37–39.

Corner, EJH (1965). Check-list of Ficus in Asia and Australasia with keys to identification. *The Gardens' Bulletin Singapore* 21, 1–186.

Corner, EJH (1967). *Ficus* in the Solomon Islands. *Philosophical Transactions of the Royal Society of London, Series B: Biological Sciences* 253, 23–159.

Corner, EJH (1969). *Ficus* (A discussion on the results of the Royal Society expedition to the British Solomon Islands Protectorate,

Sources

1965). *Philosophical Transactions of the Royal Society of London*: *Series B, Biological Science* 255, 567–570.

Corner, EJH (1981). *The Marquis, a Tale of Syonan-to*. Heinemann Asia.

Corner, EJH (1985). Essays on *Ficus*. *Allertonia* 4, 125–168.

Corner, EJH (1985). *Ficus* (Moraceae) and *Hymenoptera* (Chalcidoidea): Figs and their pollinators. *Biological Journal of the Linnean Society* 25, 187–195.

Corner, EJH (1992). *Botanical monkeys*. Pentland Press.

Corner, EJH (1993). I am part of all that I have met. In: S Isaac, JC Frankland, R Watling & AJ Whalley (eds.), *Aspects of Tropical Mycology*. Cambridge University Press, 1–14.

Corner, JK (2013). *My Father in his Suitcase: In Search of E. J. H. Corner, the Relentless Botanist*. Landmark Books.

Gudger, EW (1923). Monkeys trained as harvesters. Instances of a practice extending from remote times to the present. *Natural History Magazine*, May–June 1923.

Krishna, N & Amirthalingam, M (2014). *Sacred Plants of India*. Penguin.

Linnaeus, C (1753). *Species Plantarum*. Laurentius Salvius.

Mabberley, DJ (2000). A tropical botanist finally vindicated. *Gardens' Bulletin Singapore* 52, 1–4.

Mabberley, DJ & Lan, CK (eds.) (1977). Tropical Botany: Essays presented to E. J. H. Corner for his seventieth birthday, 1976. *Gardens' Bulletin Singapore* 29, 1–266.

Seemann, BC (1868). *Flora Vitiensis. A Description of the Plants of the Viti or Fiji Islands, with an Account of Their History, Uses, and Properties. Part 7*. L. Reeve.

Shanahan, M et al. (2001). Fig-eating by vertebrate frugivores: a global review. *Biological Reviews* 76, 529–572.

Vines, G (2002). King of the canopy. *New Scientist*, 21 December 2002.

Mike Shanahan

Weiblen, G D & Clement, WL (2007). *Flora Malesiana.* Series I. Vol 17, Parts 1 & 2. *Edinburgh Journal of Botany* 64, 431–437.

Whitmore, T (1996). Obituary: Professor E. J. H. Corner. *The Independent,* 21 September 1996.

SOURCES USED IN CHAPTER SIX

Ahmed, S et al. (2009). Wind-borne insects mediate directional pollen transfer between desert fig trees 160 kilometers apart. *Proceedings of the National Academy of Sciences* 106, 20342–20347.

Bain, A, Harrison, RD & Schatz, B (2014). How to be an ant on figs. *Acta Oecologica* 57, 97–108.

Berg, CC & Wiebes, JT (1992). *African Fig Trees and Fig Wasps.* Koninklijke Nederlandse Akademie van Wetenschappen.

Bleher, B et al. (2003). The importance of figs for frugivores in a South African coastal forest. *Journal of Tropical Ecology* 19, 375–386.

Burrows, J & Burrows, S (2003). *Figs of Southern & South-Central Africa.* Umdaus Press.

Compton, SG & Robertson, HG (1988). Complex interactions between mutualisms: ants tending Homopterans protect fig seeds and pollinators. *Ecology* 69, 1302–1305.

Cook, JM & Rasplus, J-Y (2003). Mutualists with attitude: coevolving fig-wasps and figs. *Trends in Ecology and Evolution* 18, 241–8.

Cook, JM et al. (2015). Fighting in fig-wasps: do males avoid killing brothers or do they never meet them? *Ecological Entomology* 40, 741–747.

Datwyler, SL & Weiblen, GD (2004). On the origin of the fig: phylogenetic relationships of Moraceae from ndhF sequences. *American Journal of Botany* 91, 767-777.

Deeble, M & Stone V (2005). *The Queen of Trees* [documentary film]. Flat Dog Productions Limited.

Sources

Galil, J & Eisikowitch, D (1968). On the pollination ecology of *Ficus sycomorus* in East Africa. *Ecology* 49, 259–269.

Galil, J & Eisikowitch, D (1974). Further studies on pollination ecology in *Ficus sycomorus* II. Pocket filling and emptying by *Ceratosolen arabicus* Mayr. *New Phytologist* 73, 515–528.

Ghara, M, Kundanati, L & Borges, R (2011). Nature's Swiss army knives: ovipositor structure mirrors ecology in a multitrophic fig-wasp community. *PLOS One* 6, e23642.

Herre, EA (1989). Coevolution of reproductive characteristics in 12 species of New World figs and their pollinator wasps. *Experientia* 45, 637-647.

Herre, EA, Jander, KC & Machado, CA (2008). Evolutionary ecology of figs and their associates: recent progress and outstanding puzzles. *Annual Review of Ecology, Evolution, and Systematics* 39, 439–458.

Jauharlina, J et al. (2012). Fig-wasps as vectors of mites and nematodes. *African Entomology* 20, 101–110.

Kerdelhué, C & Rasplus, J-Y (1996). Non-pollinating Afrotropical fig-wasps affect the fig-pollinator mutualism in *Ficus* within the subgenus *Sycomorus*. *Oikos* 75, 3–14.

Kinnaird, MF, O'Brien, TG & Suryadi, S (1999). The importance of figs to Sulawesi's imperiled wildlife. *Tropical Biodiversity* 6, 5–18.

Kissling, WD, Rahbek, C & Böhning-Gaese, K (2007). Food plant diversity as broad-scale determinant of avian frugivore richness. *Proceedings of the Royal Society, Series B: Biological Sciences* 274, 799–808.

Kjellberg, F et al. (2005). Biology, ecology and evolution of fig-pollinating wasps (*Chalcidoidea, Agaonidae*), in A Raman, W Schaefer & Withers (eds.) *Biology, Ecology and Evolution of Gall-Inducing Arthropods*. Science Publishers, Inc., 539–572

Korine, C, Kalko, EKV & Herre, EA (2000). Fruit characteristics and factors affecting fruit removal in a Panamanian community of strangler figs. *Oecologia* 123, 560–568.

Lambert, FR & Marshall, AG (1991). Keystone characteristics of bird-dispersed *Ficus* in a Malaysian lowland rain forest. *Journal of Ecology* 79, 793–809.

Leighton, M & Leighton, DR (1983). Vertebrate responses to fruiting seasonality within a Bornean rain forest. In: SL Sutton, TC Whitmore and AC Chadwick (eds.), *Tropical Rain Forest: Ecology and Management*, 181–196. Blackwell.

Machado, CA et al. (2001). Phylogenetic relationships, historical biogeography and character evolution of fig-pollinating wasps. *Proceedings of the Royal Society, Series B: Biological Sciences* 268, 685–694.

Machado, CA et al. (2005). Critical review of host specificity and its coevolutionary implications in the fig–fig-wasp mutualism. *Proceedings of the National Academy of Sciences* 102, 6558–6565.

Nason, JD, Herre, EA & Hamrick, JL (1998). The breeding structure of a tropical keystone resource. *Nature* 391, 685–687.

Rønsted, N et al. (2005). 60 million years of co-divergence in the fig–wasp symbiosis. *Proceedings of the Royal Society, Series B: Biological Sciences* 272, 2593–2599.

Rønsted, N et al. (2005). Reconstructing the phylogeny of figs (*Ficus*, Moraceae) to reveal the history of the fig pollination mutualism. *Symbiosis* 45, 45–56.

Shanahan, M et al. (2001). Fig-eating by vertebrate frugivores: a global review. *Biological Reviews* 76, 529–572.

Somjee, S (2014). The Ubuntu stratagem. Utu and peace sustaining heritage of Africa south of the Sahara. *African Peace Journal*.

Suleman, N, Raja, S & Compton, SG (2012). Only pollinator fig wasps have males that collaborate to release their females from figs of an Asian fig tree. *Biology Letters* 8, 344–346.

Terborgh, J (1986). Keystone plant resources in the tropical forest, in ME Soule (ed.) *Conservation Biology, the Science of Scarcity and Diversity*. Sinauer, 330–344

Sources

Weiblen, GD (2002). How to be a fig-wasp. *Annual Review of Entomology* 47, 299–330.

Weiblen, GD (2004). Correlated evolution in fig pollination. *Systematic Biology* 53, 128–139.

Wiebes, JT (1976). A short history of fig-wasp research. *Gardens' Bulletin Singapore* 29, 207–232.

Wiebes, JT (1979). Co-evolution of figs and their insect pollinators. *Annual Review of Ecology and Systematics* 10, 1–12.

Willdenow, CL (1806). Observations on the genus *Ficus*, with the description of some new species. In: C Konig & J Sims (eds.), *Annals of Botany*, Volume II, 312–325. R. Taylor and Co.

SOURCES USED IN CHAPTER SEVEN

Beeler, C (2015). In quest for fidelity, a model from the animal kingdom. *Newsworks: The Pulse*, 12 February 2015.

Corner, EJH (1940). *Wayside Trees of Malaya*. Government Printing Office, Singapore.

Hadiprakarsa, Y-Y & Kinnaird, MF (2004). Foraging characteristics of an assemblage of four Sumatran hornbill species. *Bird Conservation International* 14, S53–S62.

Harrison RD et al. (2012). Evolution of fruit traits in *Ficus* subgenus *sycomorus* (Moraceae): To what extent do frugivores determine seed dispersal mode? *PLOS ONE* 7, e38432.

Harrison, RD et al. (2003). The diversity of hemi-epiphytic figs (*Ficus*; Moraceae) in a Bornean lowland rainforest. *Biological Journal of the Linnean Society* 78, 439-455.

Johns, AD (1987). The use of primary and selectively logged forest by Malaysian hornbills (Bucerotidae) and implications for their conservation. *Biological Conservation* 40, 179–190.

Kemp, AC & Woodcock, M (1995). *The Hornbills: Bucerotiformes.* Oxford University Press.

Kinnaird, MF & O'Brien, TG (2007). *The Ecology and Conservation of Asian Hornbills: Farmers of the Forest.* University of Chicago Press.

Kinnaird, MF, O'Brien, TG & Suryadi, S (1996). Population fluctuation in Sulawesi Red-knobbed Hornbill *Aceros cassidix*: tracking figs in space and time. *The Auk* 113, 431–440.

Laman, T (2009). High on hornbills. *National Wildlife*, February/March 2009.

Laman, T (2010). Hooked on hornbills. *Living Bird*, Autumn 2010.

Laman, T (2013). Borneo – My rain forest roots [online article], 17 January 2013. www.timlaman.com.

Laman, T (2014). Postcards from Borneo: A family adventure begins anew. Proof: Picture stories [online article], 1 July 2014. www. nationalgeographic.com.

Laman, TG & Weiblen, GD (1998). Figs of Gunung Palung National Park (West Kalimantan, Indonesia). *Tropical Biodiversity* 5, 245–97.

Laman, TG (1995). *Ficus stupenda* germination and seedling establishment in a Bornean rain forest canopy. *Ecology* 76: 2617–2626.

Laman, TG (1995). Safety recommendations for climbing rain forest trees with 'single rope technique'. *Biotropica* 27: 406–409.

Laman, TG (1995). The ecology of strangler fig seedling establishment. *Selbyana* 16, 223–229.

Laman, TG (1996). *Ficus* seed shadows in a Bornean rain forest. *Oecologia* 107, 347–355.

Laman, TG (1996). Specialization for canopy position by hemiepiphytic *Ficus* species in a Bornean rain forest. *Journal of Tropical Ecology* 12, 789–803.

Laman, TG (1996). The impact of seed harvesting ants (*Pheidole* sp. nov.) on *Ficus* establishment in the canopy. *Biotropica* 28, 777–781.

Laman, TG (1997). Borneo's strangler fig trees. *National Geographic* 191, 38–55.

Sources

Lambert, FR (1989). Fig eating by birds in a Malaysian lowland forest. *Journal of Tropical Ecology* 5, 401–412.

Lambert, FR (1989). Pigeons as seed predators and dispersers of figs in a Malaysian lowland forest. *Ibis* 131, 521–527.

Lee, HS et al. (2002). Floristic and structural diversity of mixed dipterocarp forest in Lambir Hills National Park, Sarawak, Malaysia. *Journal of Tropical Forest Science* 14, 379–400.

Lee, HS et al. (2002). The 52-hectare Forest Research Plot at Lambir Hills, Sarawak, Malaysia: Tree distribution maps, diameter tables and species documentation. Forest Department Sarawak & the Arnold Arboretum–CTFS Asia Program.

Leighton, M (1982). Fruit resources and patterns of feeding, spacing and grouping among sympatric Bornean hornbills (Bucerotidae). PhD thesis, University of California, Davis.

National Geographic photographer profile: Tim Laman [online article]. www.nationalgeographic.com

Peart, DR (2003). The Road to Cabang Panti. Unpublished manuscript. Dartmouth College.

Poonswad, P & Tsuji, A (1994). Ranges of males of the Great Hornbill *Buceros bicornis*, Brown Hornbill *Ptilolaemus tickelli* and Wreathed Hornbill *Rhyticeros undulatu*s in Khao Yai National Park, Thailand. *Ibis* 136, 79–86.

Porter Brown, N (2013). Paradise found. *Harvard Magazine* (January–February 2013), 62–65.

Shanahan, M & Compton, S (2001). Vertical stratification of figs and fig-eaters in a Bornean lowland rain forest: how is the canopy different? *Plant Ecology* 153, 121–132.

Shanahan, M & Compton. S (2000). Fig-eating by Bornean treeshrews: evidence for a role as seed dispersers. *Biotropica* 32, 759–764.

Shanahan, M (2000). *Ficus* seed dispersal guilds: ecology, evolution and conservation implications. PhD Thesis. University of Leeds.

Shanahan, M et al. (2001). Fig-eating by vertebrate frugivores: a global review. *Biological Reviews* 76, 529–572.

Wallace, AR (1863). The Bucerotidæ, or hornbills. *The Intellectual Observer*, June 1863, 309–316.

SOURCES USED IN CHAPTER EIGHT

Ahmed, S et al. (2009). Wind-borne insects mediate directional pollen transfer between desert fig trees 160 kilometers apart. *Proceedings of the National Academy of Sciences* 106, 20342–20347.

Al-Khalaf, A, Quinnell, RJ, & Compton, SG (2015). Influence of temperature on the reproductive success of a fig-wasp and its host plant. *African Journal of Agricultural Research* 10, 1625–1630.

Bryan, JE et al. (2013). Extreme differences in forest degradation in Borneo: Comparing practices in Sarawak, Sabah, and Brunei. *PLOS ONE* 8, e69679.

Davenport, WH (2000). Hornbill carvings of the Iban of Sarawak, Malaysia. *RES: Anthropology and Aesthetics* 37, 127–146.

Fredriksson, GM, Danielsen, LS & Swenson, JE (2007). Impacts of El Niño related drought and forest fires on sun bear fruit resources in lowland dipterocarp forest of East Borneo. *Biodiversity and Conservation* 16, 1823–1838.

Gaveau, DLA et al. (2014). Four decades of forest persistence, clearance and logging on Borneo. *PLOS One* 9, e101654.

Harrison, RD & Shanahan, M (2005). Seventy-seven ways to be a fig: An overview of a diverse assemblage of figs in Borneo. In: DW Roubik, S Sakai, & AA Hamid (eds.), *Pollination, Ecology and the Rain Forest Canopy: Sarawak Studies*. Springer Verlag, 111–127.

Harrison, RD (2000). Repercussions of El Niño: Drought causes extinction and the breakdown of mutualism in Borneo. *Proceedings of the Royal Society, Series B: Biological Sciences* 267, 911–915.

Sources

Harrison, RD (2001). Drought and the consequences of El Niño in Borneo: a case study of figs. *Population Ecology* 43, 63–75.

Harrison, RD (2005). Figs and the diversity of tropical forests. *BioScience* 55, 1053–1064.

Harrison, RD (2005). A severe drought in Lambir Hills National Park. In: DW Roubik, S Sakai, & AA Hamid (eds.), *Pollination, Ecology and the Rain Forest Canopy: Sarawak Studies.* Springer Verlag, 51–64.

Harrison, RD (2011). Emptying the Forest: Hunting and the extirpation of wildlife from tropical nature reserves. *BioScience* 61, 919–924.

Harrison, RD et al. (2003). The diversity of hemiepiphytic figs (*Ficus*; Moraceae) in a Bornean lowland rainforest. *Biological Journal of the Linnean Society* 78, 439–455.

Janzen, DH (1979). How to be a fig. *Annual Review of Ecology and Systematics* 10, 13–51.

Jevanandam, N, Goh, AGR & Corlett, R (2013). Climate warming and the potential extinction of fig-wasps, the obligate pollinators of figs. *Biology Letters* 9, 20130041.

Johns, AD (1987). The use of primary and selectively logged forest by Malaysian hornbills (Bucerotidae) and implications for their conservation. *Biological Conservation* 40, 179–190.

Kinnaird, MF & O'Brien, TG (2007). *The Ecology and Conservation of Asian Hornbills: Farmers of the Forest.* University of Chicago Press.

Mohd-Azlan, J & Engkamat, L (2006). Camera trapping and conservation in Lambir Hills National Park, Sarawak. *The Raffles Bulletin of Zoology* 54, 469–475.

Nakagawa, M et al. (2000). Impact of severe drought associated with the 1997–1998 El Niño in a tropical forest in Sarawak. *Journal of Tropical Ecology* 16, 355–367.

Redford, K (1992). The Empty Forest. *BioScience* 42, 412–422.

Shanahan, M & Compton, S (2001). Vertical stratification of figs and fig-eaters in a Bornean lowland rain forest: how is the canopy different? *Plant Ecology* 153, 121–132.

Shanahan, M & Compton. S (2000). Fig-eating by Bornean treeshrews: evidence for a role as seed dispersers. *Biotropica* 32, 759–764.

Shanahan, M & Debski, I (2002). Vertebrates of Lambir Hills National Park, Sarawak, Malaysia. *Malayan Nature Journal* 56, 103–118.

Shanahan, M, 2000. *Ficus* seed dispersal guilds: ecology, evolution and conservation implications. PhD. Thesis. University of Leeds.

Shanahan, M et al. (2001). Fig-eating by vertebrate frugivores: a global review. *Biological Reviews* 76, 529–572.

SOURCES USED IN CHAPTER NINE

AAAS (2009). Interview of Tim White by Ed Lempinen. SciPak / American Association for the Advancement of Science, 30 September 2009.

AAAS (2009). Oldest hominid skeleton unveiled. Press backgrounder 'Ardipithecus'. SciPak / American Association for the Advancement of Science, 1 October 2009.

Alba, DM et al. (2015). Miocene small-bodied ape from Eurasia sheds light on hominoid evolution. *Science* 350, aab2625.

Bassie-Sweet, K (2008). *Maya Sacred Geography and the Creator Deities*. University of Oklahoma Press.

Black, J (1998). *Reading Sumerian Poetry*. Cornell University Press.

Black, JA et al. (1998–2006). The Electronic Text Corpus of Sumerian Literature [online reference]. Faculty of Oriental Studies, University of Oxford. www.etcsl.orinst.ox.ac.uk

Cappers, RTJ & Hamdy, R (2007). Ancient Egyptian plant remains in the Agricultural Museum (Dokki, Cairo). In RTJ Cappers (ed.) *Fields of Change: Progress in African Archaeobotany*. Barkhuis, 165-214.

Sources

Chan, H (2007). Survival in the Rainforest: Change and resilience among the Penan Vuhang of Eastern Sarawak, Malaysia. *Research Series in Anthropology*. University of Helsinki.

Denham, T (2007). Early fig domestication, or gathering of wild parthenocarpic figs? *Antiquity* 81, 457–461.

Dominy NJ et al. (2016). How chimpanzees integrate sensory information to select figs. *Interface Focus* 6, 20160001.

Galil, J & Eisikowitch, D (1968). On the pollination ecology of *Ficus sycomorus* in East Africa. *Ecology* 49, 259–269.

Galil, J (1968). An ancient technique for ripening sycamore fruit in East-Mediterranean countries. *Economic Botany* 22, 178–190.

Galil, J, Stein, M & Horovitz, A (1977). On the origin of the Sycamore Fig (*Ficus sycomorus* L.) in the Middle East. *Gardens' Bulletin Singapore* 29, 191–205.

Gopukumar, ST & Praseetha, PK (2015). *Ficus benghalensis* Linn – the sacred Indian medicinal tree with potent pharmacological remedies. *International Journal of Pharmaceutical Sciences Review and Research* 32, 223–227.

Handcock, PSP (1912). *Mesopotamian Archaeology: An introduction to the archaeology of Babylonia and Assyria*. Macmillan and Co.

Hopkin, M (2005). Ethiopia is top choice for cradle of *Homo sapiens* [online article]. *Nature*, 16 February 2005.

Ipulet, P (2007). Uses of genus *Ficus* (Moraceae) in Buganda region, Uganda. *African Journal of Ecology* 45, 44–47.

Janečka, JE et al. (2007). Molecular and genomic data identify the closest living relative of primates. *Science* 318, 792–794.

Janmaat, K et al. (2014). Wild chimpanzees plan their breakfast time, type, and location. *Proceedings of the National Academy of Sciences* 111, 16343–16348.

Janzen, JM (1978). *The Quest for Therapy in Lower Zaire*. University of California Press.

Janzen, JM (2012). Teaching the Kongo transatlantic. Newsletter, The African Diaspora Archaeology Network, Spring 2012.

Jolly-Saad, M-C et al. (2010). *Ficoxylon* sp., a fossil wood of 4.4 Ma (Middle Awash, Ethiopia). *Comptes Rendus Palevol* 9, 1–4.

Kislev, M, Hartmann, A & Bar-Yosef, O (2006). Early domesticated fig in the Jordan valley. *Science* 312, 1372–74.

Kislev, ME, Hartmann, A & Bar-Yosef, O (2006). Response to Comment on 'Early Domesticated Fig in the Jordan Valley'. *Science* 314, 1683.

Kunwar, RM & Bussman, RW (2006). *Ficus* (fig) species in Nepal: a review of diversity and indigenous uses. *Lyonia* 11, 85–97.

Lev-Yadun, S et al. (2006). Comment on 'Early domesticated fig in the Jordan Valley'. *Science* 314, 1683.

Liu, W et al. (2015). The earliest unequivocally modern humans in southern China. *Nature* 526, 696–699.

Lovejoy, CO (2009). Re-examining human origins in light of *Ardipithecus ramidus*. *Science* 326, 74–74e1–74e8.

Martin, EA et al. (2009). Conservation value for birds of traditionally managed isolated trees in an agricultural landscape of Madagascar. *Biodiversity and Conservation* 18, 2719–2742.

Masi, S et al. (2012). Unusual feeding behavior in wild great apes, a window to understand origins of self-medication in humans: Role of sociality and physiology on learning process. *Physiology & Behavior* 105, 337–349.

Maspero, G (1903). *History of Egypt, Chaldea, Syria, Babylonia and Assyria*. The Grolier Society.

Maundu, P et al. (2001). Ethnobotany of the Loita Maasai: Towards Community Management of the Forest of the Lost Child. Experiences from the Loita Ethnobotany Project. People and Plants Working Paper Number 8. UNESCO, Paris.

McDougall, I, Brown, FH & Fleagle, JG (2005). Stratigraphic placement and age of modern humans from Kibish, Ethiopia. *Nature* 433, 733–736.

Sources

Merlin, M (2015). *People and Plants of Micronesia: Database of economic plants of Micronesia.* University of Hawai'i at Mānoa.

Morales, J & Delgado, T (2007). Figs and their importance in the prehistoric diet in Gran Canaria Island (Canary Isles). In: RTJ Cappers (ed.) *Fields of Change: Progress in African Archaeobotany.* Barkhuis, 77–85.

Nicholson, PT & Shaw, I (eds.) (2000). *Ancient Egyptian Materials and Technology.* Cambridge University Press.

Normand, E & Boesch, C (2009). Sophisticated Euclidean maps in forest chimpanzees. *Animal Behaviour* 77, 1195–1201.

Normand, E et al. (2009). Forest chimpanzees (*Pan troglodytes verus*) remember the location of numerous fruit trees. *Animal Cognition* 12, 797–807.

Oakley, KP (1932). Woods used by the ancient Egyptians. *Analyst* 57, 158–159.

O'Leary, MA et al. (2013). The placental mammal ancestor and the post-K–Pg radiation of placentals. *Science* 339, 662–667.

Plutarch. *Moralia,* trans FC Babbitt (1931). Harvard University Press.

Porteous, A.(2005). *The Lore of the Forest.* Cosimo Classics.

Prentice, R (2010). *The Exchange of Goods and Services in Pre-Sargonic Lagash.* Alter Orient und Altes Testament 368. Ugarit-Verlag, Münster.

Renne, P et al. (2015). State shift in Deccan volcanism at the Cretaceous-Paleogene boundary, possibly induced by impact. *Science* 350, 76–78.

Sayers, K, Raghanti, MA & Lovejoy, CO (2012). Human evolution and the chimpanzee referential doctrine. *Annual Review of Anthropology* 41, 119–138.

Schulte, P et al. (2010). The Chicxulub asteroid impact and mass extinction at the Cretaceous–Paleogene boundary. *Science* 327, 1214–1218.

Shi, J et al. (2014). An ethnobotanical study of the less known wild edible figs (genus *Ficus*) native to Xishuangbanna, Southwest China. *Journal of Ethnobiology and Ethnomedicine* 10, 68.

Stanford, CB (2012). Chimpanzees and the behavior of *Ardipithecus ramidus*. *Annual Review of Anthropology* 41, 139–149.

Theophrastus. *Enquiry into Plants*, trans. A. Hort (1916). W.Heinemann.

Watts, DP et al. (2012). Diet of chimpanzees (*Pan troglodytes schweinfurthii*) at Ngogo, Kibale National Park, Uganda, 1. diet composition and diversity. *American Journal of Primatology* 74, 114–129.

White, TD et al. (2009). *Ardipithecus ramidus* and the paleobiology of early hominids. *Science* 326, 75–86.

White, TD et al. (2015). Neither chimpanzee nor human, *Ardipithecus* reveals the surprising ancestry of both. *Proceedings of the National Academy of Sciences* 112, 4877–4884.

White, TD, Suwa, G & Asfaw, B (1994). *Australopithecus ramidus*, a new species of early hominid from Aramis, Ethiopia. *Nature* 371, 306–312.

WoldeGabriel, G et al. (2009). The geological, isotopic, botanical, invertebrate, and lower vertebrate surroundings of *Ardipithecus ramidus*. *Science* 326, 65–65e1–65e5.

Wrangham, RW et al. (1993). The value of figs to chimpanzees. *International Journal of Primatology* 14, 243–256.

Wrangham, RW et al. (1994). Seed dispersal by forest chimpanzees in Uganda. *Journal of Tropical Ecology* 10, 355–368.

Zohary, D, Hopf, M & Weiss, E (2012). *Domestication of Plants in the Old World*. (4th edn). Oxford University Press.

SOURCES USED IN CHAPTER TEN

American Public Media (2011). Wangari Maathai – Planting the Future [transcript]. *On Being with Krista Tippett*. 29 September 2011.

Sources

Anderson, D (2005). *Histories of the Hanged: The Dirty War in Kenya and the End of Empire*. Weidenfeld.

Beech, MWH (1913). A ceremony at a mugumu or sacred fig-tree of the A-Kikuyu of East Africa. *Man* 13, 86–89.

Beech, MWH (1913). The sacred fig-tree of the A-Kikuyu of East Africa. *Man* 13, 4–6.

Berman, B & Lonsdale, J (1992). *Unhappy Valley: Conflict in Kenya & Africa. Book 2: Violence and Ethnicity*. Ohio University Press.

Biles, P (2012). Mau Mau massacre documents revealed [online article]. BBC Online (30 November 2012).

Cagnolo, C (1933). *The Akikuyu. Their Customs, Traditions and Folklore*. Mathari Press.

Chappell, S (2011). Airpower in the Mau Mau conflict: the government's chief weapon. *RUSI Journal* 156, 64–70.

Davidson, B (1994). The motives of the Mau Mau. *London Review of Books*, (24 February 1994), 12.

Films Media Group (2009). *Wangari Maathai: For Our Land* [documentary film].

Gathogo, J (2013). Environmental management and African indigenous resources: echoes from Mutira Mission, Kenya (1912-2012). *Studia Historiae Ecclesiasticae* 39, 33–56.

Henderson, I & Goodhart, P (1958). *The Hunt for Kimathi*. Hamish Hamilton.

Hewitt, P (2008). *Kenya Cowboy: A Police Officer's Account of the Mau Mau Emergency*. 30 Degrees South Publishers.

Hughes, L (2002). Moving the Maasai: A colonial misadventure. DPhil thesis. University of Oxford.

Huxley, E (1991). *Nine Faces of Kenya*. The Harvill Press.

Kamenju wa Mwangi, JW (2008). Gikuyu origins [online article]. 13 November 2008). www.mukuyu.wordpress.com.

Karangi, MM (2008). Revisiting the roots of Gĩkũyũ culture through the sacred Mũgumo tree. *Journal of African Cultural Studies* 20, 117–132.

Karanja, J (2009). *The Missionary Movement in Colonial Kenya: The Foundation of Africa Inland Church*. Cuvillier Verlag.

Kenyatta, J (1965). *Facing Mt. Kenya: The Tribal Life of the Gikuyu*. Vintage.

Leakey, LSB (1977). *The Southern Kikuyu before 1903. Volume 1*. Academic Press.

Maathai, W (2006). *Unbowed: A Memoir*. Alfred A. Knopf.

Maathai, W (2010). *Replenishing the Earth: Spiritual Values for Healing Ourselves and the World*. Doubleday.

Merton, L & Dater, A (2008). *Taking Root: The Vision of Wangari Maathai* [documentary film]. Marlboro Productions.

Muiruri, S (1999). MPs, Maathai beaten at forest. *Daily Nation*, 9 January 1999.

Mwangi, E (1998). Colonialism, self-governance and forestry in Kenya: Policy, practice and outcomes. *Research in Public Affairs*. University of Indiana.

National Assembly (Kenya) (1995). Parliamentary Debate. Points of Order: Protection of mugumo tree in Thika. *Kenya National Assembly Official Record (Hansard)*, 20 July 1995, 1631–1632.

National Assembly (Kenya) (1996). Parliamentary Debate. Question 022: Maintenance of worshipping places. *Kenya National Assembly Official Record (Hansard)*, 9 May 1996, 737–738.

National Assembly (Kenya) (2002). Parliamentary Debate. *Kenya National Assembly Official Record (Hansard)*, 6 August 2002, 2082.

Ng'ang'a, W (2006). *Kenya's Ethnic Communities: Foundation of the Nation*. Gatundu Publishers Limited.

Ngugi, T (2013). Mugumo trees and the odd ambivalence of Kibaki. *The East African*, 19 January 2013.

Njagih, M (2010). KWS to market Kimathi tree 'mailbox' as historic tourist attraction [online article]. *Standard Digital*, 3 June 2010.

Njagih, M (2010). Secrets of old tree that was Mau Mau post office. *East African Standard*, 3 June 2010.

Nthamburi, Z (ed.) (1991). *From Mission to Church: A Handbook of Christianity in East Africa*. Uzima Press.

Ofcansky, TP & Maxon, RM (2000). *Historical Dictionary of Kenya*. Scarecrow Press.

Overton, JD (1990). Social control and social engineering: African reserves in Kenya 1895–1920. *Environment and Planning D: Society and Space* 8, 163–174.

Sandgren, DP (1982). Twentieth century religious and political divisions among the Kikuyu of Kenya. *African Studies Review* 25, 195–207.

Truth, Justice and Reconciliation Commission (2013). *The Final Report of the Truth Justice and Reconciliation Commission of Kenya*.

Walker, ES (1962). *Treetops Hotel*. Robert Hale Publishing.

Wamagatta, EN (2009). *The Presbyterian Church of East Africa: An Account of Its Gospel Missionary Society Origins, 1895–1946*. Peter Lang Publishing.

SOURCES USED IN CHAPTER ELEVEN

Ahmed, S et al. (2009). Wind-borne insects mediate directional pollen transfer between desert fig trees 160 kilometers apart. *Proceedings of the National Academy of Sciences* 106, 20342–20347.

Anon. (1885). The results of the Krakatoa eruption. *Science* 6: 291–293.

Ball, EE & Johnson, RW (1976). Volcanic history of Long Island, Papua New Guinea. In: RW Johnson (ed) *Volcanism in Australasia*. Elsevier.

Blong, RJ (1982). *The Time of Darkness: Local Legends and Volcanic Reality in Papua New Guinea*. University of Washington Press.

Compton, SG et al. (1988). The colonization of the Krakatau islands by fig wasps and other chalcids (Hymenoptera, Chalcidoidea). *Philosophical Transactions of the Royal Society B* 322, 459-490.

Cook, S, Singadan, R & Thornton, IWB (2001). Colonization of an island volcano, Long Island, Papua New Guinea, and an emergent island, Motmot, in its caldera lake. IV. Colonization by non-avian vertebrates. *Journal of Biogeography* 28, 1353-1363.

Dampier, W (1729). *A Continuation of a Voyage to New Holland, Etc. in the Year 1699 by William Dampier.* John and James Knapton.

Guevara, S, Laborde, J & Sanchez-Rio, G (2006). Rain forest regeneration beneath the canopy of fig trees isolated in pastures of Los Tuxtlas, Mexico. *Biotropica* 36, 99–108.

Hefferan, D & Hess, B (2013). Can *Ficus* sp. forests be restored through vegetative propagation? [research poster]. Drake University.

Johnson, RW (2013). *Fire Mountains of the Islands. A History of Volcanic Eruptions and Disaster Management in Papua New Guinea and the Solomon Islands.* The Australian National University.

Lomáscolo SB et al. (2010). Dispersers shape fruit diversity in *Ficus* (Moraceae). *Proceedings of the National Academy of Sciences* 107, 14668–14672.

New, TR, Smithers, CN & Marshall, AT (2005). Ian Walter Boothroyd Thornton (1926-2002). *Historical Records of Australian Science* 16, 91–106.

Schipper et al. (2001). Colonization of an island volcano, Long Island, Papua New Guinea, and an emergent island, Motmot, in its caldera lake. III. Colonization by birds. *Journal of Biogeography* 28, 1339–1352.

Shanahan, M et al. (2001). Colonization of an island volcano, Long Island, Papua New Guinea, and an emergent island, Motmot, in its caldera lake. V. Colonization by figs (*Ficus* spp.), their dispersers and pollinators. *Journal of Biogeography* 28, 1365–1377.

Shilton, LA & Whittaker, RJ (2010). The role of pteropodid bats in re-establishing tropical forests on Krakatau. In: *Island Bats: Evolution, Ecology, and Conservation*. University of Chicago Press, pp. 176–215.

Shilton, LA et al. (1999). Old World fruit bats can be long-distance seed dispersers through extended retention of viable seeds in the gut. *Proceedings of the Royal Society of London*, B 266, 219–223.

Smithsonian Institution National Museum of Natural History Global Volcanism Program: Long Island [online report]. http://volcano.si.edu/volcano.cfm?vn=251050.

Thornton, IWB (1996). *Krakatau: The Destruction and Reassembly of an Island Ecosystem*. Cambridge, MA: Harvard University Press, 346.

Thornton, IWB, Compton, SG & Wilson, CN (1996). The role of animals in the colonization of the Krakatau islands by fig trees (*Ficus* species). *Journal of Biogeography* 23, 577-592.

Thornton, IWB (2001). Colonization of an island volcano, Long Island, Papua New Guinea, and an emergent island, Motmot, in its caldera lake. I. General introduction. *Journal of Biogeography* 28, 1299–1310.

Zahawi, RA (2008). Instant trees: Using giant vegetation stakes in tropical forest restoration. *Forest Ecology and Management* 255, 3013–3016.

SOURCES USED IN CHAPTER TWELVE

Blakesley, D & Elliott, S (2003). Thailand, restoration of seasonally dry tropical forest using the Framework Species Method [online report]. Forest Restoration Research Unit, Chiang Mai University.

Elliott, S & Kuaraksa, C (2008). Producing framework tree species for restoring forest ecosystems in northern Thailand. *Small-Scale Forestry* 7, 403-415.

Elliott, S et al. (2003). Selecting framework tree species for restoring seasonally dry tropical forests in northern Thailand based on field performance. *Forest Ecology and Management* 184, 177–191.

Elliott, S, Anusarnsunthorn, V & Blakesley, D (1998). *Forests for the future: Growing and Planting Native Trees for Restoring Forest Ecosystems.* Within Design Co. Ltd, Chiang Mai.

Goosem, SP & Tucker, NIJ (1995). *Repairing the Rainforest: Theory and practice of rainforest re-establishment in North Queensland's wet tropics.* Wet Tropics Management Authority, Cairns, Australia.

Hansen, MC et al. (2013). High-resolution global maps of 21st-century forest cover change. *Science* 342, 850-853.

Kim, D-H, Sexton, JO, & Townshend, JR (2015). Accelerated deforestation in the humid tropics from the 1990s to the 2000s. *Geophysical Research Letters* 42, 3495-3501.

Kuaraksa, C & Elliott, S (2012). The use of Asian *Ficus* species for restoring tropical forest ecosystems. *Restoration Ecology* 21, 86–95.

Pakkad, G et al. (2001). Forest restoration planting in northern Thailand. *Proceedings of the SE-Asian Moving Workshop on Conservation, Management and Utilisation of Forest Genetic Resources,* Thailand, 25 February 2001.

Sinhaseni, K (2008). Natural establishment of tree seedlings in forest restoration trials at Ban Mae Sa Mai. Chiang Mai Province. MSc Thesis, Graduate School, Chiang Mai University.

Toktang, T (2005). The effects of forest restoration on the species diversity and composition of a bird community in Doi Suthep-Pui National Park, Thailand, from 2002 to 2003. MSc Thesis, Department of Biology, Faculty of Science, Chiang Mai University.

Toktang, T, Elliott, S & Gale, G (2005). The effects of forest restoration on the species diversity and composition of a bird community in Doi Suthep-Pui National Park. *Natural History Bulletin of the Siam Society* 53, 156–157.

Sources

SOURCES USED IN THE EPILOGUE

Anadolu Agency (2016). Muğla's historic structures threatened by trees, plants. *Hurriyet Daily News* 19 February 2016.

Cook, BI et al. (2012). Pre-Columbian deforestation as an amplifier of drought in Mesoamerica. *Geophysical Research Letters* 39, L16706.

Cooke, K (2016). Climate helped trigger Angkor's fall [online article]. climatenewsnetwork.net, 4 March 2016.

Cottee-Jones, HEW (2014). Isolated *Ficus* trees and conservation in human-modified landscapes. DPhil. University of Oxford.

Cottee-Jones, HEW (2015). Isolated *Ficus* trees deliver dual conservation and development benefits in a rural landscape. *Ambio* 44, 678–684.

Cottee-Jones, HEW et al. (2015). Are protected areas required to maintain functional diversity in human-modified landscapes? PLOS One 10, e0123952.

Cottee-Jones, HEW et al. (2016). The importance of *Ficus* (Moraceae) trees for tropical forest restoration. *Biotropica* doi: 10.1111/btp.12304.

Dixit, Y, Hodell, DA & Petrie, CA (2014). Abrupt weakening of the summer monsoon in northwest India 4100 years ago. *Geology* 42, 339–342.

Marris, E (2014). Two-hundred-year drought doomed Indus Valley Civilization [online article]. nature.com, 3 March 2014.

Masson, C (1842). *Narrative of Various Journeys in Balochistan, Afghanistan and the Panjab Including a Residence in Those Countries from 1826 to 1838*. Richard Bentley.

Lansky, EP (2008). *Ficus* spp. (fig): Ethnobotany and potential as anti-cancer and anti-inflammatory agents. *Journal of Ethnopharmacology* 119, 195–213.

Lansky, EP & Paavilainen, HM (2010). *Figs: The Genus* Ficus *(Traditional Herbal Medicines for Modern Times)*. CRC Press.

Turner, BL & Sabloff, JA (2012). Classic Period collapse of the Central Maya Lowlands: Insights about human–environment relationships for sustainability. *Proceedings of the National Academy of Sciences* 109, 13908–13914.

Supporters

Unbound is a new kind of publishing house. Our books are funded directly by readers. This was a very popular idea during the late eighteenth and early nineteenth centuries. Now we have revived it for the internet age. It allows authors to write the books they really want to write and readers to support the writing they would most like to see published.

The names listed below are of readers who have pledged their support and made this book happen. If you'd like to join them, visit: www.unbound.co.uk.

Thomas Adams

Barbara Adolph

Catherine Airlie

Annabelle Aish

Mohamed Alian

Anthony Allen

Charles Alpren

MJM Annett

Argaw Ashine

Johanna Aspel

Shardul Bajikar

Sharon Bakar

Catherine Baker

Mel Bale

Chris Bartlett

Stephen Bass

Lesley Bassford

Philip Bearfield

Alice Bell

Jamie Bell

Michael and Carol Bell
Paul Bigmore
Emma Blackmore-Evans
Jeremy Blott
Margaret Bluman
Steve Blundell
Bill Bold
Charles Boot
Christina Booth
Ron Borchmann
Mary Borders
Dylan Bould
Jaime Martinez Bowness
Maxwell Boykoff
Catherine Brahic
Victoria Brandon
Rania Bratberg
Nick Britton
Chris Brody
Elly Brosius
Catherine Brouwer
Emma Palmer Brown
Joshua Brown
Marie Browne
Dan Burgess
Renata Byrne
Roser Cabré-Verdiell
Jim Cameron
Liz Carlile

Andrew Carter
Andy Carter
Gary Chamberlain
Yun-Peng Chiang
Daniela Chiaretti
Kerry Churchill
Mathew Clayton
Garrett Coakley
Liz Cobain
Soti Coker
Steve Compton
Philip Connor
Emma Cooper
Teresa Corcoran
Michael Cosby
Eden Cottee-Jones
Colin Crewdson
K D
Geoffrey Darnton
Edward Davey
Shoroobini David
Stuart Davidson
Helen de Jode
Márcia de Lucena
 Washington
Susan Deakin
Igor Debski
Benny Declerck
David Charles Dewsnap

Mark Diacono

Hans Dols

Wendalynn Donnan

Joanna Eden

Markus Eichhorn

James Fahn

Ian Ferguson

Suzanne Fisher-Murray

David Fogarty

Charlotte Forfieh

Francesca Forrest

Jale Forrest

Carol and John Forward

Leif John Fosse

Isobel Frankish

Edward Franks

Emanuela Furiosi

Laura Furones

Lucia Galvez-Bravo

Mark Gamble

Mark Garner

Rose George

Khurshid Ghani

Barbara Giovanardi and
  David Lewis

Carol and Mick Glasson

Rosalind Goodrich

Gabby Grandison

Clair Grant-Salmon

Oli Greenfield

Nick Greenwood

Maryanne Grieg-Gran

Jonah Gubbay

Joydeep Gupta

John Guthrie

Stephen Hampshire

Harriet and Chris

Clay Harris

Jane Harrison

Rhett D. Harrison

Caitlin Harvey

Luke Hasler

Jonathan Haynes

Sophie Hebden

Caspar Henderson

Liz Hensor

Ced Hesse

Marcus Hickson

Sarah Hill

Dan Hoare

Elizabeth Hodge

Peter Howard-Dobson

Jacob Howe

Marie Hrynczak

Nicola Hughes

Saleemul Huq

Richard Ingleby

Johari Ismail

Paul Jabore
Franke James
Charlotte Jandér
Robert Jazwinski
Angela Jeanne
Peter Kavanagh
Nicole Kenton
Fozia Khanam
Matthew Kidd
Dan Kieran
Kevin Kieran
Jaspreet Kindra
Margaret Kinnaird
Alex Kirby
David Koehne
Ido L
Maureen Laverack
Jimmy Leach
Garth Leder
Daren Lee
Eric and Noelle Leigh
Anna Lewington
Kate Lewis
Mun-Keat Looi
Pauline Loven
DeAndra Lupu
Lucy MacDonald
J MacGregor
David Mackay

Duncan Macqueen
Kali Madden
Yvonne Maddox
Marion Mako
Martina Manna
Elliott Mannis
Jeremy Marchant
Josephine Marchant
Emma Marris
Ehsan Masood
Christine Maxwell
James Mayers
Gordon McGranahan
Sandra McGuire
Jerry Meislik
Chris Menzel
George Micallef
Lenard Milich
Simon Milledge
Chris Mills
Laurence Mitchell
Paul Mitchell
John Mitchinson
Essam Yassin Mohammed
Duncan Moir
Kris Montague
Simone Moore
Iris Mueller
Judy Munday

Kate Munro
Declan Murphy
Stu Nathan
Beverly Natividad
Carlo Navato
Jocelyn Newmarch
Tom Fig Newton
Tess Nicholson
Micah Nilsson
Dave Nimmo
Gregory Norminton
Sakthi Norton
Dave Nunn
Damon O'Driscoll
Georgia Odd
Jeff Ollerton
Michael Opoku-Forfieh
Sarah Chalmers Page
Coralie Palmer
William Palmer
Rosamund Annett Parnell
Vish Patel
Sarah Patmore
Antony Peattie
Yan-Qiong Peng
Rodrigo Pereira
Rory Perkins
John Pettitt
Michel Pimbert

Lucy Calderón Pineda
Ross Piper
Justin Pollard
Alan Precious
Alan Precious and Family
Simon Preuveneers
Frank Quain
Marie and Arthur Quinn
Wasantha Kumara
 Ramanayake
Jean-Yves Rasplus
Kate Raworth
Robert Zhao Renhui
Philippa Richards
Darren Roberts
Mari Roberts
Lucile Robinson
Lucy Robinson
The Robinson Family
Dom Rodgers
Stian Rødland
Nina Rønsted
Elizabeth Rowlands
Angharad Ruttley
Otilene Santos
David Satterthwaite
Sebastian Schrader
Leslie Scott
Karen Sellwood

Supporters

Jennifer and John Shanahan
Noah Shanahan
Shelly Sharon
Rosie Sharpe
Sue Sharpe
Kelly Shemirani
Vineeta Shetty
Linda Siegele
Moira Simpson
Susan Sluglett
Mark Smedley
Sam Smit
Kate Smith
Lynn Smith
Nigel Smith
Peter James Smith
Stuart Snaith
Valerie Sonnenthal
Richard Soundy
Neil Starr
Elspeth Steel
Kathryn Stevenson
Lindsay Stewart
David Stokes
Martin Storey
Krystyna Swiderska
Geraldine A Sylver -
  O Malley
Padma T V

Cecilia Tacoli
Elspeth Tavaci
Rianne ten Veen
Frances Tew
Branden Thomas
Jeff Tollefson
Adrian Tompkins
Paul Tompsett
Margaret Tongue
Camilla Toulmin
Matthew Toy
Catrin Treadwell
Steve Trent
Nick Turner
Lea Turunen
Maria Valencia
Gary Vernon
Bas Verschuuren
Linda Verstraten
Gaia Vince
Paolo Viscardi
Richard Visick
Halina Ward
Angharad Westmore
Doug White
David Whitmer
Thomas Wigley
David Wildgoose
Andrew Wille

Kate Wilson
Jeneni Withers
Gretchen Woelfle
Piyaporn Wong
Shadia Wood
Jamie Woolley

Sharon Worrell
Matt Wright
Rachel Wright
Linda Youdelis
Steven Zwick

hamlyn

THE
Rescue Dog

Gwen Bailey

Foreword by
Katie Boyle

'For Beau – who helped me realise how much could be achieved.'

Author's note
I have referred to 'he' rather than 'she' throughout
this book. There is no reason for this other than to save
writing he/she or it each time. There is no difference
between the worth of male and female dogs –
both have qualities that can make them rewarding,
lifelong companions.

Executive Editor: Julian Brown
Editor: Tarda Davison-Aitkins
Creative Director: Keith Martin
Design: Les Needham
Picture Research: Zoe Holtermann
Production Controller: Sarah Scanlon

First published in Great Britain in 2000
by Hamlyn, an imprint of
Octopus Publishing Group Limited
2–4 Heron Quays, London, E14 4JP

A catalogue record for this book is available from the British Library

Produced by Toppan
Printed in China

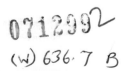

Contents

7 Foreword

8 Introduction

CHAPTER 1
10 Which is the Right Dog for You?

CHAPTER 2
28 Finding Your Perfect Rescue Dog

CHAPTER 3
44 Early Days and Introductions

CHAPTER 4
62 Building a Successful Relationship

CHAPTER 5
78 Understanding Your Dog's Needs

CHAPTER 6
90 Essential Training

CHAPTER 7
100 Coping with Shyness and Aggression

CHAPTER 8
114 Alone at Home

CHAPTER 9
130 Curing Minor Behaviour Problems

CHAPTER 10
150 Beau's Story

158 Useful Addresses and Index

Katie Boyle and her
Battersea Belles.

Foreword

Rescue dogs of all sorts, sizes and ages have always been an integral part of my own life. The only thing they had in common was that they'd all been abandoned or were victims of cruelty. This left them with loads of hang-ups, both mental and physical.

A long time ago in my native Italy, I was taught that being gentle and kind to them would, somehow, be sufficient. That loving them would make them understand us and would make them want to please us and do as they were told. This well-meaning, but amateurish attitude to dogs in need was a good start, but not enough. I learned later of the 'Think Dog' approach and how best to communicate with them. The methods and information in this book take us further and teach us what else we need to do to ensure a perfect partnership.

I've watched Gwen Bailey's rehabilitating methods in action. Her gentle, calm approach and sixth sense of understanding towards her two- and four-legged pupils are so reassuring to both dogs and people alike, and remarkably effective.

Sadly, there are still, and always will be, far too many homeless dogs to fill the number of homes available, and, every day, hundreds of healthy young animals are put to sleep. Luckily, there is also an increasing number of people who would like to give a good and happy home to an adult dog, but who are apprehensive of the problems that are likely to crop up. For them, this book will be reassuring and a much needed 'bible' to turn to for direction. I shall keep it as my permanent bedside reading too.

I am so glad what Gwen has filled a much-needed gap for dog lovers. This book is a treasure chest of information and guidance.

KATIE BOYLE

Introduction

Taking on an adult dog can be an exciting and rewarding experience that saves a dog's life and provides a family with a much loved friend. Making sure you are well prepared before taking a new pet into your home is the object of this book. It aims to give you the information you need to choose the right dog for you and your family and to make it easy to start off your relationship on the right foot. It will also provide ideas for teaching your new dog how you want him to behave, aid understanding and communication and will ease you through the early stages when you will both be adjusting to living together.

It is a sad fact that many dogs that are acquired with such high expectations as puppies do not stay with one set of owners for life. For the past 10 years, I have worked as the Animal Behaviourist for The Blue Cross, one of Britain's largest animal welfare charities. I have helped to sort out problems which have arisen between a new dog and its owner, given advice to new owners to help dogs settle in more easily and provide a back-up advice for when anything goes wrong. This book is an attempt to reach people who would otherwise not benefit from this service. Dogs and new owners are so varied that a book cannot possibly contain all you need to know, but it can give you some important guidelines to start you off on the right foot and help you avoid basic mistakes that can so easily result in the dog being returned. It will help you to select and keep a companion that will, hopefully, spend many happy years as an important member of your family.

Authors acknowledgements

I would like to thank John Rogerson, a talented and resourceful friend, who taught me so much about dog behaviour. The quality of the information he gave was such that I have been able to introduce behavioural concepts to help with rescue and rehoming at The Blue Cross and at other shelters throughout the world. Without his generosity in sharing his knowledge none of this would have been possible. I would also like to thank others who have shared their ideas and information so willingly with me over the years. They include Ian Dunbar, Tony Orchard, Peter Neville and the late John Fisher.

Several friends read the manuscript. They are Paul Barney, Katie Boyle, Andrew Edney, Elaine Grainger, Tony Orchard, Julie Sellors, Patches Silverstone and my parents. Thank you to you all for your help, encouragement and friendship.

As my employer for the past decade, The Blue Cross also deserves my thanks for allowing me to develop ways of introducing behaviour work to the rescue world. This has allowed me to help more dogs and owners than I would have thought possible and has given us new techniques and experience to pass on to others working in the field.

Publishers acknowledgements

Hamlyn would like to thank the The Blue Cross and the following people for giving up their time, lending their dogs and modelling in this book; Sally Reed; Charlotte Potts; Ginny Mabbort; Josh Perry; Linda Dixon; Tina Kew; Selina Williams; Alex Gilmore; Jo Heatherington; Lin Rogers; Georgina Parker (all from The Blue Cross); Adam Ward; Peter Burt; Mr & Mrs May; D. Millard; Carl & Louise Cross; John Stone; Kay Kentfield; Ian Shields; Diane Ward; Diane Blackburn; Samantha Visick; Andrea Fraser; T. Millard & Family; Sharon Lum; Sarah Allcock; Helen Murray; Dinah Wilkins and Katrina Moore.

The Blue Cross is one of Britain's leading animal welfare charities, providing advice, practical care, veterinary treatment and rehoming for thousands of companion animals each year.

CHAPTER

1

Which is the Right Dog for You?

A rescue dog can be a delight or a disaster. Which it is depends largely on choosing the right dog to suit your personality and that of your family. Every owner or family is different and will have different requirements. Fortunately, rescue dogs come in a wide variety of shapes, sizes and temperaments. All you have to do is put some time and thought into finding one that will be exactly right for you.

Rescue dogs come in many different shapes, sizes and temperaments.

New owners will often base their choice of dog on appearance only. They will often be persuaded by a dog that most closely resembles one they had as a child or previously owned. It is not wise to choose a dog in this way as no consideration is given to the temperament of that particular dog. A dog that attracts you instantly may bite your children or fight with your other dog, whereas a dog that has been chosen to have the right mixture of characteristics and temperament traits is much more likely to settle in easily and become a perfect pet. Having said that, appearances do count and it is also important that you are able to fall in love with the dog that you choose.

Deciding what you want

If you decide to skip this part, be warned that you may end up with a rescued dog that is less than perfect for you. A dog with traits that do not suit you, such as one with too much energy for

Small dogs are often in short supply at rescue centres as they are more popular than larger dogs.

your lifestyle, or one which is constantly harassing your cat/rabbit/child, can be awful to live with. Such dogs may make a perfectly nice pet for someone else, but you will have the wrong dog for you. Careful thought at this stage can help you to avoid the common trap of falling for the first pretty face you see. So often this results in a frustrated dog and a disappointed owner. It's a bit like finding a husband/wife/partner really!

Before you even go near an animal shelter, you need to sit down with all the people who will be involved with the new dog on a regular basis and find out what sort of dog you are looking for. There are some fundamental questions that will need answers before you can begin your search. These fall into two categories – physical attributes and temperament traits.

PHYSICAL ATTRIBUTES

You will probably find it easier to decide which physical attributes would suit you rather than what type of temperament you are looking for, but both are equally important.

Size

The size of your home and garden will limit the size of dog that it is practical for you to keep. A large dog in a small flat is not sensible and a little one that can curl up in the corner of the sofa may be more suitable. Size is often less important than how active a dog likes to be – see page 16. However, be realistic about the size of dog that may suit your home and lifestyle. Even if you have always wanted to own a Newfoundland or a Bernese Mountain Dog, you may not have the facilities to keep one properly.

Consider also what you want a dog for. If your lifestyle dictates that you often need to take your dog on a train and bus, a little dog you can tuck under your arm may be more appropriate. If you live in an area where it's dangerous to walk the streets, you may want a dog that at least looks as though it will protect you.

If you already have a dog, it is important to get one of a similar size for when they play together or fight. Boisterous play between dogs of unequal size can result in substantial injuries to

FACTORS TO CONSIDER

Before you choose your dog, you must decide which physical attributes and which temperament traits are important to you. Use the following check list to remind you what you need to consider.

Physical attributes:
- Size
- Male or female
- Neutered or not
- Age
- Type of coat

Temperament traits:
- Which breed?
- Good with children
- Good with other pets
- Good with strangers
- Good with other dogs
- Energy levels
- How strong-willed?
- How cuddly?
- How trainable?
- How independent?

the smaller dog. Similarly, if they do fight during the settling in period, the damage to the smaller animal can be potentially fatal if there is a large difference in size.

Male or female?

There is more chance of finding a dog to suit you if you decide you want a male. There are slightly more males than females in rescue centres and many potential owners tend to prefer females because they assume that bitches will be better behaved and more biddable. While it is true that male dogs are more likely to get into trouble and behave badly at some time in their lives, particularly during adolescence, female dogs also cause their fair share of troubles.

Dogs that have suffered physical or mental abuse are sometimes looking for a home. They can make wonderful pets.

Approximately six males to every four females are seen by pet behaviour counsellors. Male dogs tend to be slightly more aggressive and competitive from an early age, which can lead to difficulties if not channelled in the right direction. However, a good-natured male dog may make a much better pet than a bad-tempered female and, as the character of an adult dog is already formed, it is wise to leave your options open rather than limit yourself because of the misconception that one sex will be better than the other.

The only time when it is worth paying particular attention to whether a dog is male or female is if you already have a dog. Dogs of the opposite sex living together in a household are usually far more likely to get along than two of the same sex and will have fewer arguments. But again this depends on the individual's character (see page 15 for more information on choosing a dog to live with an existing dog).

Neutered or entire?

Many of the bigger rescue organisations neuter all their animals as a matter of course. Usually this is because they see, at first hand, the tragedy of too many pets for too few good homes. Neutering ensures that reproduction stops with the pets that go through their hands.

Generally, neutered animals have the advantage. Neutered male dogs are less likely to get into

*Young or old? Age is
often one of the easiest
criteria to decide on.*

trouble with other males, less likely to mount soft furnishings or
people, and less likely to get out and roam or be frustrated if
there is a bitch in season nearby. Neutered females do not have
the nuisance of seasons every six months. And all neutered
animals are less likely to develop hormone-related problems
later in life.

Age

More younger dogs, usually those between one and two years'
old, are given up to rescue centres than older dogs. The younger
a dog is, the more active it is likely to be as, like humans, dogs
tend to slow down as they get older. A young dog is also more
likely to have less than perfect behaviour because people often
acquire puppies that they neglect and give up to a rescue home
or turn out when the cute puppy stage has worn off.

    While a younger dog will be less set in its ways and will adapt
itself more readily to a new lifestyle, dogs of all ages are very
adaptable and most will fit in eventually. You can teach an old
dog new tricks, but it may take slightly longer than teaching the
same tricks to a younger one. Older dogs will live for fewer years,
which may be an advantage if you are elderly yourself. They will
be more likely to tolerate being left at home while you go to work
and they will hopefully have a track record of living successfully
as a pet dog. Difficult dogs are more likely to have to be
euthanased at an early age.

*'You <u>can</u> teach
an old dog new
tricks ... '*

Coat type

Coat types can be roughly divided into short (labrador),
medium (collie or spaniel), long or thick (samoyed or
bearded collie), or the type that needs to be clipped regularly
(poodle). Special care is needed for long or thick hair or hair
that needs to be clipped and you need to decide if you want
that level of responsibility.

Short coats shed hairs that may weave themselves into your clothes in a way that you never thought possible and medium length coats seem to bring back most of the mud you encounter on a walk. There are advantages and disadvantages to every type; be prepared for extra mess with whatever type of coat you choose.

TEMPERAMENT TRAITS

A dog's temperament is more important than how it looks.

Breed

The original dog breeds were developed for different jobs in the service of man and have different characteristics and abilities as a result. If you have your heart set on a pedigree dog, read about its temperament traits in the various breed books available, but do read between the lines. Such books will rarely tell you the pitfalls of the breed, but you can often work these out for yourself. Remember that every positive trait has a down side to it if it is not correctly channelled or it does not suit your household. For example, for 'lively' read 'can be exhausting', for 'determined and strong-willed' read 'can be stubborn and domineering', for 'good guard dog' read 'can be aggressive'. Ask people who already own one of your chosen breed about the good and bad traits in their dogs.

Dogs bred for working purposes, such as sheep dogs, gundogs or some hounds, often have natural energy levels that enable them to keep active all day. In an average home, this amount of energy is often too much and an owner will need to be inventive in finding outlets for it. Conversely, dogs bred for the show ring have often inherited genes that makes them lazier, but not always. Crossbreeds and

Crosses of breeds like collies usually inherit a strong desire to chase, play and be very active.

GENETIC TRAITS AND TENDENCIES

This is a general guide based on a cross-section of dogs of these breeds or crosses. It will, however, be possible to find dogs from these categories who do not fit this description.

BORDER COLLIE
Very active; prone to fears, noise phobias and nipping when scared; forms very strong bonds with owner; loyal; likes to chase; playful; needs lots of exercise and stimulation; often needs experienced owners.

COLLIE CROSS
Very reactive; prone to shyness; noise sensitive; can nip when severely frightened; easily scared; sensitive; forms very strong, rewarding bond with owner; loyal; playful; likes to chase; active and energetic.

DOBERMANN
Sensitive; can be strong willed; can be boisterous and clumsy; forms strong bond with owners.

GERMAN SHEPHERD CROSS
Likely to be good guard dog, but prone to territorial aggression, especially if shy or fearful; forms strong, rewarding bond with owner; loyal; sensitive; very loving to family; likes to chase; often quite vocal.

LURCHER/GREYHOUND
Friendly; independent and tends not to over-bond to owners; likes to run and hunt on a walk, but usually calm around the house; inclined to show predatory behaviour to smaller animals.

LABRADOR CROSS
Less reactive than collie crosses; generally good natured and tolerant; playful; can be boisterous; inclined to chew when young; can be good for a lively household.

SPANIEL
Usually very biddable; playful and willing to please; often have gentle, loving nature; good family dog if raised correctly; can be possessive of food and toys; needs lots of exercise.

STAFFORDSHIRE BULL TERRIER
Can be problematic with other dogs, but often very nice with humans; can be quite vocal; physically insensitive and may pull on lead; can be a good family dog and enjoy games with toys; can show sustained aggression if upset.

TERRIER CROSS
Lively; curious; independent; full of character; can show sustained aggression if upset; can be strong-willed.

If you have children, finding a dog that is used to them and enjoys their company is essential.

mongrels will have inherited a combination of genes and the advantage of taking on such an adult dog is that its genes have already fulfilled their potential and you can see exactly what you are getting.

Good with children

You will need to decide how important it is that your new dog will be friendly and unafraid of children. This is obviously one of the most important considerations if you have children or grandchildren, or if other children visit you on a regular basis.

Bear in mind that children vary enormously and a dog that has been brought up with older children may not be able to tolerate toddlers that fall on him, pinch him or pull his ears. Teenagers, who are often going through difficult times, may have once been intentionally cruel to a dog, which may then be very wary of people of similar ages. Or the dog who fits all your other requirements may have been teased by school-age children of which you have three at home.

Different dogs will have different tolerance levels to things that children are likely to do them. If you have loud, boisterous children, you will need a dog that can tolerate this. If you have quiet, gentle children, your dog will not need to be so tolerant. Make a family decision about what age groups your dog will need to be friendly with and tolerant of.

Good with other pets

If you have a cat or a smaller pet, such as a rabbit or bird, you will need to select a dog that does not want to chase, catch and eat it. Cats, especially, can suffer from the unwanted attentions of a new dog and may take to living outside because it is too unsafe to live inside. Selecting a dog that will quickly settle in with a cat is not easy, but it should be a major consideration if you have one.

Good with strangers

Consider how many visitors you have and how many strangers you and your family meet and interact with on a regular basis. This will tell you how important it is for your new dog to be unafraid and sociable with strangers.

   If you live a quiet life in a fairly isolated area, it will not matter if your dog is unsociable; in fact it may be advantageous since you will probably benefit from its desire to protect you and your territory from unwanted attention. However, if you run a business from home or you live in a busy household with plenty of visitors, if you like to stop and chat to other dog walkers and enjoy taking your dog everywhere with you, you will need one that is friendly and happy in the company of everyone.

A dog that barks at strangers will suit some families but not others.

Good with other dogs

There are two issues to consider when talking about other dogs: how important is it that your new dog gets on with another dog in the family or one that you have regular contact with? And how important is it that he gets on with other dogs when out on walks?

How sociable your new dog is with other dogs will determine how easily he can be taken for walks.

Most dogs will get used to and tolerate another dog that they have regular dealings with, particularly if they are introduced properly. However, being sociable with other dogs you meet outside requires your dog to have more social skills. Living with a dog that is afraid, anxious or aggressive in the company of other dogs may not be too difficult if you plan to take all your exercise in the country, but it could be very tedious if you live in a built-up area and intend to walk in a busy park.

Owning a dog that likes to run and play is ideal if you have a lifestyle to match.

Energy levels

Living with a dog that is always raring to go and that gets up expectantly whenever you make a move is fine if you are the active sort who enjoys plenty of activity and long walks. If you are not, however, it may be simpler to find a dog whose idea of heaven is a warm bed with the occasional wander up the street and back. Matching your new dog's activity level to your own will prevent your new dog becoming frustrated and a nuisance because it is under-exercised and will save you from traipsing the countryside when you would rather be tucked up in a chair with a good book. Getting this right is essential to stress-free ownership.

You will also need to match your desire to play games with your new dog to his desire to play with you. Some dogs are very playful and will constantly present you with a toy or other items in an attempt to encourage you to play. If this is not something you will enjoy, try to find a dog that is not so interested in games.

Dogs that have plenty of mental and physical energy can find it difficult to lie down all day and sleep while their owners are at work. If you have to leave your dog at home for long periods, it is sensible to look for a dog that enjoys sleeping a lot rather than getting an active dog or youngster who will become bored and cause problems when left alone.

'If, however, you are a gentle owner who is very tolerant and indulgent, find a dog that is sensitive and submissive. If you choose a stronger character, he may choose to take control once he has had the opportunity to assess your abilities.'

How strong-willed?

Pushy dogs fare much better with strong-willed owners and gentle dogs are happier with sensitive people. You need to consider how insistent you will be that your dog will conform to your rules. If you or other members of your family will be insistent and can be a bit overbearing at times, choose a dog that has a strong character as you may overpower a weaker character. Dogs with stronger characters usually have more spirit, are more confident and independent, and often learn faster.

If, however, you are a gentle owner who is very tolerant and indulgent, find a dog that is sensitive and submissive. If you choose a stronger character, he may choose to take control once he has had the opportunity to assess your abilities. Choosing a gentle dog if you are a sensitive owner will often result in a trusting and close bond that is beneficial to both parties. Dogs with gentle characters are often more tolerant of children and other animals and are often less confident of their ability to use aggression in a difficult situation.

How cuddly?

Dogs do not naturally hold and hug each other unless they are fighting or mating, whereas humans cuddle each other and other animals as an expression of love and affection. Dogs need to learn that humans do this and learn to tolerate and enjoy it. Some dogs enjoy being touched and cuddled more than others. If you are someone who likes to stroke and hug your dog a lot, find one that enjoys it or you may be disappointed when he starts to avoid you when you reach out to him.

How trainable?

All dogs can be trained once you know how, but some learn faster than others. Some dogs will know a few commands already, but the majority know only the word 'sit'. If you want a really well trained dog, it is best to

find one that is very trainable (see page 32) and acquire the skills needed to train him yourself.

How independent?

Many dogs do not enjoy being separated from their owners. All dogs will have to put up with it once in a while, but if you plan to leave your dog on a regular basis, such as while you are at work, look for a dog that is happy to be left alone. Dogs that are destructive, noisy or dirty when left alone are usually not happy and it would not be wise to take on a dog that does this if you cannot be with it for most of the time.

Finding a dog that does not mind being left alone is essential if you plan to be away from home frequently.

OTHER CHARACTERISTICS TO CONSIDER

There will be other characteristics not listed above that will be special to you and your family. Consider what an average day for your dog will be like and list all the characteristics that would enable your dog to cope easily with it. If you plan to take your dog to work every day, for example, it should enjoy travelling. Problems relating to car travel can be overcome (see page 144), but if your dog will be travelling often, it may be easier and more sensible to choose a dog that enjoys car travel.

Where to find rescue dogs

Once you have your agreed list of physical attributes and temperament traits, the next step is to choose a source of dogs available for adoption. There are many places where unwanted dogs can be found. The major sources are animal centres run by large national charities such as The Blue Cross, large dogs' homes in cities, breed rescue organisations, from friends or through an advertisement, although the latter is not recommended.

Opposite bottom: Staff at a good rescue centre will be able to give you accurate information and help you make your choice.

When you do go to see a particular dog, ensure that the whole family and anyone who will have regular dealings with your dog goes with you. It is essential that everyone likes the dog and gets on with it as much as you do.

RESCUE CENTRES AND DOGS' HOMES

There are many large rescue organisations that have centres around the country such as The Blue Cross, the National Canine Defence League, the RSPCA and the SSPCA. There is also a variety of smaller, independent charities and there is usually a large dogs' home in most major cities, such as The Dogs' Home, Battersea. The larger dogs' homes often have as many animals as the larger rescue organisations keep throughout the entire country. This gives you more choice, but it means that less information is likely to be available about each individual due to the number of dogs that pass through.

There may be more than one centre or home in your area. To find out which one is best, ask other owners of rehomed dogs about their experiences, canvas your local dog training club (which will see many of the 'problem' rescued dogs) and ask your veterinary practice for their recommendation. Excellent facilities are not as important as good management. If centre staff socialise and play with the dogs every day, the dogs will be better adjusted and will fit into your life more

TIP

Always take all of your family with you when you visit a rescue centre to look for a new pet.

Bad behaviour is more likely to be seen at centres where staff do not have the time or inclination to socialise and play with the dogs in their care.

easily. Staff will also get to know them better and will be able to help you choose the right one for you, and you will be more likely to see the true nature of a dog rather than an institutionalised version.

The advantages of obtaining a dog from a reputable rescue centre are that you will be given as much information as possible about the dog you are taking on and your dog will be healthy and will have received a health check prior to leaving. It will probably also be vaccinated, neutered and insured. You should be offered useful advice to help you settle the dog in and an aftercare service if things begin to go wrong after rehoming. If things go dramatically wrong despite everyone's best intentions, the centre will be willing to take the dog back and find it a more suitable home.

An excellent service such as this is expensive for rescue organisations and it is only reasonable to give them a generous donation when you collect your new dog. Remember that they are only able to carry out their work because of donations: none of the UK rescue centres receives any state funding.

If you visit a small rescue centre, you may be unable to find a dog that is perfect for you on your first visit. Try not to be disheartened – the turnover in such establishments is usually quite quick and if you visit a few days later, there will probably be new dogs to see. The more friendly, easy-to-home dogs will go to new homes quite quickly so if you have very stringent requirements you will need to visit the centre often to ensure that your visits coincide with the arrival of new dogs.

BREED RESCUE ORGANISATIONS

If you are determined to own a particular breed of dog and would like to take on an adult rather than a puppy, the easiest route is to contact your nearest rescue organiser for the breed in question. The Kennel Club will be able to give you details of your nearest organisation

Breed rescue organisations vary tremendously in their quality. Some are very good, but some are very poor. They are usually run by a breeder who has many years' experience with a particular breed, but this does not necessarily mean they will be good at matching dogs to prospective owners. Ask around to find out what other's experiences have been; particularly ask your local rescue centre as they will usually have had some contact with each other. Your veterinary practice may also be a useful source of information.

THROUGH A FRIEND

This may be one of the best sources since you will know the dog
and the owner. A good friend will not want to pass on a problem
to you without letting you know first. However, it is unlikely that
you will have a good friend who has to give up their dog at the
very time that you happen to be looking for one. If you take on a
dog because a friend has to give it up rather than because you
are actively looking for one, think very carefully about whether
you really do want it and consider beforehand all that dog
ownership will entail.

VIA AN ADVERTISEMENT

This is probably the worst way to find the ideal dog for you. The
'Free to good home' ads are a potential minefield for new owners
since you will have invested some emotion in the animal before
you even see it. You will have read the description, been told
about its good points over the phone and, by the time you get
there, you will be thinking about where its bed will go and what
colour collar to buy!

Unless there are very obvious flaws in a dog's character and
behaviour, it will be very difficult to make an objective decision
when you see it and you will have the added pressure from the
owner who will want to pass the dog on. If they resort to any form
of emotional blackmail, it will be difficult to resist, particularly if
you have your family with you. My advice is to steer well clear of
finding a rescue dog in this way unless you are very single-
minded and resistant to your emotions.

Why are dogs rehomed?

People give up dogs for rehoming for all sorts of reasons. Often
circumstances will dictate that they can no longer keep the dog.
Owners die, are made redundant, lose their houses, get posted
abroad, divorce and sometimes just cannot cope with life's
pressures and a dog as well. Probably about 40 per cent
of dogs go into the rescue system for these reasons rather than
because there is anything wrong with their behaviour.

That leaves about 60 per cent of dogs that have been given up
because their behaviour is less than perfect. A good proportion
of these are not too badly behaved and will probably be perfectly
all right if placed in a sensible, caring home. These dogs are
usually the young ones whose owners have not put sufficient
care and thought into their upbringing. They will need some

Dogs that are problematic in their first home may become very well behaved in the next if they are given more to do.

work, but will make perfectly good pets.

A much smaller percentage of rescue dogs have a specific behaviour problem or problems that their owners were unable to cope with. Although an owner may be able to work round a problem during the first few years of a dog's life, when dramatic life changes occur, such as divorce or moving to a new area, the dog's problem may become too difficult to cope with. A dog that is perfectly behaved can usually fit into any lifestyle despite difficult circumstances, but a dog with problems is far more likely to be given up at times of emotional or physical upheaval. Such dogs will take their behaviour problems with them into their next home. These can be redeemed, but new owners will need to be aware of the problems so they can make an informed choice. They will also need to know how to reduce and eventually eliminate the problem.

STRAYS

Dogs found straying or abandoned, which are not claimed by their owners after seven days, are often put up for adoption. Unfortunately, nothing is known about these dogs. A small proportion are likely to be genuinely lost, but the majority will have belonged to owners who cared too little or who were too irresponsible to give them up to a rescue organisation. This tells you something about the previous owners of stray animals and it is, therefore, not surprising that there is often a slightly higher number of problem animals among strays than among dogs given up by their owners.

Despite this, strays should not be discounted altogether. Most can be placed in homes and will settle well, but they need more care to determine their characteristics.

Reliability of information

Good rescue organisations will take care to collect detailed information from previous owners to pass on to the next owner, but unfortunately not all owners tell the truth about their dogs. They may be too ashamed to admit they have raised a dog that has problems, they may not be able to see the problems at all or they may feel that the best chance for their dog lies in concealing anything they feel may reduce his chances of finding a home. Good rescue organisations will have experienced staff who are skilled at getting the truth and who are able to extract plenty of information.

The better rescue organisations will also have trained kennel staff who will be able to monitor a dog's behaviour and character while it lives at the kennels. This information can be invaluable in helping to match dogs to new owners. The dog's behaviour traits and problems often become apparent as a dog settles down to life in kennels and it will soon become obvious if the previous owner's testimony was correct or not.

The reliability of any information you receive about a dog will depend on the quality of staff at the centre and will vary considerably from centre to centre and even from person to person. Whether you decide to trust the information is up to you, but even if you do it is wise to have a back up in the form of the assessment procedures on pages 27 to 41. This will help you make your own notes about the dog to compare with the information you have been given. If there is a reasonable match, the chances are that the information from previous owners and kennel staff will have been offered and collected in good faith.

If you can, try to select from any written information a centre may provide a few dogs that look as though they may suit your needs. You will then be less likely to be persuaded by the dogs' appearances. If you have found a rescue centre where the staff are well trained and seem to know what they are talking about, take their advice on which dogs may suit you as they will know their dogs' characters better than you do. Take your time to talk to kennel staff and you may be surprised by how much information they are able to give to you.

Beware of the centre that offers very limited information or none at all. The dogs in these facilities will be no more or less worthy than in any others, but you will be on your own in terms of being able to determine which dog is right for you.

The adoption process

What actually happens at a rescue centre will depend on their procedures. Sometimes you will be shown particular dogs, sometimes you will be shown all the dogs, and sometimes you will be allowed to wander around on your own. You will probably be encouraged to take a potential pet out for a walk to get to know him or to take him into a special meeting room. Although staff will be busy, do ask for their help (see above/page xx). Tell them what type of dog you are looking for and ask for all the information they have on any dogs that suit your requirements. Armed with this information, you can set about assessing the dogs you think may make a suitable pet for you (see the assessment procedures given on pages 27 to 41).

When you have chosen a dog, you will need to reserve it. This will give you and the rescue centre staff time to decide whether this particular dog is right for you. Taking a dog home on the same day you find it is not a good idea as you do need time to make an objective decision. This can be difficult in the excitement generated by the occasion, but it becomes much easier after a few days of reflection. Sadly, this thinking time may not be possible at some of the larger dogs' homes where the pressure for kennel space is great. Try not to feel pressurised into making a decision. A new dog is likely to be with your family for the rest of its life and making a mistake at this stage can lead to much emotional turmoil.

Dogs that are able to spend time with each other and with people while in rescue centres will be more contented than those who are kept isolated.

A good rescue centre will ask you lots of questions about the type of dog you want, what your lifestyle and personality is like and why you want to adopt a dog. Be prepared to answer these questions patiently and honestly since it is in your own interest as well as that of the dog. Centre staff will also want to visit your home to check that you live where you say you do and that any fences around your property are secure. It also gives them a chance to give you more information about your dog and to answer any last minute questions.

A home visit will help to satisfy the staff that your home is just right and they will be able to answer any of your last minute questions.

CHAPTER

2

Finding your Perfect Rescue Dog

Having decided on the temperament traits and physical characteristics you are looking for, the search can now begin in earnest for a dog that matches the blueprint as closely as possible. It may be unrealistic to expect that you will find the perfect dog. If you look hard enough you may do so, but it is more likely that you will find a dog that almost fits your ideal. You can then assess whether or not you can live with the traits that are less than perfect and whether you can change his behaviour sufficiently for him to fit into your lifestyle.

Be realistic about what is achievable. It is not wise, for example, to take a shy dog that is afraid of strangers into a busy, lively and noisy household where it will be the centre of attention. A shy dog can be brought out of its shell with gentle understanding, but is unlikely to ever be the life and soul of a party.

Rescue centres can evoke a variety of emotions in even the most hardened people and it can be difficult to resist what seems to be rows of pitiful eyes and pleading faces. However, if it means you end up with a dog you can be happy with and that can be happy with you, it will be worth it. Do not be persuaded by the argument that unless you take a particular dog it will be put to sleep. It is wrong for rescue centres to use this type of emotional blackmail, however understandable it may be. You cannot save all the dogs in this predicament and you will not be doing the rescue world any favours if you take on a dog only to return it later because it does not fit into your lifestyle. Be single-minded about your search until you find a dog that meets your requirements as closely as possible.

Assessing a dog's character

Before making any assessment of a dog, ensure that he has been in kennels for at least three days. New dogs go through a settling in period during which time they behave in a depressed and unusual way. Only after they have adjusted to their new environment, which takes about three days, do they begin to behave as normal.

Dogs will not behave in kennels as thay would in a home. Information from staff and the results of your own tests will help you to make a realistic assessment of his character.

ASSESSMENT CHECKLIST

You will need to take the following items with you when you assess a dog:

- The whole family
- Titbits
- Toys (ball, tug-of-war toy, squeaky toy)
- Brush
- A small towel

Even after a dog has adjusted to life in kennels, he will not behave as he would in a pet home. Kennels can be hostile places no matter how well the dogs are looked after. This saps the confidence of even the most determined dog and there are fewer opportunities to misbehave. It is possible for a dog to appear perfectly behaved when you meet him in kennels and even when you take him out for a short time, but once he settles in to your home, he will revert to previous bad habits. You will not see the true picture so follow the assessment procedure below to find out more.

The assessment procedure

When you assess any dog, remember that you will see just a brief glimpse of a complex animal's character. While assessments are useful and necessary in helping you choose a dog that will be right for you, dogs do react to whatever is happening to them at the time. A dog may be tired, bored, hungry, lonely or frightened – all such emotions will affect his apparent behaviour. A dog will also behave differently towards you depending on whether you are male or female, and if you resemble someone he knew in his past this too can influence his behaviour.

Right: An initial interested reaction indicates that this dog will enjoy meeting visitors and your friends.

Far right: A fearful aggressive reaction shows that this dog mistrusts strangers and is likely to bark at visitors.

PART ONE

ASSESSMENT IN THE KENNEL

There is no scientific validation for the following assessment procedure at present, but it works for me and I think it is worth passing on. The initial part of the assessment is quick to do and can be done on any dog that looks as though he may have potential.

Approach each dog in exactly the same way and perform the same tests and you will be able to compare their responses. After numerous approaches to different dogs, you will begin to see differences between their reactions that will help you to form some assessment of their character.

From this very simple test, you will be able to tell a lot about the dog if you are patient and observant. Every behaviour has a motivation behind it, even if it is just a backward or forward step. It takes experience to guess accurately what the reasons behind behaviour may be, but everyone can guess. Once you have thought about why a dog may have behaved in a certain way, you can begin to make some assessment of his character and predict how he may behave in the future.

Carry out this test in a small kennel with a wire-mesh door where the dog sleeps or spends a lot of time. There should be no distractions such as people walking past or other dogs barking. If the dog is hungry, looking forward to a walk or has just seen his favourite member of the kennel staff, he will not pay you full attention and your assessment may be inaccurate. Remember to ensure the dog has been in the kennels for at least three days.

Reaction to strangers

When you first see a new dog, you will be a stranger to him so this is an ideal opportunity to test how friendly or otherwise he will be with strangers. Approach the dog in his kennel and crouch down in front of the door with your body sideways on and your eyes averted. Watch the dog's reactions. Does he approach in a friendly way, tail wagging? Does he come forward slightly, but look shy and hesitant? Does he give low growls or warning barks? Does he go to the back of the kennel and look worried? Does he begin to demand your attention by barking and pawing at the wire? Or he is more interested in the other dogs and whatever else is going on than in you?

A dog that readily comes forward to meet you is likely to do this to visitors to your home once he has settled in. A dog that is wary, but looks as though he wants to be friendly will probably be a very loyal watch-dog, but not necessarily one to take into a busy household. A dog that demands attention by barking or pawing at the wire has probably learned to do this in a previous home and will need careful retraining to eradicate the bad habit.

Once you have determined how the dog behaves towards strangers, swivel round to face him without getting up and talk to him in a friendly way through the bars. Spend a few minutes talking to him and again note his reaction.

Enjoyment of body contact

If you think it is safe to do so, put your fingers up against the bars, but don't put them inside to begin with. Does he press himself up against you so that he can be stroked? Dogs that enjoy being stroked will often shift sideways so they can press their whole body against the bars for maximum contact with you. Little dogs that are used to being picked up and cuddled will often bounce up and down excitedly at this point. Dogs that are more aloof will keep their distance. This could be through shyness, their lack of motivation to be touched or because they have not been stroked much in the past. Love and affection is often in short supply at rescue

This dog enjoys being stroked and has positioned herself so that it is easy for the person to touch her.

This dog feels uneasy and is licking his lips to try to stop someone staring at him.

kennels despite the attempts of dedicated staff, so if a dog does not respond to you at this stage and you want a dog that will enjoy lots of body contact, you may need to look elsewhere.

You may find that it takes a while for the dog to trust you enough to come forward to be stroked. If you are patient and are rewarded by the dog presenting his neck area to be touched, you will have found a dog that will be loyal and trusting with its owner, but aloof and reserved with strangers.

Hand-shy?

At this stage, you may like to judge his reaction to sudden hand movements. Dogs that have been smacked too much will either take evasive action or become aggressive. Raise your hand suddenly above the dog's eye level. A dog that has had no mistreatment will probably blink and then wag his tail. A dog that has been hit is likely to cower with his eyes closed, move away, or show aggression towards you. One that shows aggression to a suddenly raised hand is not likely to be safe around children. If you have children at home and the dog stiffens up and stares when you raise your hand suddenly, it may be worth repeating this movement several times to see if you can push it into using aggression. This may seem unfair to the poor dog, but it would be more unfair if he was to bite your children and had to be returned.

Afterwards talk to the dog kindly until he has relaxed and you have reassured him that your intentions are good.

Strength of character and sociability

Remove your hands and make eye contact with the dog. Observe his reaction. Does he stare back, look away quickly, retreat or show a range of submissive gestures, such as licking his lips? How he responds can tell you a lot about him.

In a dog's language, prolonged staring can be a threat of intended aggression. A dog that has been well socialised and is friendly and unafraid will have learned that human staring is safe and a signal to approach. If the dog you are assessing stares back at you with a happy expression and a wagging tail, it is a sign that he will get on well with most people.

Dogs that are less well socialised will avoid direct eye contact by looking away. Most dogs will do this. Staring may induce a sense of unease in the dog and he may yawn, suddenly become interested in something else, scratch or turn away and move to the back of the kennel. Some dogs may become aggressive with a warning growl, a display of teeth or sometimes, though rarely, an explosive display of anger. Through these responses, you will be able to see how the dog copes with a mild threat from a human and whether his future behaviour is likely to be suitable for you and your family.

Prolonged eye contact will often evoke signs of appeasement and submission in the form of lip licking or paw raising. If the dog displays extreme submission, such as rolling onto his back or continuous paw movements and wriggling soon after you begin to stare, he will probably have little confidence in his ability to deal aggressively with difficult situations, preferring instead to choose appeasement. Such a dog may be ideal for a family with children, but may not tolerate isolation from the safety of other pack members very easily.

Dogs with strong characters will often stare back at you if you stare at them. Dobermanns and rottweilers are renowned for this. They seem to weigh up your next move and have the confidence to hold their ground while under threat. This is an ideal characteristic for a guard dog. These dogs will often learn quickly and be quite independent. However, they may be more likely to react with aggression when seriously threatened and, unless you are sure about their past history, it may be better to avoid such dogs if you have children.

TIP

Staring and raising your hands quickly in front of a dog's face are very threatening to him and should be done only when he is safely behind bars. It is not pleasant for the dog being tested and you should do this only with dogs that you are genuinely interested in. If you have any doubts about the friendliness of the dog after your test, look elsewhere.

Trainability

It is possible to train all dogs, but some will learn faster than others. Offer the dog a titbit. If he takes it and eats it greedily, you can test him to see if he will be easy to train. Hold the next titbit just out of his reach and keep it still. He will probably sit down. As soon as he does something else to try to get the titbit, such as pawing at the wire or pressing his mouth to the bars, reward him immediately by feeding the titbit. Offer another in the same way and wait for the same behaviour to be shown before giving it to him. After a few repetitions, you will notice that the dog has worked out exactly what he has to do to get the titbit. Very smart dogs will learn after just a few attempts while it will take the less able longer.

Trainable dogs are also likely to be inventive about displaying behaviours that increase their chances of getting the titbit. If a dog just sits there waiting for a long time, he may be a very patient, steady dog who does not do the unexpected, but he will probably not be as smart as a dog that is constantly inventing novel behaviour.

Right: A titbit is held just out of reach. Be patient while the dog thinks of what to do.

Opposite: The dog raises a paw in an attempt to get the titbit. Give the titbit immediately and it is likely that he will repeat the behaviour next time.

Other traits to look for

Throughout the tests in part one, you will have seen how active
or lazy a dog is. One that is constantly leaping up and down or
pacing to and fro will be one that likes to be kept active. One that
has only just enough energy to plod over to you and sit down
may be quite happy to lie around all day while you get on with
your life.

Other dogs in adjoining kennels will probably be barking or
walking past during the assessment. Watch how the dog you are
assessing reacts. Does he behave aggressively? If so, he is likely
to behave like this to some other dogs in your environment once
he has settled in. Is he more interested in other dogs than in
you? If so, he may have grown up with other dogs and it may be
difficult for him to become a human-oriented dog.

SIGNS TO WATCH FOR

Anxiety or uneasiness:
- Looking away
- Lip licking
- Ears held back
- Weight on back legs
  ready to run
- Growling

Appeasement:
- Lip licking
- Raised paw
- Rolling onto back

Once you have made an initial assessment, a member of staff will give you more information and will help you take the dog out of the kennel.

PART TWO

ASSESSMENT OUTSIDE THE KENNEL

Once you have found a dog or dogs that seem to have potential from your tests, the second part of this assessment procedure will help you decide which is your perfect rescue dog. You will need to take the dog out of the kennel so ask the permission of the kennel staff before doing so.

Taking an unknown dog out of his kennel always carries with it a slight risk. You will not know what treatment the dog received from strangers in the past and so you should proceed with caution. However, the kennel staff would be unlikely to allow you to take out a problematic dog. If you treat him with respect, handle him gently, take things slowly and do not expect too much of him at first, you are unlikely to experience problems. A dog cannot tell you if he is unhappy with something so watch for signs that he is anxious. Growling or lip curling signal the intention to bite so if either happens stop what you are doing at once. Do not try to discipline him, just accept that you took things too far with this particular dog too soon.

General observations

From the moment you begin to interact with the dog, you need to make observations that will help you build up a picture of his character. It is easy to get a lead on to his collar? Does he begin to bark frantically as soon as he knows he is going out? Does he leap up and down so much that it is difficult to calm him down enough to clip the lead on? Is he just very pleased to see you and not as interested in going out? Once out, does he pull hard on the lead and insist on going through doorways first (see page 70) All of these observations will help you assess the dog's character and predict its future behaviour.

Behaviour with other dogs

As you walk the dog out of the building, watch his interaction with other dogs. Does he try to avoid most dogs and hide behind you if another dog barks at him? Is he quite tolerant of other dogs barking at him, but cannot resist having a go back at the most ferocious? Does he keep his head down and try to get away from them as quickly as possible? Or is he aggressive to every dog that he comes across?

Kennels can be very hostile places as far as dog interactions are concerned. There are almost always a few dogs that do not like other dogs and these will bark and threaten the others as they go past. Such hostility can push even the most mild-mannered dog into self-defence and you will probably see your chosen dog behaving at his very worst in this environment.

If you have the opportunity to take him for a walk, take it. You will then be able to see how he interacts with other dogs when out

In the face of such an angry demonstration from the little dog, this big German Shepherd puts out his tongue and licks his nose to try to calm the aggression

on walks. Does he ignore other dogs and concentrate on the walk or on the humans? Does he lunge aggressively at all dogs? Is he very keen to play and interact with other dogs? Aggression towards other dogs is usually caused by fear and most dogs can be brought out of it with patience (see pages 108 to 111). You may not have the time, commitment or experience to embark on such a project, so it is best to know in advance if there are any problems in this area.

While he is looking towards another dog, see if you can distract him with a tasty titbit or a game with a toy. If he cannot be distracted, walk away from the other dog and try again. How distracted he is will indicate how easy it will be to teach him to come back to you when he is out playing in the park and has become interested in other dogs.

Playing with toys

Once you have taken the dog out and given him some exercise, find an undisturbed place, preferably enclosed so that you can get to know him a bit better. Let him off the lead and allow him to explore the room or area for a while. Sit down quietly and wait for him to come to you. How long it takes will indicate how people-oriented he is and how much he enjoys their company.

When he has settled down, produce a toy, tease him with it briefly in an excited way and throw it for him. Does he rush after it? Does he pick it up? Does he come back and drop the toy for you to throw again? If so, this indicates that chase is his favourite game and he is not a possessive dog. Dogs that play like this often make very nice pets. How obsessive about playing chase is he? If he plays for a long time and is still keen for more, you will need to think about whether you are prepared for this level of game playing on a regular basis.

This dog enjoys playing with toys and waits patiently for the toy to be thrown.

Try to take the toy away from him. Does he growl or go rigid? If he does, it is not wise to proceed further unless you are very experienced. Does he tease you with the toy and hang on to it when you try to take it? Does he like to play tug-of-war? If he does, it may indicate a strong character. Try to get him really excited by rushing about and waving the toy wildly. Does he play gently or roughly after this? If you have children, especially small ones, this will be a useful exercise as it will tell you how careful he is with his teeth and how inhibited his biting is.

Encourage him to play with a squeaky toy. Does he back away from it or squeak it gently? Does he squeak it hard and try to tear it to pieces? Dogs that enjoy 'killing' squeaky toys often enjoy catching small animals. Their predatory instinct tends to be well defined – many of the terriers and hounds fall into this category. If you have a cat or other small pets at home and this dog enjoys 'killing' small, squeaky things, it may not be wise to choose him.

If the dog will not play, it could be that he does not know how to or it may be that he is not feeling relaxed enough to try. Give him more time to settle down and feel at ease. If he is still not playful, take special care to note how he behaves with other dogs. If he prefers their company to yours, it may be that he has been raised with another dog and has never had to learn to play with people. Such dogs can make good pets, but it takes a while to focus their attention onto people and to teach them to play properly.

This dog is comfortable about being handled and is happy and relaxed while being groomed.

Handling and grooming

Allow the dog to settle down again after the play session. Sit on the floor and encourage him to come closer. If he comes to you, stroke and handle him gently. If you feel it is safe to do so, run your hands gently over his body, down his tail and down each leg. Let him walk away if he wants to and watch for signs of unease such as yawning, ears back, the whites of the eyes showing and a lowered, still tail. Do not proceed if you see any of these signs. If he appears happy and relaxed, try gently restraining him and repeating the procedure. Finally, try some gentle brushing. If all goes well, try picking up each foot in turn and wipe them with a towel.

All of these procedures will allow you to judge how much the dog has been handled in the past and how comfortable he is with it. It will also enable you to assess how much he enjoys body contact. A dog that is not comfortable with handling and grooming can be brought round with care and patience, but such a dog may not be ideal to have around children unless they are very gentle and reserved.

This dog enjoys the company of children and remains calm and relaxed when they try to touch him.

Response to commands

When the dog is standing, ask him to sit. Most dogs know this command. How quickly does he respond? Does it take two or three repetitions? If he responds, praise him, encourage him to stand again and ask him to sit. Does he sit willingly and quickly a second time? And a third? If he understands the command, how willing he is to obey will give you an indication of his biddability. Many dogs will not respond well to someone they have yet to get to know, but the easy-going, responsive ones will.

Behaviour with children

Before taking any dog out with your children, question the centre staff closely about the information they have from previous owners. Try to make an estimate of how reliable this information may be based on your knowledge of the dog so far. Assessing whether a dog will be good with children is one of the most difficult things to do, which is why you need to rely on information from the previous owners.

Make sure your children are present throughout the assessment procedures so you can observe the dog's reaction to them and his friendliness towards them. Watching them play together with toys will give you further insight into the dog's suitability. If your handling and grooming exercises went well, you may like to allow your children to try some gentle brushing and see how the dog responds. Allow him to approach the children when he is ready and to move away if he wishes. An ideal dog for a family with children will tolerate all their attentions well and should appear to be enjoying them. If you have any doubts, it is probably better to go with your intuition.

If you have children, it would be unwise to consider stray dogs, those for which there is no background information or those that are known to be difficult around children. Sadly, many dogs will have been teased into being aggressive to children. These dogs would probably make very good pets if living with decent children, but it is wise to give them a miss and let them go to families of adults instead. If your children are older teenagers, you will not need to be so careful and you will have a wider choice than those families with younger children.

If you do not have children living at home, but have grandchildren or children who visit regularly, try to get them to visit the centre with you. If this is not possible, you will have to rely on previous information and the observations of the kennel staff who may have witnessed interactions with children.

Other factors to consider

There are many things you will not be able to tell from meeting the dog and the assessment procedure, such as how good a traveller he is. However, you will have a much better idea of his character after the assessment and this will enable you to predict future behaviour. For example, if he is nervous and seems scared by many things, it is likely that he will also be afraid of travelling in the car.

GOOD WITH SMALL ANIMALS?
One of the most difficult areas to find out about is how good the dog is likely to be with cats and other small animals. If you are lucky, the rescue centre will have a few worldly-wise cats about the place that can be used to gauge the dog's response. Unfortunately, these cats are used to dealing with unruly dogs and usually have so much confidence that new arrivals do not dare to tackle them. When faced with a cat that is preparing to flee, however, the same dog that turned away from the rescue centre cat will often take great delight in giving chase.

All you can really do is use the interactions to give you a general impression of the dog's excitability when faced with a cat. If he pays a great deal of attention to the centre cat and becomes very excited, especially if he is a terrier type or a hound, it may be best to avoid him if you have cats and other small animals. Ask the staff for their advice and try to find out if he lived with a cat in a previous home. An adult terrier or a greyhound/lurcher type who has not lived with cats before is not a good prospect. Some collies are so keen to chase that they can make life miserable for any cats they live with, but this does depend on the individual's character and how they have been brought up.

MEETING YOUR OTHER DOG(S)

Once you have chosen a dog, you will want to see if he can get along with any other dogs you may have. If there is a large open area at the rescue centre, get them together a few times before you decide to take the new dog home. The dogs will then be more familiar with each other before one has to move into the other's territory.

The worst way to introduce two dogs is head to head in a small space. The intensity of such a meeting can often result in a defensive display of aggression from one of the dogs. Instead,

'The worst way to introduce two dogs is head to head in a small space.'

When introducing your dog to a new dog, start off some distance apart and gradually get closer together. This will allow the two dogs to get used to each other slowly.

walk them in a large, open space in parallel with each other, keeping them apart initially. Keep walking so that the interest of the walk takes the pressure off the meeting. Gradually allow them to get together and interact with each other. Try to keep their leads as slack as possible so you are not influencing the body signals they give each other. If you are very lucky they will play together, but most dogs will ignore each other at this stage. Consider this a successful meeting as it will take them time to get to know each other – at least there was no fighting (see page 51).

Success at this stage, and on subsequent meetings, does not guarantee that the dogs will live happily together. They will still need to establish a hierarchy and this can be a source of friction between them. However, if they have been all right together during the first introduction, it is more likely that they will settle down eventually.

Taking on a challenge

In every rescue centre, there will be several dogs that need experienced owners. They will have difficult behaviour problems that need to be overcome. These dogs are incredibly rewarding to rehabilitate and there are some owners who take pleasure in taking a difficult dog and turning it into a decent member of society. It is possible to turn the majority of difficult dogs around, but it takes skill and experience to know which dog to choose. You run the risk of being heartbroken if you fail and the dog has to be returned or put to sleep. However, if you succeed, you will have the satisfaction of knowing that without your help that dog may not have survived. Such dogs are not ideal for first time owners, but the more experience you have, the more difficult a case you will be able to take on. Always consider the people you have contact with (family, friends and neighbours) before you take on a problem dog and get their agreement first.

This dog is large, lively and afraid of strangers. He will need experienced owners to help him overcome his fear and settle down.

CHAPTER

3

Early Days and Introductions

Arrange to collect your new dog in the middle of a weekend so you have just one day before everyone goes out to work or school and the everyday routine begins. If you spend a week at home to settle him in, he will get used to having you around all the time and will find it very difficult to cope when normal life resumes. Many dogs will sleep a lot during the first few weeks in a new house. Whether this is a reaction to stress or just because the dog is warm and comfortable and enjoying the luxury of being able to sleep all day is unclear, but if you take a week off work to be with him, he is likely to be quite unresponsive anyway.

Preparations

Before bringing your new dog home, everyone who will be looking after him should agree on the house rules that you will expect him to stick to. Decide whether he should be allowed upstairs, in the bedrooms, on the furniture or to be fed from the table. You also need to decide who is going to walk him, feed him, play with him and groom him?

Choose his name and draw up a list of commands you will use. If everyone uses the same words and keeps to the same rules it will be a lot less confusing for your dog and he will learn your house rules much more quickly. Decide also where he should sleep and, if you have young children, make it clear to them that he is not to be disturbed when he goes to lie there. The area around his bed should be a no-go zone for children so that he can be left alone if he needs rest.

Buy a good collar and a leather or nylon lead. Do not buy a chain or rope lead as this can hurt your hands and his neck. Buy toys, brushes and a bed. You should already know what kind of toys he likes and you will need brushes to suit his coat type. Do not buy an expensive bed at first in case he chews it. A strong cardboard box with the front cut down and a thick blanket inside will be fine to begin with and can be replaced with something more comfortable later.

The first day

How well your new dog travels in the car will probably be one of the first things you will find out about him unless you are walking home. If you are collecting him in a car, make sure whoever comes with you gets into the car first and put the dog in last. Start by placing him in the spot where you always intend him to travel so that he begins good habits straight away. Ensure he has got enough room and is not squashed in too tight with too many children. Fasten him or put up a barrier so that you do not have to start off by correcting him if he tries to jump into the front to join you. Ignore any bad behaviour in the car as this is something you will need to tackle later on (see pages 144 to 147).

Take him straight home (unless you have another dog, see page 49) and walk him into the garden. Let him off the lead to run around and explore. Sooner or later he will go to the toilet. It is worth waiting for him to do so, even if it is cold and wet outside. Praise him profusely as soon as he has been and feed him two or three small titbits while you do so. This will get him into a good habit from the beginning. When he needs to go to

Encourage your new dog to jump into the car if possible. If necessary lift him slowly and gently, holding him firmly in case he struggles.

Allowing your dog to explore the garden before going into the house will enable him to go to the toilet after the journey.

the toilet again later, he will remember where he went and this will help to keep the house clean.

Once he has been to the toilet, or has made a thorough investigation of the garden, allow him inside to explore the house. From the moment he goes inside, begin to explain the house rules to him. He will not know what they are at first and may behave as he used to in his previous home. If he does something you do not wish him to do in your house, correct him quietly and calmly and gently show him what you want him to do instead. Try to make it clear that he has done something wrong, but do not sound angry or be too aggressive or he may become fearful and defensive, which will slow up the learning process. If he is shy or sensitive, be gentler with him so that you do not frighten him. As soon as he does something you approve of praise him warmly. In this way, he will quickly begin to learn what you expect of him.

After he has had about an hour to get used to the house, it may be a good idea to take him for a walk. He may have settled down enough to need to go to the toilet again and the pleasurable experience of walking with you will help him feel more at home. Take some toys with you as you may be able to entice him into a game that will help to get your relationship off to a very good start.

Remember, though, that he does not know you or your home. You cannot tell him that this is his new home and there is nothing he should worry about. He will feel displaced, unsure and unsettled for a while and you should try to ensure that he has the time and space he needs to adjust during that time. Try to be sympathetic to how he feels, but do not allow any bad habits to begin that you may later want to correct.

Introducing children

Your new dog will probably have met your children at the rescue centre, but first impressions of them at home are very important. If you left your children at home while you collected your new dog, they will be excited at the prospect of his arrival. It is essential that your dog is not crowded by the children or forced to interact with them until the excitement of being somewhere new has worn off.

It is probably best if the children are asked not to touch the dog while he is let into the garden. This will give him time to explore and to go to the toilet. Hold on to toddlers so they cannot suddenly rush forward towards the dog. Ask the children to go into the house first and sit down. Give them a few small dog food treats each and ask them to wait while he makes his initial exploration of the house. They can then call him one at a time, giving him one titbit on the flat of the hand when he goes to them.

Keep children restrained while your new dog explores the garden. If your dog is playful, a quick game with a toy will help settle him in and get rid of excess energy before going into the house.

Dogs will take to children more easily if they are sitting down, and if they stroke them on the chest rather than the head.

TEACH YOUR CHILDREN WHAT TO DO

Teach them in advance how to give food treats by placing it on their palm, keeping their fingers together, putting their hand down beneath the dog's mouth level and keeping it still. Also teach them how to stroke a dog safely by touching him under the chin and throat rather than by patting his head. Putting hands onto a dog's head covers up his sense organs and can be misconstrued as an aggressive act if the hands approach too fast. Be prepared to move the dog away if your child becomes overwhelmed or the dog is about to jump up. A big dog at face level may seem huge and can be a bit frightening.

Dogs do not always appreciate being hugged or cuddled unless they have been familiarised with it from an early age. It is very tempting for children to do this, especially if they have been used to hugging a previous dog. You will need to find out gradually what your dog will accept from the children, supervising constantly at first to ensure that neither is feeling overwhelmed by the actions of the other.

Once the initial introductions in the house have been made and the excitement has died down, this may be a good time to introduce a new game or toy for the children, which will keep them occupied and take their minds off the new arrival. This takes the pressure off your new dog who can then get to know the children in his own time.

Once everyone has had a chance to settle down and your new dog has had some rest, take them all out into the garden or out for a walk. Take the dog's toys out with you and try to get children and dog playing happily together. Eventually, both dog and children will need to learn certain rules if the games are to be successful (see page 48), but these initial games should be as much fun as possible for all concerned. Take a light-hearted approach and intervene only if the situation seems to be getting out of hand.

GO AT THE DOG'S PACE

For the first two weeks at least, insist that your children let your dog approach them rather than the other way around. They can call him to them if they want to, but should be taught not to go to him if he does not want to go to them. This will give him the time and space he needs to build his confidence with them. Keeping to this regime may be more difficult with younger children, but it will be your responsibility to ensure that they are constantly supervised so that no harm comes to either children or dog.

If your children have not had a dog before, they will need to be taught to respect him and not treat him as a toy. The high-pitched squeals of excited children can upset a dog until he is used to them, so try to keep play as calm as possible and

Titbits given on the flat of the hand help to give a good first impression.

interrupt it before it begins to get out of hand. Some dogs, such as collies, have a strong herding instinct and may nip at children's ankles when they run. This usually causes them to squeal and run away, which excites the dog more. Be ready to step in at once to stop the behaviour, which will otherwise quickly become a habit.

LEARNING THE BASICS

Children have to learn not to tease or bully your dog; the dog has to learn not to jump up, be too boisterous or nip them in play. It is important to supervise all their activities until they have both learned the rules. It is not advisable to leave children under the age of 10 alone with any dog. Until you are sure that your new dog does not guard its food from children, it would be wise to give him bones and chews when they are in bed or put him into another room that can be locked to ensure that young children do not wander in unexpectedly. Teach your children never to approach a dog when it is eating or chewing a bone or chew.

Follow the same rules and procedures for introducing any visiting children to your dog. If your dog has a pleasant first encounter with them, if he is not crowded by them or approached when he wants to be left alone and if he sees them as a source of titbits and games he will begin to enjoy having them around and they will soon become friends (unless he has been badly frightened by children in his past).

BE VIGILANT

If you do not have children and you have chosen a dog that has an unknown history with them, you will need to proceed cautiously when any children visit or if you meet any outside the home. It is safer to assume that your new dog is not good with children until you have had time to observe his reactions to them. If you are still unsure, it may be wise to muzzle him to begin with. This will tend to make him a little more fearful if he was afraid to begin with, but it will prevent him biting. Make sure that your dog is used to the muzzle beforehand (see page 104) so he does not associate it with the presence of children.

CHILDREN

- Make sure children don't overwhelm your new dog.
- Let the dog approach the children rather than the other way around.
- Teach children how to give titbits safely.
- Teach children how to stroke a dog properly.
- Buy your children a new game or toy to take the attention from your new dog.

Give the two dogs time to get to know each other in the garden, where there is more space and the desire to 'defend the territory' is less strong.

Introducing other dogs

If you are taking your new dog home by car, keep him separate from your existing dog. Try to find an area that is unfamiliar to both dogs on the way home where there is plenty of space for their first walk together. The interest of the walk will make the introduction less intense and they can get to know each other as they walk. Keep them walking in parallel and try to avoid head to head encounters. Walk them for as long as possible, gradually letting them have more and more contact with each other. Don't worry if they ignore each other at this stage.

After the walk, when they are both well exercised, take them home and let them both into the garden. If your new dog is shy and you have more than one existing dog, take it in turns to let each dog meet the new dog so that he does not get overwhelmed.

Before allowing them into the house, remove anything they are likely to fight over such as toys, bones, beds and bowls. Allow time for the new dog to explore the house and then separate them while any children are introduced. If you are using titbits, take the new dog out of the room once he has met all of the children and allow the existing dog back in to get some treats. Make sure all the food has gone before the two are let back in together so there is nothing to fight over.

ESTABLISHING A HIERARCHY

Try to ignore any small disagreements or scuffles between the two dogs at first. If you see both dogs stiffening up and staring at each other, distract them by pretending something much more interesting is going on elsewhere. If they look as though they may fight, attach short leads to their collars so you can use these to break up an incident. If a fight ensues, do not grab at the dogs to break it up as you may get bitten by accident or make the fight worse. Use the leads to part them or a sudden surprise, such as throwing a bucket of water over them, banging tin trays together loudly just above their heads or throwing a heavy coat over them. Afterwards, be ready to lead each dog away and isolate them until they have calmed down.

Usually, introductions go smoothly and the new dog is treated, and acts, like a visitor. The hierarchy between them is usually sorted out during the first few weeks and disagreements are possible during this time. Try to avoid situations that may cause aggravations between the two. Feed them separately, for example, until they are used to each other and do not make such a fuss of the new dog that the existing dog feels excluded. Take care not to leave them alone together until it is obvious they have become friends.

Dogs that live together will always form a hierarchy. Initially, the existing dog will be leader of the pack and it is important that you, as the owner, is seen to reinforce this. This means treating them not as equals, but instead favouring your existing dog by putting him first in most things, such as feeding, giving attention, playing and going through doorways. This should be easy as you will have a stronger bond with him anyway.

Opposite: Attaching a long line to your dog's collar when he is in the presence of your cat will enable you to stop him quickly should he decide to give chase.

Gradually over the following two weeks the dogs will make their own assessment of who should be in charge. If the new dog is mentally stronger and more ambitious, he may well end up taking over. This could happen without any problems or the existing dog could resist which may lead to scuffles and fights. Try not to interfere in this natural process unless they begin to fight. If it becomes obvious that the new dog has taken control, you will have to reinforce this by putting the new dog first in everything instead. This may be difficult to do, particularly if your sympathies lie with your first dog. However, not to do this will interfere in the natural pack order and could lead to fights between the dogs.

Be particularly careful not to do anything that may aggravate a situation between your dogs during the settling-in period. Shut them into two separate rooms when you give them chews and bones and take the treats away before they are allowed back together. Be careful with them at moments of excitement such as when you are about to take them out for a walk, if someone has returned home, if the doorbell rings or the postman delivers letters. This is a time when annoyance with each other is likely to flare into a fight. If they are small dogs, be particularly careful not to lift one above the other and, in doing so, unwittingly give the underdog a height advantage that can trigger the top dog into aggression.

Not all dogs fit in well to a life with other dogs. Dogs that have been doted on by previous owners, for example, may be too obsessive about their humans to allow any other dogs near. Watch out for signs of bullying by the strongest dog. If, after one month, either dog is very unhappy with the situation or there are often fights and scuffles between them and the situation is not getting better, it may be kinder to let the new dog go to another home.

BREAKING UP A DOG FIGHT

- Never attempt to separate fighting dogs with your hands.
- If the dogs are wearing leads, use these to separate them.
- Try to defuse the situation by throwing water or a heavy coat over them.

Introducing cats

Cats and dogs living in the same household can become friends and enjoy each other's company. How you introduce them and how they take to each other on the first few meetings is critical for future success. It is essential that your cat does not become frightened of the dog or the dog learns that it can chase the cat. If

Allow the cat to come and go as it pleases but ensure that the dog is restrained so that he cannot give chase.

either of these things happen, the time taken for them to live happily together will be greatly extended.

It is best to shut the cat away upstairs or in a different room while the dog comes in and explores the house. The two animals will quickly become aware of each other's presence because of their keen sense of smell. Wait until all excitement has died down and the dog has had a chance to recover from all the new experiences. It may be better to wait until the evening when everyone is more relaxed and younger children are in bed.

Put the dog on his lead, sit down with him at the opposite end of the room to the door and wait until the dog is lying down and relaxed. Get another family member to let the cat out and encourage it to come into the room adjacent to where the dog is. Once the cat is in this room, ask someone to shut the doors so that the cat can only be in this room and the room where the dog is. Encourage it to come in to the room where the dog is by tempting it with food, but do not force things at this stage. Keep the dog as still as possible, insisting that it sits or lies down.

The cat is more likely to be brave if it feels it has an escape route or it can get up high. Your cat will not put itself in a dangerous situation that it cannot get out of. It needs to learn that the dog is safe before it can come closer so be patient and let things take a natural course. The more shy the cat and the more boisterous or vocal the dog, the longer it will take. Forcing things at this stage will result in more fear in the cat that will take longer to overcome. If your cat is bold or used to dogs, he may come straight in. If he begins to approach the dog, let the dog get up and greet the cat, but hold on to his collar just in case.

How many attempts it will take will depend upon the two animals in question. Keep the dog under complete physical control until there is no excitement generated by the cat's arrival. You can then gradually begin to allow the dog more freedom, but be sure you can prevent any chasing should it arise. Leave a trailing line on the dog that you can stand on in a hurry should a chase begin. This is a useful way of getting control quickly, but be careful with this if you have small children or elderly people in the house.

Ensure you supervise all encounters between your dog and cat for several weeks. They will get to know each other at their own speed. Sometimes it can take many months. Only by being in control of the meetings and by being calm and patient will you enable their friendship to develop as quickly as possible. Never leave them alone together until it is obvious that they are happy with each other.

If your cat is very timid, it may be wise to confine him to the house for the first week to prevent him running away when the dog arrives and refusing to come back. Lock the cat flap and give your cat an area of the house where the dog cannot go, such as upstairs. Put a litter tray in a convenient place and feed the cat somewhere away from the dog's territory so that it can eat undisturbed. This will enable the cat and dog to co-exist comfortably in the same house until you have the time to supervise their encounters.

Keep a new dog restrained and under close observation until you have seen how he behaves with small pets. A terrier and a rat is not a good combination.

Introducing smaller pets

Keep your new dog away from smaller pets for a few days until you have had time to develop a stronger bond with him. This will make him more responsive to you and he is more likely to take notice when you try to teach him how to behave around small, delicate animals. Small, active, fluffy or furry animals usually bring out the predatory instinct in the most placid of dogs. Some dogs have a stronger instinct than others do and certain types of dog, such as terriers and lurchers, are more likely to respond unfavourably.

Throughout all early introductions, keep your dog on a lead, under control and confine the small pet to its familiar cage. Allow the dog to approach slowly, but do not allow the small pet to be frightened. This is unfair and it may cause it to run, which will make your dog more excited. Insist that your dog sits or lies down. Talk calmly to your dog and praise him if he remains still. Be aware of things

The instinct to chase is very strong in many dogs. Quick, erratic movements of smaller pets can prove irresistible.

TIP

Before leaving your dog alone in the house, make sure small animals in cages are well out of reach or behind a secure door.

going on around you as any sudden excitement, such as a child running towards you, may cause your dog suddenly to lunge forward. Take time to allow your new dog to get used to the small pet, but end the session after about five minutes. Repeat as often as you can for the first week, taking care never to allow your dog to rush up to any cage.

You can repeat this procedure with the dog fastened securely while you handle the small pet. Again, insist that he sits or lies down. Get someone to help you to do this if necessary. By doing this, you will be able to gauge your dog's reaction to small creatures. Predatory dogs will become interested whenever the small animal moves, despite being given time to become familiar with them. Dogs that are scared and unfamiliar with small animals will gradually become used to them over time and, eventually, should take little notice of them. Whatever the reaction, remember that a dog's instincts often lie just below the surface and never put your dog in a position where he can grab at the smaller pet should it decide to make a sudden, unexpected movement.

The first night

It is a good idea to put your new dog to bed half an hour before going to bed yourself for the first few nights. This allows him to get used to the idea of being alone while your reassuring presence is nearby. It also allows you to judge how well he is likely to cope with the isolation. Make sure he has had a chance to go out to the toilet before putting him to bed.

If your dog is in any way pushy or strong-willed, insist that he stays in the kitchen at night and ignore all his attempts to get you to go back in to him. If you do so you will be rewarding his behaviour and it is likely to increase in intensity. Warn the neighbours that there may be a few sleepless nights and put something up against the door and over the carpet near the door so that he cannot damage it if he scratches while attempting to get out. Go into the room in the morning only if your dog is quiet. If you go in when he is barking, your appearance will reward his behaviour and he is likely to wake you up earlier in future. Wait until there is a pause in the noise before going in.

If your dog has a shy, gentle or submissive nature, you may find that he copes with his first few nights better if he can sleep closer to you. Put his bed outside your bedroom and close the door so he cannot disturb you in the night. You may hear him sniffing underneath the door during the night as he tries to reassure himself that you are still there.

If your new dog wakes up during the night and makes frantic attempts to attract your attention, he may want to go to the toilet. Get up and take him out, but do not speak to him or make a fuss of him. If you do, he will probably try to get you up again next time he is feeling a bit lonely. Wait with him in the garden until he has relaxed, and praise him if he does anything. If he doesn't go, bring him back in and leave him alone for the rest of the night. Once he has settled in and his body adjusts to your routines, these nightly exercises should disappear. (See page 135 for how to solve the problem of dogs that persistently have 'accidents' at night.)

Gentle or shy dogs may prefer to sleep closer to you at night. Putting a bed outside the bedroom door will help to settle him and to teach him that he cannot come into your room.

The early days of life together

After the first day with your new dog, introduce your house rules and continue with your normal daily routines as if your dog is already part of the family. Start as you mean to go on and your dog will adapt more quickly to your lifestyle. In particular, make sure you leave him alone in the house for a period of time on each of the first few days. This will have to happen eventually and he is more likely to accept it if it happens straight away. Rescue dogs are renowned for getting very attached to new owners very quickly and you may find it becomes impossible to leave him if you do not get him used to it at once. How long you leave him for will depend on the character of the dog. Shy, gentle, submissive dogs usually find it harder to cope without you. This is especially important if you go out to work. He will quickly get used to your routines and to being left and will see it as a bonus when you are around rather than becoming anxious whenever you cannot be with him. See chapter 8 for how to teach your dog to be left alone.

During the first few days of your new life together, try to introduce him to people outside your immediate family who will be visiting often. Relatives and close friends should be encouraged to visit so they can meet your new dog. Anyone he meets often during these early weeks is likely to be treated as part of your extended pack and will be greeted accordingly.

Do not keep him isolated during this time, particularly if he is shy, as this is likely to make him insular and suspicious of anyone outside his immediate family. Try to ensure that he enjoys his encounters with new people. Give them titbits to give him, or toys to throw for him. Let him approach them rather than the other way around and watch his body language for signs of stress. If he is too boisterous, keep him on a lead while he greets people so you can control his actions. Allow him to go forward only when he is behaving sensibly and not jumping up.

BATHING

A good rescue centre will ensure that your new dog has been bathed prior to you picking him up. If, for some reason, he has not been bathed and he is very smelly, it may be best to wait for a few days before washing him rather than add to the stress he is already under. When the time comes, lift him into a dry bath or shower tray onto a non-slip mat and add water afterwards. He will then be less likely to panic and splash water everywhere than if you try to put him into a full bath. Talk to him quietly to reassure him while you are washing him, and dry him thoroughly with a towel afterwards.

Insist on good manners from day one when greeting visitors.

HOUSE-TRAINING AND THE IMPORTANCE OF ROUTINES

During the early days with your new dog, try to stick to a schedule for feeding, walking and sleeping. This will help your dog adjust more quickly to your routines and will help him readjust his body from the routine he was used to in kennels.

Until he has had time to adjust, leave newspaper on the floor by the back door whenever you leave him so that he can go to toilet on this if necessary. Place polythene underneath the newspaper to prevent any leakage on to the floor. This is important as dogs have such a strong sense of smell, which will attract them back to use the same place next time.

Leaving your new dog alone for short periods during the first few days will help him learn to accept isolation.

Most adult dogs will have been house-trained, but some may have been in kennels for a long time and may need reminding. Take your dog outside to the garden on numerous occasions and on regular walks during the first few days to remind him of the right place to go (see page 136 for advice on house-training problems). When taking him to the garden, make sure you stay with him for reassurance and so you can praise him and let him know he has been good when he goes to the toilet.

Your dog is likely to be excited and slightly anxious during the first few days of his new life. This may cause his immune system to be depressed and may allow any minor ailments that his body was just coping with in kennels to come to the fore. Your dog may develop loose bowels, which may cause him to have house-training accidents. Try not to be upset by this or react adversely towards your dog. Clean up the soiled area with biological washing powder solution or special products available from your veterinary practice. Many other household cleaning products will not remove all of the smell and your dog may be attracted back to the area. Do not let symptoms persist for longer than 24 hours before consulting a veterinary surgeon.

You can reduce the chances of your new dog developing diarrhoea by acquiring at least a week's supply of the food your dog was eating in kennels so that you can implement any dietary changes slowly. The last thing your dog needs when he is adjusting to his new home is changes happening inside his body as his system adjusts to the new food. If you want to change your dog's diet, make changes slowly once he has settled into the family by gradually increasing the proportion of new food to old over a few days.

During the first few days, accompany your dog when he goes out to the garden to go to the toilet.

CHAPTER

4

Building a Successful Relationship

All good relationships are based on trust and friendship. Your dog has to learn that you will do what is best for him and to trust you. This can be particularly difficult for dogs that have had a rough time with their first owners. In a similar way, you have to learn to trust that your dog will not bite you under any circumstances. This will take time and you will need to have many experiences together before you can both be really sure of your ground. The less you resort to punishment to get your own way and the fewer times you get angry with your new dog, the quicker he will learn to trust you.

If he is the right dog for you and you take time to understand him and treat him well, a strong bond of friendship will gradually grow between you. You cannot expect this to happen overnight, but the more reasonable your behaviour is towards your dog, and the better you understand him, the quicker it will happen. Don't expect miracles too soon. It takes about six months for a dog to really settle down in a new home, for you to get to know him and all his faults, and for him to learn about you. While you should be able to develop a good working relationship long before this, it is likely to take quite a while before he is truly your dog.

As well as trust and friendship, a dog needs to have firm guidelines on what is acceptable behaviour and what is not. As long as he knows his boundaries and the ground rules of life with you, he can be free to be himself and to have fun without overstepping the mark. When your new dog comes home with you for the first time, he will have his own rules for life with humans based on his previous experiences. These rules are unlikely to be the same as yours and so you will need to be prepared to teach him a new set of boundaries from day one. How you treat him in the first six months will set the scene for the rest of your time together. Getting it right from the outset will be easier than backtracking later.

'Don't expect miracles too soon. It takes about six months for a dog to really settle down in a new home, for you to get to know him and all his faults, and for him to learn about you.'

Setting ground rules

It is important that you show your dog what is required from him and reward him for showing the correct behaviour. So often owners chastise or punish new dogs for breaking their rules, but as a new dog will have no idea that he is doing something wrong, this comes as a surprise to him and he can begin to resent and distrust his new owners if it happens too often. A much better way to train your dog is to try to anticipate and prevent any unwanted behaviour. If you know he was allowed on furniture in

Provide your dog with a suitable place for resting and teach him to go there when he is sleepy.

HOW DOGS LEARN

- Dogs learn by trial and error. If they are rewarded for doing something, they are more likely to do it again. If their actions bring no success, they are less likely to repeat them.
- A dog needs to be rewarded as soon as he does a required action. Although he can remember earlier actions, he cannot associate praise or correction with an action unless it follows immediately. Consequently, if you want your dog to continue to do what it is he is doing, praise and reward him for it at once and it is more likely to happen in future.

his first home, for example, attach a lead to his collar before you let him into your lounge so you can prevent him from jumping on the sofa. When he is looking for a place to settle, tap the carpet or his bed and encourage him to lie there instead. Reward him well for lying in the right place.

In the early days, remember to reward him whenever you catch him being good so he knows he is doing the right thing. It is easy to forget to do this when everything is going well, but it will help to let him know that you are pleased with him and will give a sharp contrast to times when you may need to correct him. If you make sure that good behaviour is rewarded, it will soon become a habit. Extreme unwanted behaviours, such as jumping up at small children, should be stopped at once. Take hold of your dog's collar and tell him off. Then immediately lighten your tone and show him how you want him to behave instead. As soon as he does this, praise and reward him.

What's in a name?

Strays or dogs that have not had good relationships with people will not know their name. Test whether your new dog knows his by waiting until he faces away from you and saying his name clearly, but quietly. If he responds, it is likely that he has learned to associate the sound of his name with pleasant experiences with humans and you may like to continue to use it, particularly if he is an older dog. If, however, he does not have these associations or looks worried when you say his name, it may be a good idea to change it, particularly if you do not like it very much.

Choose a name that is easy to say and that all family members will be happy to yell loudly in a public place. What you choose is not important, but there is a theory that the name you choose indicates the type of relationship you want from your dog. Calling the dog a human name such as Ben or Sally, for example, indicates that you want a closer relationship than if you choose Fido or Mutt. Use the new name as soon as you get your dog and make sure everyone calls him the same thing. Often names get shortened or lengthened, but it will be quicker for him to learn if you all keep to the same name for a while.

You can speed up the process by saying his name often whenever he is looking the other way or concentrating on something else and producing a titbit or playing a game whenever he looks at you. He will quickly begin to link the sound of his new name with something very pleasant and will begin to respond and orientate towards whoever calls him. If you use his name too often, however, or you are cross with him when you call him, he will steadily become more and more unresponsive.

Calling your dog's name and seeing how he responds is a good test of the relationship between you. If he responds happily and comes to you wagging his tail, he has a good relationship with you. If he ignores you or looks worried, you will need to work harder to gain his affection and confidence.

The 'honeymoon' period

During the first two weeks, your dog is likely to feel like a visitor and behave extraordinarily well. Try not to be taken in by this best behaviour – it is likely that there is bad behaviour to come. As your dog begins to see the home as his territory and the family as his pack, his confidence level will rise and you are likely to see behaviours appearing that were not present at first. Some of these behaviours, such as guarding the house or being less

It may take up to two weeks before your new dogs feels that he belongs to the territory and that he needs to defend it.

responsive to commands, may be unwanted. It is for this reason that rescue societies usually receive requests for advice approximately two weeks after adoption.

Be aware that this 'honeymoon' period occurs and have realistic expectations otherwise you may be very disappointed when your perfect dog turns out to have a bad side after all. If you have been warned of possible problem behaviours this period also gives you a chance to put in some work with the problems before your dog becomes confident enough to assert himself. For example, a shy dog may not bark or be aggressive for the first two weeks. This gives you time to socialise him and make him feel more comfortable with people so that, hopefully, he will view them in a different light by the time he has developed sufficient confidence to be difficult with them.

Some very confident dogs may settle down more quickly. Dogs that were never corrected or suppressed in their first home may walk in as if they own the place and take control of the situation immediately. However, other dogs may take more time, particularly those that were badly treated in their previous home. Dogs that were kept very suppressed or were ill or under-nourished in their previous home may take months before they find their feet and gain confidence.

Why is hierarchy so important to dogs?

All domestic dogs have descended from wolves – creatures that live in a structured society governed by a strong hierarchical system. The animals at the top of the pack get access to more resources than their subordinates and they are ones who will produce the puppies. In an established hierarchy pack members rarely need to fight – most pack members know their place and are careful not to overstep the mark. This ensures that injuries are minimised and they are all fit to help each other hunt.

This natural hierarchy system has been passed down via genes from their ancestors to our domestic dogs. The ambition to be pack leader will be stronger in some dogs than others and it will have been encouraged to different degrees in the dog's previous home. Until you are sure about your dog's view of the world from a hierarchical perspective, it may be best to assume that he

Only high ranking wolves produce puppies and pass on their genes to the next generation. This is a privilege lower ranking wolves do not have.

Wolves have a natural hierarchy system that has been passed down via their genes to our domestic dogs.

needs to be firmly placed at the bottom of the pack. Doing this from day one will ensure that you achieve your goal to become his pack leader. Leaving it a few weeks until you have found out how strong-willed he is will make it much harder to regain control once you have lost it. It is easier to relax the pressure that keeps him at the bottom of the pack if you find he does not need it, rather than apply pressure to him if he thinks he has the upper hand.

BEING A GOOD PACK LEADER

A dog that thinks he is pack leader will make his own decisions, will be out of control and, in general, will act like a spoilt child who will try all manner of things to get his own way. He will not obey commands or do anything he does not want to and will always want to be the centre of attention.

If you are pack leader, you will have the right to make decisions that affect members of your pack and your dog will have enough respect to abide by those decisions. Dogs that think they are at the bottom of the pack will be compliant and biddable. They will be under your control because they view you as a parental figure rather than as a slightly older brother or sister or, worse, a younger sibling.

No one can afford to have a dog that is out of control. Life in the house with a dog that thinks he is the boss is no joke. A well-behaved, obedient dog is a pleasure to own and is usually much happier than one that is in constant conflict with its owners.

YOUR RESPONSIBILITIES AS PACK LEADER

As a pack leader, it will be your responsibility to make decisions about who does what and when, including sorting things out when they go wrong, protecting the pack and making sure everyone is comfortable and happy. As your dog's pack leader, you are taking on total responsibility for his welfare. This means you have a duty to understand him, to find out what makes him feel happy and safe and to learn how he thinks and sees the world.

The best pack leaders are benevolent and tolerant, but can be tough when they need to be. You should make it clear you will stand no nonsense, but are happy to be the dog's friend. A good pack leader does not constantly bully the dog to force him to stay inferior. Once your dog understands who is in charge, he will be more than happy to accept his position in life. In fact, dogs who have had the responsibility of pack leadership taken off their shoulders are usually more puppy-like and playful.

The dog you take on will have a predetermined view of humans based on his previous experiences with them. Despite this view, how he is treated during the first few weeks in a new home will make a considerable impression on him. From the very first encounters with members of his new pack, he will be assessing them to find out where his position lies.

Winning a small contest, such as who will get out of the gate first, can help to prevent challenges over larger issues.

THE RIGHT ATTITUDE

It is important to show your dog that you are fit to be a pack leader and to resolve to will win contests and challenges with your new dog, however small these challenges are. If you are a gentle, easy-going person, you may need to steel yourself to be strong for the first few weeks while your dog settles in and learns your strengths. It is important that you manage all encounters well during this time. Ultimately, you cannot fool your dog forever, but you may be able to do so for long enough to get the upper hand. This is why it is so important to choose the dog with a character most suited to you (see Chapters 1 and 2).

Consider a situation where you meet a friend in the street and stop to talk to them. Your dog notices a lamp post close by that he wants to

investigate and he tries to pull you towards it. If you give in and allow him to move, he has got his own way and you have lost a small contest. If, however, you make him sit and wait until you have finished talking, then allow him to go there as a reward for his good behaviour, you have won the contest and increased your status in the dog's eyes. Insisting on good behaviour is all important. Winning small contests like this from the outset will help to ensure your dog does not try to challenge you over the bigger issues.

While establishing yourself as leader, do not issue commands that you are not in a position to enforce should your dog decide to ignore them. Nothing will lower your status quicker than your dog learning that he does not have to respect your wishes. If your dog ignores your first command, manoeuvre him gently, but firmly, into place before rewarding. Do not give four or five commands that he ignores, which makes you so angry you feel you want to punish him. Punishing a dog will not accelerate your promotion to pack leader status. The respect has to be earned and you will not increase your chances if you bully your dog. Dogs that are punished in an effort to train and dominate them are likely to react by becoming defensively aggressive.

THE NATURAL WAY TO ACHIEVE PACK LEADER STATUS

The easy way to achieve status as pack leader is to use the techniques that wolves use for maintaining their hierarchies. This is a natural way and one that dogs seem to understand instinctively. The techniques centre on situations and events on which your dog will place more significance than you. These are sleeping places, territory and movement of the pack around the territory; winning of games and possession of toys; order of feeding; and attention and grooming from other pack members.

Sleeping place and territory

The dominant wolves in a pack will choose the best den in the territory to raise their puppies. They will also choose the best places to rest and will move others out of their chosen spot if necessary. Movements around the territory are instigated by the dominant animals. In your house, you have chosen the bedrooms as the best places to sleep. If you allow your dog to sleep on your bed, you will encourage him to think that he is on an equal footing with you. Ambitious dogs should sleep in their own bed away from the bedrooms. You will also rest on

Leading the way helps your dog realise you are the one that makes the decisions.

Preventing your dog from going into your bedroom keeps him off the bed and gives you a higher status.

sofas and chairs. Allowing him on these will raise his status. It is best to keep ambitious dogs off the furniture. It is also a good idea to control movements of your dog around the territory/home by going through doorways, up stairs and through narrow openings first. Leaders should lead, followers should follow. This also prevents your dog charging ahead and dragging you through doorways and down steps at speed.

Playing to win

In the wild, the stronger animals are those that are able to maintain their positions at the top of the hierarchies. To be an 'alpha wolf', you need to be both physically and mentally strong. As a subordinate, your dog will depend on you, his pack leader, for leadership and protection – no one wants to be led by a weak leader.

Tug-of-war games are a trial of strength between dog and owner. During such games, both players find out who is physically and mentally stronger. The individual who wins most of the time is the one who, in the dog's eyes, is the best equipped to lead the pack. If your dog enjoys these games, it is important that you win more often than not. If you cannot win because your dog is too strong for you, it is better not to play possession games at all. Playing and losing will give an ambitious dog the wrong message.

Always take a toy away from your dog at the end of a play session. This will make you seem like a possessive animal and will give you higher status.If your new dog hides under tables or races round and round so that you cannot get the toy back, attach a long line to his collar before you play so that you can pull him over and remove the toy from him. If it is difficult to get the toy out of his mouth, hold a tasty titbit under his nose so that he drops the toy to eat the titbit. As he begins to let go, give him a 'leave!' command so he begins to associate the action of letting go with this command.

If you find that your new dog is stealing items and running away with them to challenge you, attach the long line again and deliberately leave things down for him to steal. When he does so, pick up the end of the line, ask him to come to you and use the line to enforce your command. Continue to pull him to you until you can remove the object he has stolen from his mouth. Put it back where he found it. Repeat if necessary and, sooner or later, your dog will realise that there is no advantage in trying to challenge you by stealing things because you always win.

'Always take the toy away from a strong-willed dog at the end of a play session. This will make you seem like a possessive animal and will give you higher status.'

*Playing to win will help a
strong-willed dog to learn that
you can take control of
the possession in the territory
if you want to.*

Order of feeding

In the wild, the dominant animals will usually eat first, keeping others away until they have had enough. This helps to ensure that the biggest, strongest animals stay fit and healthy in times of famine.

In your household, dogs should be fed after the rest of the family has eaten. This may seem relatively unimportant to you, but for many pet dogs feeding is one of the highlights of their day and it can be very significant.

Attention and grooming from other pack members

Dominant wolves will decide when they wish to have attention from their subordinates. At other times they will remain aloof and independent. In order to maintain high status with an ambitious dog, humans in the pack should initiate most of the interactions with him, rather than the other way around. Do not always respond to your dog's demands for attention.

Grooming your dog helps to strengthen the bond between the two of you and teaches him to accept being held and handled.

If you choose to ignore him, do not speak to him, look at him or touch him so that he gets the message. When he has gone away to lie down, call him to you and give as much affection as you like. Being aloof with a pushy dog helps him get the message that he is lower in status and helps to foster a more independent attitude in a dog that is likely to become over-attached to his new owners.

GROOMING

It is important for your dog to accept being touched, handled and groomed all over. Some dogs will not have learned to cope with this and will need to be familiarised with it gradually. Dogs that are happy with human contact will be more trusting and are more likely to allow veterinary attention, even with un-comfortable procedures. If you cannot handle your own dog without a struggle, your veterinary surgeon will not be able to either.

Try to groom your dog every day for the first few weeks. Even short-coated dogs need to accept being touched all over and it gives you a chance to do a quick health check at the same time. Keep sessions short at first and follow them up immediately with a treat, game or walk so your dog will learn that if he stands still and tolerates the attention he will be well rewarded.

If your dog is afraid, take things very slowly at first, brushing 'safe' areas such as down his back and on his shoulders. Work up to brushing underneath and between his hind legs. Some dogs have a very low pain threshold and tugging long hair or digging brushes into their skin can distress them. Previous rough handling may have made them terrified of brushes. It is important to persevere with such dogs and to work slowly and gently to gain their trust.

Some dogs will not let you groom them because they consider themselves too high in status. For dogs that try to wriggle away when they have had enough, who try to turn it into a game, try to bite the brush or nibble your fingers, insist on grooming until you have finished. Keep going until your dog gives in and allows you to groom him without making a fuss. Then break off and offer a big reward. It may be easier to place such a dog on a table where he will have less confidence. Put the table in the corner of a room so that you only have to prevent him from jumping off on two sides. Hold his collar with one hand and groom with the other. If there is too much resistance you may need to tie him. Ask a professional groomer to show you how to restrain a difficult dog.

KEEP FRINGES TRIMMED

If your dog jumps when you touch him on his side or back, it may be because he cannot see well as he has long hair covering his eyes. Sudden movements or touches that seem to come out of the blue could cause him to snap in self-defence. If your dog has a long fringe, carefully clip the hair from this area or tie it up out of the way. It may look less appealing but it is much more pleasant for your dog to be able to see where he is going.

Parents should always be on hand to help out if the dog likes to play tug-of -war.

For a pushy, self-confident dog, it is important to have complete physical control in case he behaves badly and continue grooming until he has accepted it.

If you groom your dog a little every day, even the most difficult dog will become more compliant and trusting. Continue to build this up gradually until you can look at his teeth, in his mouth, in his ears, lift up his legs and hold his paws. Do not overwhelm him with too much at first, but gradually introduce these exercises as he learns to trust you.

High status for children

It is important that your new dog learns that his position in the pack lies below that of any children in the family. Make sure that your children follow the guidelines given above, especially during the early days with your new dog. Do not allow them to sneak the dog up to their bedroom, either to sleep or play, until you are satisfied that the dog will not attempt to take over. Feed the children before the dog and keep him away from toddlers while they are eating to prevent him from stealing food from their hands. Encourage your children to join in the grooming process, but wait until your dog completely accepts being groomed and touched by all adults in the house first.

For dogs that enjoy tug-of-war games, ensure that an adult is on hand at all times to help a child win if necessary, especially if the child is small and your dog is big. If your dog feels that the family forms a coalition at such times to assist the children, he will feel that he cannot win against them and will consider himself lower than they are in the pack. If your dog is rough during play, avoid such games altogether when the children are present and play chase games instead.

CHAPTER

5

Understanding Your Dog's Needs

Dogs are usually able to fit into our families extremely well and it is sometimes easy to overlook the fact that they are from a completely different species. They view the world differently from humans, have a different way of communicating with each other and have different motivations for the things they do. If your dog is to behave well, it is important that you understand these differences and make allowances for them during interactions with him. Providing for his special species needs will ensure that he does not behave badly in an attempt to fulfil innate urges.

Dogs gather as much information by sniffing as we do by looking. Deposited scents around this post seem irresistible.

A world full of scent

When we go into a new situation, we use our eyes to gather information about what is happening around us; for humans, sight is our most important sense. When a dog enters a new environment, it sniffs as it moves about. The sense of smell is his most important way of gathering information.

Dogs' sense of smell is far superior to ours – they can easily follow the route taken by a person or animal who passed by

Humans will look around when entering a new situation, whereas dogs will use their nose to find out what goes on there.

hours or days earlier, leaving no visible signs, and they can sniff out minute amounts of drugs or explosives through layers of packaging and containers. Their sense of smell is known to be at least 100 times more acute than ours and may be even better. The area inside a dog's nose that detects scent is about 14 times larger than ours and the nerves from this go to a part of the brain that is larger and further developed than the area of the human brain that processes information from the nose.

This amazing sense of smell allows dogs to detect odours that are lost to us completely. We should not be surprised that they spend hours investigating lamp posts where other dogs have left urine or when they put their noses in all the wrong places when investigating new people. They are doing as nature intended and gathering information. Being able to tell the age, sex, state of health, reproductive status and even state of mind from one sniff is a remarkable ability.

Knowing that dogs live in a world of scent rather than sight helps to explain why dogs sometimes do unusual things. For example, your dog may bark at you if he sees you approaching from a distance and only change this to a greeting response when you get within sniffing distance or if the wind blows your scent in his direction.

Dogs see shape, form and movement, whereas humans see detail and texture.

Sound sensitivity

Dogs are more sensitive to sounds than we are and can hear sounds that we cannot. This explains why they will sometimes appear to be listening intently when we can hear nothing – they can hear sounds from four times farther away than we can, so there is no need to shout when asking your dog to do something. Unless his hearing is impaired, your dog will easily hear what you are saying even if you are some distance away and if he is ignoring you it will have more to do with his motivation to listen and whether he is paying attention rather than his ability to hear.

Dogs of some breeds are likely to be more sensitive to sound than others. Those used for herding, such as collies and German shepherd dogs and their crosses, are likely to react to loud noises and are more prone to developing noise phobias than others.

They can also hear a high range of frequencies that allows them to hear ultrasonic sounds, such as mice squeaking. This explains a dog's ability to hear 'silent' dog whistles when we hear nothing and may help to explain why they get excited when they hear their owner's car approaching but will ignore others of the same make.

A physical feature that affects dogs' ability to hear is whether it has pricked ears or whether his ears hang down. Pricked ears will catch more sound and they are more mobile, which allows them to be rotated to pinpoint the source of the sound. A spaniel that runs in all directions to find his owner when called finds it hard to determine where the call came from because of his heavy ear flaps.

Selective sight

Dogs are not colour blind as used to be believed, but their colour vision is not as good as ours. This means that they will detect objects on a contrasting background better than if they blend in.

A dog is more likely to see a yellow ball on green grass, for example, than a red one. Dogs also see detail and texture less well and recognise objects by shape and form instead.

They are also much very sensitive to movement, especially movement at ground level, than we are as they evolved to catch moving animals. This makes it more likely that they will see a moving object, whether it is a rolling ball or a running cat, than a stationary one. They can also see at night and in dim conditions because they have a reflective layer at the back of their eyes. This traps light and allows them to make more use of it and is the reason a dog's eyes shine when caught in the beam of a car's headlights. The ability to see better at lower light levels helps wild dogs to hunt at dawn and dusk and allows domestic dogs to run off at top speed in darkness without crashing into things.

SEEING FROM A DIFFERENT PERSPECTIVE

A dog sees the world from a much lower perspective than we do. While this may seem obvious, it is often overlooked. This is why dogs jump up to greet their owners or to see out of windows. It becomes an important point when a dog is particularly small and has short legs. Thinking what it must be like for dogs to be in our giant world can help to explain some of their behaviour.

Jaws, paws and the sense of touch

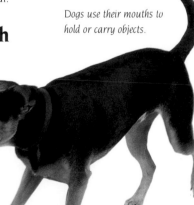

Dogs use their mouths to hold or carry objects.

Another obvious difference between humans and dogs is that dogs do not have hands. Instead they use their mouths to pick up objects, to explore and for defence. Experienced dogs can be as accurate with their mouths as we are with our hands – if an adult dog bites and misses, it probably meant to!

It is also worth knowing that paws, neck and whisker areas around the sense organs can be particularly sensitive to touch. If dogs are being attacked, these are the areas they need to guard the most. A dog cannot run if one of his paws is injured; it is important to protect his vulnerable jugular vein in his neck when fighting;

and the organs with which he senses the world are particularly vulnerable and important.

Appreciating these sensitivities can help to prevent you startling your dog by touching him on these areas unexpectedly or when he is asleep. You may notice that he jumps a little when

The dog in the middle of the picture above is not enjoying the attention and sits dowm and licks its nose to signal this to the others.

touched in these places so avoid these areas until he has learned to trust you. As your relationship with him develops, get him used to having his paws touched and held, and to being held around the neck. Many dogs are very sensitive around the head area, but they begin to tolerate and enjoy being touched there as they begin to relax and trust their humans.

Body language

Dogs usually communicate with each other using body language. This involves the use of the tail, ears, eyes, posture and facial expression to signal their intentions. They will automatically try to communicate with their owners using these signals too and if you can learn to read them you will be able to decipher what your dog is trying to tell you.

Learning body language is not difficult. The most important thing to do is to watch your dog in different situations. Look at his posture, at what his tail is doing, how he carries his ears, where he is looking and what he is doing with his mouth. Watch how he behaves and try to work out a reason for the action. You will soon be able to guess at how he is feeling just by looking at him if you watch him enough.

Why do dogs do that?

Having evolved from wolves, dogs are driven by similar needs to those that kept their ancestors alive. These are the need to live in a social group, the need to stay safe, the need to maintain their bodies and the need to reproduce.

All dogs are different, just as all people are different, and some will place different emphasis on certain behaviours and enjoy doing different things more than others. However, dogs are all basically the same and learning about their special species needs can help you to provide an outlet for their natural behaviour that will result in a contented, well behaved pet.

LEARNING BODY LANGUAGE

Hand signals
Dogs use vocal communication very little when 'talking' to each other and consequently find it difficult to learn words. They will learn hand signals much quicker because it taps into to their natural method of communication.

Tail wagging
A wagging tail is a sign of excitement, not just of happiness. A happy dog will wag his tail, but so will an excited dog that is about to bite. A stiff body posture and a wagging tail signals something very different from a body that is relaxed with a wagging tail.

Play bow
A play bow, with elbows on the floor and bottom in the air, is an invitation to play.

Head high
A confident dog holds his head high, his tail erect and looks directly at the source of interest. His ears are up and his mouth is relaxed.

Flattened body, tail down
A shy dog will flatten his body, keeping most of his weight on his back legs ready to run if necessary. The tail is often tucked under or held down. His ears are held back and his eyes are open wide so that the whites of his eyes can be seen. He will avoid looking at the person or animal that makes his feel shy but will glance in their direction and look away quickly.

All dogs need social contact, whether from humans or other dogs.

THE NEED FOR SOCIAL CONTACT

If wolves are to survive, it is important for them to live in a social group. This enables them to hunt, stay safe and reproduce. Pet dogs have retained this need for social contact, which is why they make such good pets. All dogs need to feel that they are part of a pack. This need can sometimes be overlooked if everyone in a household leads a busy life. Lack of attention and affection can become a problem if it persists as a dog will begin to behave badly just to get attention. Bad behaviour then becomes a nuisance and, sadly, it is often punished rather that treated as a symptom of an underlying need.

Lack of love and attention is unlikely to be a problem with a new dog. However, as the novelty begins to wear off and the family returns to normal routines, you need to reassure your dog that he is a valued member of your family. Try to set aside a quiet time each day to give your dog the undivided attention he needs. Play with him, stroke him, talk to him and let him know that he is important to you and the family. This should not be a chore, but it is often something that we need to consciously make time for with our busy lives.

Many of the behaviours displayed by dogs come from the need for social contact. Greeting rituals when you arrive home, face licking, pawing for attention or noses pushed under your hand, tail wagging and other gestures are all designed to keep us close and are done instinctively by the dog to promote the bond of friendship between us.

THE NEED TO STAY SAFE

All animals need to feel safe as the penalty for not being safe in the wild is death or injury. As it is so important, it takes priority over all other behaviour.

A new dog may take a long time to settle in, particularly if he was frightened in his previous home. He may feel very vulnerable at first and he may not want to play or even eat very much because he is on red alert all the time. In addition, he will be more likely to be defensive when approached or when his safety zone is breached. Growling, raising his lips or hackles, or hiding under tables or behind chairs will all be signs that he is not feeling safe. As he gains more confidence he may decide that the family is safe, but intruders are not and may show territorial behaviour designed to keep visitors away.

Some dogs are worse than others. Collies and German shepherd dogs and their crosses are particularly prone to being fearful and any dog that has had bad experiences or not enough socialisation as a puppy will take a long time to feel safe in a new environment. It takes time to build up the trust a dog needs to feel safe. Be a considerate owner who gives him the space he needs, but who works with him gently and gradually until he can overcome his fears to help him come round faster.

The desire to stay safe overrides all others. Getting away into a small space, which is easy to defend can help a dog feel less afraid.

*Playing with toys is
domestic dogs' substitute for
hunting. It helps to keep
their bodies fit and active.*

Some dogs are fine at home with the family, but are very scared of things they encounter when out for a walk. Things that move and make a noise, such as big lorries, children on bikes or skateboards, other animals or people can all frighten a dog that is unfamiliar with the world we live in. Take care not to overwhelm him with too much at first and keep your distance from these scary things to help him realise that these things will not hurt him.

Try not to expect a dog to lose his fears overnight. Fears are nature's way of keeping him safe and a dog will not lose the feeling of being afraid until he has had many positive experiences with whatever it was he is worried about. See Chapter 7 for more information.

Many other behaviours associated with staying safe may be displayed by a new dog. Tearing up items that smell of their owner, scratching at doors to get out of the house when left alone or marking the territory with urine to make themselves feel more secure are common behaviours in recently rehomed dogs. If your dog does something unusual during its first few days with you, it is likely that he is trying to make himself feel safer.

THE NEED TO MAINTAIN THEIR BODIES

A healthy body requires food and water and our dogs' ancestors had to travel to find both. This desire to exercise has been passed on to our domestic dogs. In addition, wolves have to hunt to eat and although most of our dogs no longer do this they have retained the motivation to behave in a similar way. Playing with toys is an acceptable substitute for hunting and fulfils the instinctive desire for dogs to chase and capture. It can also help to ensure that your dog is so busy concentrating on you that he is not getting into trouble chasing other things that move, such

Chewing is necessary for healthy teeth and jaws. Dogs like to do this throughout their lives not just as puppies.

DIFFERENT GAMES

- Chase games: the most popular game played particularly by herding breeds. Most dogs love the thrill of the chase and the desire to stop the 'prey' from moving is strong.
- Possession games: it is important for dogs to keep hold of items in their possession. Once these would have been pieces of meat or hide, but we can substitute pieces of rubber or rope.
- Squeaky toy games: these stimulate a very primitive instinct to bite and 'kill' a squeaking object. Terriers, bred to catch and kill small animals, usually enjoy this game. How excited a dog gets when it plays this game will give you an indication of how strong its predatory instinct is.

DOGS THAT WON'T PLAY

If your dog will not play with toys, it might be because he has not learned to do so or has played too much with another dog rather than humans. Begin with soft toys, particularly those covered in fake fur, to stimulate his instincts. Keep it moving quickly and erratically, concentrating on the toy rather than your dog. Have fun yourself throwing it to a partner or throwing it in the air until he begins to want to join in the game. Allow him to catch it and end the game while he is still wanting more. He will gradually begin to have more fun playing with you and the toy and you will be able to play for longer.

as cats, sheep, wild animals, cars or children on bikes.

Domestic dogs also display other behaviours associated with body maintenance. They will often clean themselves by licking and self grooming, they may bury excess food to keep it safe for later or dig out to a cool or warm place to lie. Chewing to maintain the teeth and jaws is something that dogs like to do throughout their life. As commercial pet food is often not chewy, provide suitable items that they can chew on to fulfil this desire.

THE NEED TO REPRODUCE

Animals have evolved a desire to pass on their genes to the next generation. An entire dog will instinctively try to mate with receptive members of the opposite sex. Male dogs will take any opportunity to mate, particularly when there is a bitch in season nearby, whereas bitches have a 'season' or 'heat' period about twice a year.

Dogs do vary, however, in the effort they are willing to make to achieve their goal. Some entire dogs will happily remain at home if there is a bitch in season down the road, while others will escape and camp outside until the season is over. Similarly, bitches will differ in their desire to escape during seasons. Male dogs that have a strong desire to mate may show other unwanted behaviours such as escaping and roaming, and mounting cushions, blankets, peoples legs and small children. If you own a male dog that does this have him castrated to take away the urge and the unwanted behaviour. This is ultimately kinder to him than keeping him in a frustrated state or punishing the unwanted behaviour as it occurs. Similarly, spaying bitches will prevent them from escaping at the critical time in their season and presenting you with a litter of unwanted puppies a couple of months later.

What happens when you frustrate canine needs

Ignore these basic needs at your peril! Frustrating a dog's desire to maintain social contact with his group, stay safe, run, jump, play and chew will usually have unpleasant consequences as he tries to find fulfilment anyway.

A dog denied social contact will persistently seek attention or will try to escape to find social groups elsewhere. A dog that feels unsafe will show a range of unwanted defensive behaviours. A

dog denied the opportunity to exercise fully is likely to move about constantly and get in your way or will look for things to do that you may not approve of. Outside, he is likely to run off and not return and, if he is not playing appropriate games with toys, he will be playing inappropriate games with other things that move. A dog denied the chance to chew appropriate items will select your best shoes or anything accidentally dropped on the floor instead.

Knowing your dog's special species needs and giving him an outlet for them all will create a dog that is content and well behaved. Suppressing his basic needs or ignoring them will create a frustrated dog and bad behaviour.

Playing with toys out on a walk can help to keep your dog interested in you. He is then less likely to wander off and get into trouble.

BUILDING A FRIENDSHIP

There is nothing as effective as playing with toys to develop the bond between you and your new dog. Playing exposes strengths and weaknesses and allows you to get to know each other better. It is important to play a lot with your new dog, teaching him to do so first if necessary.

6

Essential Training

Teaching your dog to come back when called, walk well on the lead and sit and lie down when told makes life easier, safer and more pleasant for you both. He may know some of the commands already and it would be wise to test out a variety of words and hand signals to check. Unfortunately, many dogs know the word 'sit' and little else, but if you use positive methods, training should be fun and rewarding.

A well trained dog makes everyday tasks easier and more pleasant.

Progression towards good manners and behaviour should begin as soon as you get your dog home, but training him to respond to commands can be left until a good relationship has developed between you. He will be more willing to please you if you are established as the leader of his social group and a friend, and this will take time to develop.

POINTS TO REMEMBER WHEN TRAINING

- Keep lessons short. Ten three-minute sessions are much better than one 30-minute session.
- Always end on a good note. Ask for something you know your dog can do and reward him well.
- Stop immediately if you feel yourself becoming frustrated or angry.
- Reward the correct action immediately.

Hand signals are easier than words

A dog will find it much easier to read your body language than listen to the words you speak. You can help your dog to learn words by giving hand, arm or body signals at the same time as you say the command. Once he responds every time, you can gradually reduce the body signals until just the spoken word remains.

Dogs can't be trained in a day

It will take a couple of months of regular teaching and many, many repetitions before what you are teaching will become permanently fixed in your dog's mind. Try not to expect too much of him too soon, particularly if you want him to respond to spoken words only.

Although he is a sophisticated and complex animal, he is not designed to learn to respond to spoken words and it is quite hard for him to learn them. If in doubt, always assume he has not quite understood it yet and show him what to do.

Different circumstances, different places

Remember that all dogs learn a set of associations surrounding an event. In order for your dog to learn that the word you say equals an action he performs, which equals a reward given to him by you, you will have to repeat the teaching process in many different locations under altered circumstances. Eventually, your dog will realise that all the associations surrounding the action other than the word itself are irrelevant and that you will give the reward whenever he does the required action when he hears the word wherever he is.

Distractions

Dogs learn better if they are taught in a quiet, calm environment with no distractions. However, once your dog has learned what you require, you will need to slowly increase the level of distraction and teach your dog that he has to respond to your requests even if he would prefer to do something else. This will require you to keep him controlled at first so that he cannot run off to be 'rewarded' by the distraction instead. Continue to build up the distractions until he will work for you even when he has very powerful urges to do something else.

Close control

Until you can more or less guarantee that your dog will respond to your requests, keep him under physical control so that he cannot be rewarded by running off and doing what he wants to do.

Above: Take titbits and toys out with you so that you can incorporate short training sessions throughout your walks.

Kind and effective ways to train

Dogs learn more quickly and remember more if they are rewarded for doing the right thing rather than punished for doing something wrong. The most effective training involves rewards and incentives and is fun and enjoyable for both parties.

Find out what motivates your dog. What does he like to do most – eat, chase balls, tug on toys, kill squeaky toys, be stroked, be praised? If he likes to do one or all of these things you can use them as an incentive and reward for responding to your requests. If, instead, he prefers to run free or hunt, life will be more difficult for you because you will need to teach him to enjoy playing and interacting with you first. This will take time and it should be done before you start any training. There is nothing more frustrating than trying to teach a dog that has no interest in you or your incentives. If you are not succeeding in getting him to play with toys, try feeding him by hand for a week so that he learns that you are a source of what he needs to survive. Once he is focusing on the food, begin to put some inside toys so that he starts to see these as a source of interest too.

Rewards can be made more enticing by withholding them for a period before training. Who wants another chocolate biscuit when you have just eaten a whole packet? This is difficult to do with affection and is a good reason why pet dogs need other incentives to encourage them to make the extra effort to learn what you want them to do.

COMING BACK WHEN CALLED

Being able to call your dog back to you ensures that he can be let off the lead safely and it is one of the most important things to teach your dog.

STEP I

Step 1: Begin in the house and garden. Call your dog enthusiastically and make sure you have a good reward ready for him when he reaches you. Gradually build this up, practising frequently throughout the day and rewarding well each time, until he is rushing to you at top speed whenever you call, even if he is busy doing something else.

STEP 2   STEP 3

STEP 2: Take your dog, on a long lead or piece of line, to a quiet area and wait until he has explored his surroundings. When he is looking away from you, but is not too engrossed in something else, call him enthusiastically using the same words and tone you did at home and reward him well if he comes to you. If he does not, tug the lead praising him well when he moves a few paces towards you. Run backwards and enthusiastically encourage him to move with you. Reward him well when he gets to you.

STEP 3: If your dog enjoys chase games, make a toy obvious to him then throw it behind you to encourage him to run up right up to you next time. Don't throw it too far or he will pull you over as he runs to get it.

STEP 4: Once he has the toy, use the lead to bring him back to you and let him know how pleased you are. Praise him while he is holding the toy for a few moments first and then take it from him. Do not touch the toy or the area around his head for a while or he will begin to avoid coming back in case you take the toy.

STEP 4

Practice makes perfect

STEP 5: When he responds readily to your call, practise when your dog is engrossed in something else. Use the lead to pull him away from whatever he is doing and enforce your command if necessary. Doing this will begin to make him more reliable about coming when called even when he would rather be doing something else. Once he has come back to you, let him go back to what he was doing to reward him.

STEP 5

STEP 6: Continue to practise regularly until he responds every time despite any distractions going on around him. Use a washing line or similar long line as a lead to increase the amount of freedom he has and continue to practise in different areas until he is reliable. When you have this mental control, find a quiet area away from traffic, other dogs or livestock and let him off the lead (but make sure he is wearing a collar and identity disc just in case he runs off). Allow him freedom for a while before practising your recall. Reward him well and let him run free again.

STEP 6

WALKING ON A LOOSE LEAD

If your dog walks nicely on the lead, family members will be more willing to take him out for walks. He will be better exercised and, consequently, better behaved. There are two ways to achieve this: one is to fit a specially designed head collars and the other is to teach him not to pull when on the lead.

Wearing a headcollar

If you do decide to use a headcollar, follow the fitting instructions carefully and ignore your dog's attempts to scratch it off. Some dogs will seems quite frantic at first, but they will soon overcome their worries if you persevere. Most dogs learn to tolerate these devices very well and they are an ideal way to prevent pulling. Remember, though, not to tug or pull the lead sharply as this can damage your dog's neck. Once your dog has got used to the feel of something fitted around his nose and behind his ears, you can use it to control the position of his head so that he cannot pull.

TEACHING YOUR DOG NOT TO PULL

Dogs learn quickly and will soon realise they cannot pull when wearing a headcollar.

Most dogs pull on the lead because they want to go faster. If your dog learns that each time he pulls you stop, he will eventually walk without pulling. This method works well for all dogs, but takes considerable perseverance, particularly for dogs that have

been pulling their owners around for years. Practise at first in a quiet area when you do not need to get anywhere in a hurry. You can speed up the process by tiring your dog before you begin. Throw a toy for him in the garden until he tires or allow him to let off steam by giving him access to an open area before attempting to train him.

The key is to be persistent. Never allow the lead to go tight without stopping. If you have to be somewhere in a hurry, use a head collar so you do not set back your training. Begin training as soon as you put the lead on and do not allowing your dog to pull you as you leave the house. The first few walks may take a long time, but it will get easier and quicker as he learns.

STEP 1

STEP 2

STEP 3

STEP 1: If the lead begins to tighten, stop and stand still. For very boisterous dogs or persistent pullers, use your weight to bring them to an abrupt halt with a tug on the collar.

STEP 2: Keep your hands quite close to your body to give you maximum stability as your dog pulls. As he turns to find out why you have stopped, encourage him to come back to you. If he continues to pull away from you, give little tugs on the lead so that he cannot lean on it and encourage him to come back to you when he stops pulling.

STEP 3: TRY TO encourage him to return to his position beside you.

STEP 4: As soon as he is in position, praise him well and begin to walk forward at a fast pace. Praise him and continue to walk forward for as long as the lead remains loose.

STEP 5: Walking without pulling does not mean your dog must stay close to you all the time. With a long lead, or a flexi-lead, your dog can have quite a lot of freedom. However, as soon as the lead goes tight, begin again from Step 1 and repeat the exercise as frequently as necessary.

STEP 4

STEP 5

'SIT', 'DOWN' AND 'STAY'

These are three useful words for your dog to know and they are easy to teach. He may know them already, but could need a refresher course to sharpen his responses.

STEP 1

STEP 2

STEP 3

'Sit'

STEP 1: Offer a reward and ask your dog to sit. If he does not, hold a tasty titbit in front of his nose.

STEP 2: Move the titbit up and backwards. As his nose follows it, his bottom should go down. If your dog moves backwards instead, position him in the corner of the room so that he is unable to do so.

STEP 3: Feed the titbit as soon as your dog's bottom touches the floor and praise him well while he remains sitting.

Continue with this sequence over several sessions until your dog begins to understand what he is expected to do. Eventually you will find that he will begin to learn what is expected and will sit when you hold the titbit above him. Practise in different locations and circumstances until he sits reliably when you ask.

STEP 1

STEP 2

'Down'

STEP 1: Ensure your dog is in the sitting position. Offer something that he wants and move it down towards the floor. It is usually easier if you offer a titbit instead of a toy as you can hide food in your hand and your dog cannot get it until you release it.

STEP 2: Keep his attention on whatever it is, but do not allow him to take it. Eventually, he will become tired of holding his head down and will begin to lie down to get more comfortable.

STEP 3: As soon as he lies down, give him the reward and praise him well.

STEP 3

STEP 1

STEP 2

'Stay'

STEP 1: Ensure your dog is sitting. Ask him to stay and stand
still beside him. Wait for a short time then praise him gently for
remaining in position. If he gets up at any time, replace him in
the position in exactly the same spot and repeat. If he gets up
repeatedly, you may need to exercise him more before the next
training session or spend more time teaching him how to sit or
lie down on request.

STEP 2: Once he has learned to stay still when you are beside
him, ask him to stay and take a step to the side. Use the lead to
stop him from getting up if you can and put him in the same
place if he moves. Wait a short time and then move back to him
and praise him gently while in position as before. Progress until
you no longer need to keep him on the lead.

STEP 3: When he is happy to stay while you move to the side,
progress to moving in front of him. A hand signal will help him to
understand what you mean and can be used to supplement the
word if he looks as though he may move. Move back to him and
praise him gently as before.

Gradually build up this exercise until your dog will stay still for
longer periods and in different positions. These exercises are

STEP 3

Tip

Never ask your dog to stay without tethering him when you leave him unattended in public places. There are many distractions that may cause him to move, which could result in a nasty incident.

useful for times when you want him to stay in the car when you open the door until you have attached a lead, for example, or you want him to settle down and lie still beside you while you visit a friend. The word 'stay' can then be used to help him to understand what he is supposed to do in these situations.

DOG TRAINING CLASSES

Training classes can help you solve training problems and bolster your enthusiasm for training until your dog has reached a suitable standard. However, many rescue dogs are afraid of other dogs or people and being in a crowded hall full of both may push him into behaving aggressively. If your dog is shy or already aggressive with people or dogs, it may be better to train him at home or arrange individual tuition first.

   If you do decide to attend dog training classes, go along without your dog first to see if you approve of their methods. The trainer should use rewards rather than punishment: toys and titbits should be used rather than choke chains. Ask your veterinary surgeon for a recommendation or contact the Association of Pet Dog Trainers, which monitors the methods used by its members and ensures they are kind, fair and effective.

CHAPTER

7

Coping with Shyness and Aggression

If you have chosen your dog carefully using the methods suggested earlier, you are unlikely to see real aggression from your dog unless you have been unlucky or have deliberately taken on a problem dog as a challenge. However, as dogs cannot talk to us and tell us what is wrong and if we ignore their body language, as we so frequently do, they have only one way of telling us to stop what we are doing. While most dogs settle into their new homes without problems, it helps to know some of the causes of aggression so you can heed any warning signs.

Reasons for aggression

Dogs do not become aggressive without reason. Most aggressive incidents happen because the dog is afraid and is acting defensively. Sometimes he may be guarding resources, such as food or the territory, which he thinks he needs to protect. Or he may be trying to raise his status within the pack. Some dogs will be aggressive to other smaller animals because their predatory instincts are triggered. If your dog is being aggressive, seek professional help from a pet behaviour counsellor (see Chapter 9).

FEAR AND SHYNESS

Most fears arise from a lack of socialisation with people and other animals when the dog was a puppy. Unsocialised dogs are also unfamiliar with many things in their environment, which adds to their fears. Dogs that have this problem are usually shy and fearful when taken to new places. They are often suspicious of new people, especially those in dark clothes or wearing or carrying anything unusual. Men are often mistrusted more than women as puppies are often raised by women and may have limited contact with men in their early weeks.

An unpleasant experience, whether frightening or painful, can ensure that the dog becomes fearful when the same circumstances occur again and bad treatment from owners or others can result in fears of certain types of people. Mother dogs who are fearful themselves can pass on their fears to their puppies.

A frightened dog will often appear crouched, ready to run and may pant rapidly.

WARNING SIGNS

If your dog is upset with you, he will usually try to let you know before he takes the drastic action of biting. These are the warning signs:

- He will use obvious body language, such as slight crouching, flattened ears and lowered tail, and will look intently at you.
- If this is ignored he will growl and raise his lips to show his teeth.
- He may stiffen and stare.
- Often he will snap in the air, close to your skin, to show you that he means business.

Ignoring any of these signals is not wise as it may result in a real bite. Punishing these behaviours is also counterproductive as the dog will learn not to give warnings before it bites, which results in an unpredictable dog. This may have happened to your dog in the past and you may find that a slight change in his body language is all that precedes a bite.

It is essential that you avoid situations where your dog may become aggressive. If, however, he exhibits any of these warning signs, defuse the situation by stopping what you are doing immediately (see page 108).

A dog showing defensive
aggression does not look
frightened even though he
is. This dog is putting up a
good display to make
the recipient back down.

Four defence strategies

If an animal feels under threat, it can adopt one of four strategies for dealing with the threat and can switch between them rapidly and without warning. These strategies are fight, flight, freeze and appease.

Fight: dogs may make lots of noise and frightening visual displays to try to prevent a threat from coming closer. When this fails, or if a threat is approaching too fast, it can choose to fight and bite to make a threat retreat. Dogs will often use biting only as a last resort as the penalties of being injured in any retaliation are usually seen as too high. However, once a dog is forced to use this strategy, it will quickly discover how effective it is and is more likely to use it again. In order to use this strategy, a dog needs a certain amount of self-confidence. Confident dogs, especially those on home ground, near other members of their pack and in small, easily defendable spaces are more likely to choose this strategy than dogs on their own in a strange place.

Flight: running away is the safest form of defence if a dog has somewhere to run to and if he is not fastened to his owner or a fixed point by a lead. The 'flight' option is not as effective for a dog in a small territory, such as a car, cage or small fenced garden, and so it will often choose the 'fight' option instead.

Freeze: keeping still and hoping the threat will go away is a strategy that sometimes works. However, dogs in the freeze position will be ready to adopt one of the other strategies if this one fails. Gentle, shy dogs are likely to adopt this strategy.

Appease: when faced with another animal, which appears higher in rank or dangerous, puppies or young dogs will often show appeasement gestures. They may lick their muzzles, flatten their ears, raise a paw, roll over, lift a hind leg to expose the groin area, produce a small amount of urine or some or all of these. These gestures are designed to show the stronger animal that they are no threat and, hence, that there is no need to use aggression. Some dogs carry this strategy into adulthood, but most reserve it for members of their own pack as they mature.

Physiological changes

When an animal is under threat hormones and other chemicals are released into the blood stream, the heart rate and breathing get faster and the blood supply to vital organs increases. A dog under threat may tremble or shake, pant in short rapid breaths, sweat through his pads and will probably want to go to the toilet soon after it detects a threat.

TIP

Be jolly rather than sympathetic if your dog is scared. If he sees that you are not worried, he will be more likely to forget his own fears.

Tasty titbits offered by a stranger can help shy dogs to overcome their fear.

These bodily changes will subside quite quickly after the initial fright, but the physiological changes persist for some days afterwards so that if the threat returns, the dog is prepared. Remember this if your dog is shy or fearful. An experience that upsets him, such as being taken to a new home or being treated by the veterinary surgeon, can be enough to activate these changes. For some days after a fright, and possibly during the early days of his new life in your family, your dog may be more easily triggered into defensive behaviour than normal.

Coping with shyness

Many dogs are shy and afraid of the unfamiliar. If your dog is like this when you get him, he may take a while to settle down. If you keep him relatively calm and expose him to new situations slowly, never going beyond what he can cope with, he should begin to get braver. However, if you take things too fast, particularly if you force him to have encounters with things that scare him, he is likely to get worse and may even begin to be aggressive in his own defence.

In order not to overwhelm a shy dog, watch his body language and learn to tell when he is enjoying an experience and when he is becoming afraid (see page 81). Watch his ear and tail carriage particularly as these will give you the first clues. Identify what scares him most – is it strangers, other dogs or new environments? Once you know the cause, give him a controlled exposure to small amounts of whatever it is that scares him.

Combine this with activities that he enjoys, such as playing or eating, and he will become more confident more quickly. If your dog is frightened of traffic, for example, take him to where he can see traffic in the distance, but is not afraid. Play with him and make it fun to be in that place and then move a little closer to the traffic. Continue until you think your dog is on the edge of what he can cope with. End on a positive note and finish for the day. If you do this every day, keeping away from close encounters with traffic until he is cured, he will soon realise that it will not hurt him. It will take some time to overcome the problem completely, as with all fears, but you should begin to see results quite quickly.

It is important that owners of shy dogs take charge to ensure that their dog feels safe at all times. Once your dog begins to trust that you will be there to help him out of difficulties, he will relax and enjoy himself.

This dog is worried and is moving away so that he feels safer. Forcing him to confront his fear by pulling him closer could result in him using aggression instead.

Aggression to strangers

Nearly all aggression to strangers is caused by fear. Even common territorial aggression to postmen and other visitors is caused by a mistrust of people coming onto the property. If your dog has bitten anyone, it is up to you to ensure it never happens again. It is essential to keep complete control of your dog at all times and it is important to get professional help to identify the cause of the problem and to work our a treatment programme.

Tackling the problem alone can be frightening and fraught with difficulties so ask your veterinary surgeon to refer you to a member of the Association of Pet Behaviour Counsellors (see page 158). You can also ask the rescue centre that rehomed your dog for help.

If your dog is likely to snap, accustom him to wearing a muzzle. Although they look cumbersome, basket muzzles are less restricting than the tube style and allow more circulation of air around the tongue.

INTRODUCING YOUR DOG TO A MUZZLE

If your dog is likely to be aggressive, buy a well fitting muzzle and get him used to wearing it. To do this, put the muzzle on him a few minutes before something nice is going to happen to him, such as dinner time, someone arriving home or a game with a toy. Ignore any of his attempts to remove the muzzle and praise him when he accepts it. During one of the acceptance periods, remove the muzzle and immediately reward him. After a few days he will begin to accept the muzzle and you will be able to leave it on for longer. If you do this, your dog will associate the muzzle with pleasant things about to happen, and you will have no trouble in getting it on him in future. If he associates it only with unpleasant things, such as a trip to the veterinary surgery, he will be very intolerant of it.

Make sure he is wearing the muzzle whenever there is a chance that he may be aggressive. Muzzles are restricting and do tend to make fear-biters more fearful, but they do at least prevent a bite. If you have a large dog you are not sure of, it is safer to muzzle him when he goes to the veterinary surgeon, at least for the first few times, just in case. Even the most docile dog can become aggressive in defence if he is in pain so accustoming your dog to a muzzle may be a wise precaution.

FEAR OF STRANGERS

If your dog barks at people or shows signs that he may be frightened, it is possible to change his attitude to strangers. To do this, arrange for your dog to meet strangers one at a time in a calm atmosphere so he can get used to them gradually.

Begin by putting your dog into a back room when a visitor arrives so he does not meet them on the doorstep where his excitement levels will be greatest. Ask the visitor to sit down and arm them with toys and titbits if they are willing to help. When all is settled, bring your dog in on a lead and sit away from the visitor. Wait until your dog has settled down before asking the visitor to encourage him to come forward to receive titbits and, perhaps, a game with a toy. If there is any doubt about your dog, prevent him from going too close and ask your visitor to throw the titbits or toys. Ask your visitor not to stare at your dog or make sudden movements that may scare him. End on a positive note and take your dog out of the room before your visitor gets up to leave.

Introductions made in this way will teach your dog to look forward to the arrival of that particular person, but they may have

Yawning can be one of the first signs that your dog is uneasy about his situation.

to visit several times before your dog goes forward to greet them. Keep the visitor sitting down at first and gradually work up to them getting up and moving around as your dog begins to accept them. You can speed up this process by arranging to meet on neutral territory and trying to get some gentle interaction going between the two of them, such as a game.

When your dog has got to know one person, try again with another. It may be a good idea to start with women as they are usually better accepted by shy dogs, and work up to introducing men. Increasing your dog's circle of friends in this way will build his confidence in people and he will begin to see them as a source of interest and fun rather than being afraid.

Throughout the process, ensure that your dog approaches each visitor first rather than the other way around. Try to keep to one visitor at a time until he can cope with more. Never punish or scold unwanted behaviour, but distract him instead by, for example, asking him to come to you and sit, and praising him. Try to relax and make sure you are in control of the situation so that your dog is not overwhelmed at any stage. If you have a number of people visiting at any time or anyone who is frightened of dogs, it may be best to keep him shut in another room until they have gone.

FEAR OF CHILDREN

If your dog is aggressive towards children, you sould seek professional help from a pet behaviour counsellor and keep him under control and muzzled until he has changed his attitude towards them.

If your dog is worried about children, take great care to ensure that they do not crowd him or get too close, which may make him feel threatened. Watch carefully when children are around and move him to a safe place if you see that he is becoming worried. Always insist that your dog approaches the children rather than the other way around and if he does not want to go to them, don't force him. Try to get him playing with the children in the garden and give them tasty titbits to throw to him. This will help to change his attitude towards them, but ensure they do not accidentally go near him and scare him until he has begun to see them as friends.

Many dogs are unfamiliar with toddlers and smaller children and find it difficult to cope with them because they squeal, move erratically and can pinch and pull fur when up close. If you have very young children or they visit you, it may be best to use a stair gate so that your dog is not isolated, but is kept out of the room that the children are in.

Aggression to owners

When your dog first comes home he will not know the people in the household and may not trust them at first. He may be particularly mistrustful if he has been punished or mistreated by previous owners. In addition, the stress of all the changes will make him more reactive and defensive. Any growls or warnings that happen in the first few days should be accepted as part of the settling in process. Try not to retaliate or be disappointed by your new dog, but try to avoid the same situation happening again. Make an extra effort to win your dog's trust and affection.

COLLAR SHYNESS

Many dogs are wary of being held by the collar and may bite if grabbed suddenly. A dog's neck is a sensitive area and it is where dogs will bite each other when they begin fighting. In addition, many dogs have learned that when they are held by the collar, there is no escape. They may have been grabbed in the past and held while they were punished or dragged somewhere they were afraid of going.

If your dog has a tendency to be worried when held by the collar, get him used to being held by approaching slowly and in a friendly way. Talk to him and try to let him know that your intentions are good. You may need to get him to come to you at first, rather than you approaching him. Hold his collar, feed him a tasty treat and release him. Continue to do this on a regular basis, gradually increasing the speed with which you approach him until he begins to trust you.

PAIN-RELATED AGGRESSION

If your dog is in pain, he may not trust you enough to let you help, particularly if he is new to the family. If your dog has an accident or needs to be given treatment, such as ear drops in a sore ear, it may take a while before you both trust each other enough to do it easily.

Take things slowly and muzzle him if necessary. If necessary, put the muzzle on a few minutes in advance of any treatment so he does not associate the two procedures and begin to resent being muzzled. Do not get cross with him or punish him for showing aggression as this will aggravate the problem. Try not to be disappointed that he is acting in this way. You cannot tell him that you are doing what is best for him – trust is something that comes only with time.

REDIRECTED AGGRESSION

Dogs sometimes bite humans without meaning to when they are in a frenzy about something else. If you try to break up a fight between two dogs, for example, your dog may bite by accident. Similarly, if your dog has seen another dog that it would like to be aggressive to and you are restraining it, he may turn and bite without really thinking he is biting you. It is therefore best to keep away from dogs that are highly aroused and use a lead or other means, such as a cushion, to take them away from the situation to calm down.

DOMINANCE AGGRESSION TO OWNERS

Some dogs are ambitious and want to lead the pack. If you chose your dog well and put in place all the suggestions in Chapter 4 as soon as you got your dog home, he should realise that his place is below all the humans in the household. However, as his confidence gradually increases, he may begin to get more pushy with whoever he perceives as being the weakest member of the household. If he begins to get aggressive, seek professional help from a pet behaviour counsellor. If he is just starting to get pushy, enforce all the rules in Chapter 4 rigorously and ensure that you and all in your family win all encounters with him for the next few months.

Aggression to other dogs

Some dogs are aggressive when on the lead, but are all right if they are loose because they know that they are able to run away if necessary. If your dog is aggressive to others, it is important that you take control of him and keep other dogs safe. Even if he does not hurt other dogs, he can scare them, which can in turn cause other dogs to become afraid and aggressive with others. You are also likely to get into trouble with other owners if you do not keep your dog under control. Get professional help from a pet behaviour counsellor if your dog is seriously aggressive.

DEFENSIVE AGGRESSION

As with aggression towards humans, most aggression towards other dogs is caused by fear. This may be due to a lack of socialisation with other dogs at an early age or it could be caused by an unpleasant experience in the dog's past.

Dogs often do not have enough confidence to use aggression as a way of coping with the fear they feel when they are new to an area so you may begin to see a change in your dog after the first few weeks. The best way to deal with any displays of aggression towards other dogs is to focus his attention on you.

Practise at first in an area where you can put a distance between you both and other dogs. Take out his favourite toys and treats, stand still and let him explore. When he begins to look at the other dogs, call him to you and play enthusiastically or offer tasty treats. Move steadily closer to the other dogs, repeating this procedure each time he looks at them. Gradually, after several sessions, you will find that he begins to look towards you whenever he sees another dog. Reward him well when he does.

If he will not play or eat, or if he begins to get agitated, you may be too close to the other dogs. Move farther away and try again. If your dog will not play or eat when out on a walk, even in

The dog on the left has chosen the 'fight' option in an effort to scare away the other dog, which has come too close for comfort.

the absence of other dogs, you will need to teach him to do this first (see below).

Avoid close encounters with other dogs if possible until he is feeling more confident as bad experiences will set back your progress. If, however, you can't avoid other dogs, cross the road if you see one approaching, put your body between your dog and the other one, ask your dog to sit and try to keep him focused on the reward. Keep working with him until the other dog passes, reward him well and continue with your walk.

He will gradually learn that you become a source of interesting, pleasant things when other dogs are about and will prefer to concentrate on these rather than deal with the fear he feels when concentrating on the other dog. He will learn that you keep him safe and out of trouble and that when, he is with you, he has no need to try to keep other dogs away by using aggressive behaviour. This takes time and perseverance, as with the treatment of all fear-based problems, but you should see improvements gradually. If you do not progress, seek advice from a pet behaviour counsellor.

One of the worst things you can do for dogs that are afraid of other dogs is to take them to a conventional dog training class. Here they will be in close contact with many of the creatures they fear the most and it will make them worse rather than better.

FRUSTRATED PLAY

Some dogs enjoy playing with other dogs so much that they can become very frustrated when prevented from doing so by their lead. These dogs will have grown up playing with other dogs instead of playing with humans and will consider it a very important part of their life. For the more boisterous and determined, this frustration can develop into aggression that may appear to be directed towards other dogs. When allowed off the lead, they will often play nicely, if sometimes roughly, with others.

Such a dog will need to be taught that he cannot play with all the dogs he meets and that you will select those he can play with. Withdrawing all opportunity to play at first is likely to make him slightly worse, so he should have regular access to another playful dog if possible. After this, take him out and teach him how you want him to behave in the presence of other dogs. Teaching a dog how to play with people is difficult, but can be very rewarding as he will then begin to focus on you when outside rather than trying to get to every other dog he sees. You will need to be as determined about this as he is about trying to play with other dogs, but you will begin to see results and his behaviour should improve in time.

Predatory aggression

Predatory instincts are present to a greater degree in some dogs than others. Terriers and lurchers tend to have strong instincts for catching and killing, but not all dogs will be like this and some other breeds may also have these tendencies. Predatory aggression is likely to be directed at anything that is small, that squeaks or cries and moves quickly or erratically. Anything appearing injured or weak is more likely to be targeted.

Owners often find it difficult to believe that the dog they cuddle and that appears so loving is capable of killing, but they forget that dogs do not have our sense of what is right and wrong. A dog that shows this type of aggression is no more prone to other forms of aggression. There is no need to worry that, as a result of catching and killing next door's rabbit, he is likely to try to sneak up the stairs and grab you by the throat in the night. Dogs with a strong predatory drive are only dangerous to animals that look and behave like prey animals. This does, sometimes, include new born babies, but attacks on babies are, thankfully, very rare.

Dogs that chase livestock are usually more interested in the 'thrill of the chase' than in predation.

If your dog has a predatory nature, there is little that you can do other than be very aware of the problem and prevent contact with vulnerable creatures. Be careful never to leave him alone anywhere he can get to small pets' cages. Predatory behaviour can be inhibited in some dogs with firm handling, but it is safer to keep them away from trouble altogether.

Alone at Home

Some dogs will find it difficult to cope with being left alone in their new house at first. For some, the rehoming experience may have been quite traumatic and they will need time to settle down. Others may have had separation problems in a previous home or may have never have been left alone at all before.

Many dogs wait patiently for their owners to return, but some become very distressed when separated from their pack.

Whatever the reason, dogs that are destructive, make a noise or are dirty in the house can be difficult to live with. It is important that a speedy resolution is found to the problem. It is encouraging to know that most dogs gradually improve as time goes on, but it is also worth knowing that there are things you can do to speed up the process. You first need to find out why your dog is behaving in this way.

Punishment does not work

Never punish your dog when you return home regardless of what he has done. Punishment after the event will not prevent it happening again. If the problem was caused by anxiety, punishment will probably make it worse. Sadly, owners often punish their dogs, partly because they are angry that their belongings have been ruined and partly because they think their dog looks 'guilty'. What the dog is actually doing is showing submission in response to their anger. Dogs are very sensitive to our moods and body language, and your dog will notice immediately if you are not pleased by what you have discovered upon opening the door. A natural display of submission to this posture is often seen by us as guilt and evidence that 'he knows he has done something wrong'.

The truth is that your dog does not know his behaviour was wrong since no one stopped him at the time. He was just acting in a manner appropriate to his motivations. Punishing him when you return will not work because he will not understand what you are punishing him for. He can remember what he did, but you have no way of linking the action with the punishment, even if you take him to the scene of the crime. The intelligent way forward is to put him in another room while you clear up the mess or until you are ready to greet him in a friendly way and then think about what you can do to make him feel more comfortable about being left alone next time.

Will another dog help?

Getting another dog to solve a separation problem will probably mean that you will end up with two dogs with the same problem. This is particularly true for anxiety or fear-based problems as these are very easily passed on to another dog. Unfortunately, in most cases a second dog is no substitute for a human and so the 'problem' dog continues to have the problem.

A second dog will really help only in cases where the 'problem' dog has been used to living with another dog and now finds itself on its own. If you are lucky, and the second dog proves to be a suitable substitute for the dog that is missing, the problem may well subside.

It is natural for dogs to want to be with their pack leader. Rescue dogs need time to learn that you have not abandoned them and that you will return.

Leaving calmly and without a big fuss can help your dog remain at ease.

Establish a good departure routine

It is important to start as you mean to go on and this is especially true when it comes to leaving your dog alone. Some owners will take a week or two off when they first get their new dog to help him settle in. However, they usually find that on their first day back to work their dog has been unable to cope with the sudden isolation and they return to a chewed or messy house or complaining neighbours.

From day one, it is important for your new dog to learn that he cannot be with you all the time. Begin by leaving him in the room where you intend him to sleep several times for a short period on his first day while you are elsewhere in the house. Leave him alone in the house on the second day for several short periods if possible. This will mean that if you go out to work your dog will be better able to tolerate your absence because it has been part of what he has become used to. Some dogs will take longer to settle than this and, if you find your new dog will not tolerate being isolated from you without panicking, you may need to take things more slowly.

TIP

Leave a tape or video
recorder running to
help you discover what
your dog does when
you leave and to help
you to identify the
exact nature and
cause of his problem.

Over-attachment to new owners

Being taken from a home where everything is familiar, left in
kennels for a period of time and then finding yourself in a
different home where everything is new and strange can be a very
unsettling experience. Upon finding themselves in a new home,
many dogs want to stick like glue to their new owner and find it
very difficult to cope when they are left behind at first.

Dogs most likely to become over-attached are those that feel
vulnerable for some reason and those with very little self-
confidence. Very young and very old dogs may feel vulnerable,
dogs that have been abused or punished a lot may lack
confidence and those with gentle, submissive natures who would
not want to use the fight option as a means of defence are often
worried when left.

Many dogs come in to rescue centres when they reach
adolescence. This is a time when dogs would be dispersing from
the nest in the wild and becoming more independent. In a pet
home, dogs will go through this process with owners, gradually
becoming less dependent as they mature. However, if you
enforce the separation between owner and dog, as happens
when a dog is given up to a rescue centre, it seems to set back
the process and the dog is likely to develop separation problems
in their next home.

New dogs will often follow their owners from room to room
at first, even when they go to the bathroom, not wanting to be
out of sight in case they should be left behind. This is a
perfectly normal response of any social animal to adversity. In
the wild, it makes sense to stay with other members of your
group when life is dangerous as you have more chance of
survival. Consequently, when all your surroundings are new and
you are not sure how safe life is, it is sensible to stay with other
members of your new pack.

SYMPTOMS

Over-attached dogs want to stay with you. They follow you
obsessively when you are in the house and, in severe cases, may
want to be in physical contact with you most of the time. Or they
may not want to go to sleep unless they are resting against you
so they can be ready to follow when you move. If they do become
separated from you, they begin to panic and show all the usual
symptoms of fear, such as an increased heart rate, dilated pupils,
rapid panting and increased activity. This panic tends to subside
after the first few minutes, but they will often remain anxious

until reunited with you. Dogs that are anxious when left will not want to eat. Chews and food left down will remain untouched until you return.

When left alone in the house, different dogs will cope in different ways. Some may try to scratch and chew at doors and frames, others try to dig through carpet under a door and some become very active and jump up on tables and window sills to look for a way out. Most of the damage is usually concentrated around doorways and windows. If a dog does get out, it will run until it finds someone to be with. Some will bark or howl and some will become so upset that their need to go to the toilet is so great that they go in the house. Some will do nothing but sit and shake and some do all of the above. Whatever the symptoms, this problem begins as soon as you leave the house. As dogs begin to learn your routine, you will find that they begin to get agitated as you begin your preparations for departure.

Dogs that are over-attached to their owners will want to be with you all of the time. They will try to follow you and may bark or chew when they find they cannot.

Teach your dog to tolerate being alone

The only solution is to gradually desensitise your dog to being left alone. You will need to begin very slowly with very short periods of separation and gradually build up to leaving him for longer. In extreme cases you will need to begin with getting your dog to accept being away from you when you are in the same room, but most dogs can tolerate this without a problem. For most dogs, being shut in another room while the new owner is in another is the first step. Doing this throughout the day, starting with, perhaps, 20 one-minute separations will begin the process. Gradually increase the isolation period until he can cope alone while you are in the house for up to one hour. Then begin again, but this time leave the house completely. Again, gradually build up until your dog can cope with two or more hours alone.

Throughout this process, never go faster than your dog can cope with. If you leave him so long that he begins to get agitated, you will be setting back your progress. Go slowly and you will soon begin to achieve results. If you have to leave him for a longer period, try to find someone who can look after him during that time. If you can do this, you will achieve the end result much more quickly.

AN ATTITUDE THAT WORKS

Over-attached dogs get worse if you give them attention constantly when you are with them. The contrast between you being there and not being there will be so great that the dog finds it very difficult to cope alone. For this reason, it helps to give attention in doses rather than in a continuous trickle. Set aside five or 10 minutes in every hour for undivided attention and play. Make a lot of fuss of your dog during this time, but for the rest of the hour ignore him completely unless you need to interact with him for another purpose. In this way, he gets the same amount of attention, but it is given in a different way on your terms. Since he has to cope without you to some degree when you are there, it will make it easier for him to cope when he is alone.

For the same reason, say any goodbyes at least half an hour before you leave. When the time comes, just walk out the door with a minimum of disturbance. If you make a big fuss of him before you leave, there will be too great a contrast between you being there and not, which will make it more difficult for him to cope without you.

Separation problems due to fear

Fear of things outside or inside the house is another reason why dogs may be worried about being left alone. Such dogs are usually able to cope with the fear only when owners are present, but when they are left alone they begin to panic.

A classic example is a dog that is frightened of thunder. During a thunderstorm, a phobic dog left alone will panic and may try to 'go to ground' to get away from the noise. It may run around frantically and go to the toilet in the house in its distress. It may dig into a carpet under a table, try to get into a cupboard, dig into a sofa or mattress or hide under a bed. Dogs that have not experienced thunder when outside may think the noise comes from the house itself. These dogs will try to get out of the house and will damage doorways and windows.

OTHER TIPS TO HELP WITH SEPARATION PROBLEMS

- Leave a scarf that you have been wearing recently on the outside handle of the door through which you exit. Your dog will sniff under the door to find out if you are still close and may be reassured by your scent.
- Leave a radio playing or a tape recording of family activity. This may help block out other noises that may cause your dog to worry and may provide a more familiar background sound in the house.
- Feed your dog a small meal a short time before leaving so he will be more sleepy.
- Leave your dog in the place where he will feel most secure, but where he can do least damage. Keep him away from valuable items and furniture and anything that may damage him, such as electrical wires. Leaving him in the centre of the house may help him to feel more secure and, if he barks or whines, may limit the noise that your neighbours can hear.
- Leave your dog inside the house rather than outside. Leaving him outside will make him more insecure and will make the problem worse. It will also make it more likely that he will bark and upset your neighbours.

Scared dogs often try to find a dark, safe place when left alone and may chew up items that carry your scent.

FEAR OF THINGS OUTSIDE THE HOUSE

Dogs can be frightened of a whole range of things that may worry them while their owner is away. They may be worried about other dogs or people entering the house – they don't know the door is locked – or unfamiliar noises outside. It may be a constant fear that lasts all the time the owners are away or it may be triggered by certain events such as the postman delivering letters. This type of problem may therefore occur every time your dog is left alone or it may happen sporadically when triggered by an external event. It may occur immediately because he is anticipating being scared and is getting worried about being left or it may be triggered by an event later.

Dogs that are afraid of things coming into the house from outside may take objects that smell of their owner, chew them up into small pieces and curl up in the debris so they are surrounded by a nest of their owner's scent. Being such scent-oriented animals, one can only assume that they think other animals and people will smell the scent of the pack leader and go away and leave other pack members alone. They will often choose the items that smell most strongly of their owners, such as the TV remote control, underwear, the arm of a favourite chair or other items recently touched or worn. They will often select items that carry the scent of the person in the household who they perceive to be the strongest.

Another way dogs may cope with their fear of things coming into the house is to mark their territory with urine. If your dog does this, you will often find that strategic points in the house have been marked. These are specially positioned so that an intruder cannot fail to walk past them as they enter. The dog is hopeful that the 'intruder' will smell his presence, appreciate that they are on someone else's territory and go away.

FEAR OF THINGS INSIDE

Dogs may also be worried about noises that occur within the house, such as fridges or heating switching on and off, wind in the chimney or cellar or noises from next door. These dogs will try to get out of the house if they can and will damage doors and windows as they attempt to do this. If they do get out they will often sit on the doorstep waiting for you to get back rather than run away.

TREATMENT

The key lies in discovering exactly what such a dog is afraid of and desensitising him to it. It is not always easy to find the cause, particularly if it is something that happens inside the house. You could leave a tape or video recorder running when you go out to help you to detect noises and movements and find out when the problem begins so you may be able to link it to some external occurrence. You could also leave your dog in a different room to find out where he is less worried, but this could lead to more damage in rooms previously untouched.

Once you have found out what it is that scares him try to desensitise him to it. You will need to do this slowly and, preferably, he will need to be left with someone until he has got over his fears. Introduce him very slowly to a reduced form of whatever it is that scares him and make sure he has a happy experience with it by playing with his favourite toys and feeding him exciting treats. Gradually increase the amount of exposure he gets to the frightening thing, never going beyond what he can cope with, until he is happy and coping in its presence. When he is no longer frightened, it will be safe to leave him alone again. For dogs that are afraid of people or other dogs, a gradual socialisation programme will be needed to make him more settled in their presence (see page 105).

TIP

Never leave anxious dogs shut into an indoor kennel as they can cause terrible damage to their paws and mouth in their panic to get out.

FIRST AID MEASURES

Until you have found the cause of the fear, there are various first aid measures that can help should you have to leave your dog alone. For a dog with mild problems, these may be all that is necessary for him to feel calm again.

● Leave a large article of clothing, preferably made from natural fibre, which you have recently worn for your dog to curl up in. Only leave something that you do not mind being chewed! Leave it where he is most likely to lie while you are out. To find out where your dog likes to lie, feel for the warm patch on the floor or furniture when you return. Replenish your scent on the clothing each time you go out – wear it again, rub it on your skin or keep it in the laundry basket with your dirty clothes.

● If your dog urinates in the house, put down pieces of kitchen towel down, which you have wiped on your own skin, in the areas he has marked in the past.
If he continues to mark these areas, put polythene down so it is at least easy to clean up.

● It may help to provide your dog with a den-like area for him to crawl into to feel safe. A strong cardboard box may work or try an indoor kennel with a blanket over it and the door left open. Put the 'den' under a table or in the place where your dog lies when you are out. You may also be able to cover a table with a blanket to provide a small, dark place for your dog to go when he is scared.

● Exercise your dog well in advance of leaving him so he has time to settle down again before you go out.

DRUG THERAPY
There are drugs available through veterinary surgeons that can help some dogs with very severe cases of anxiety. However, these do need to be used in conjunction with treatment recommended by a pet behaviour counsellor. If your dog has a very severe problem when left alone, ask your veterinary surgeon to refer you to a good pet behaviour counsellor in your area.

Bored dogs

Young dogs or those with lots of energy will become bored when left alone for too long and will often find unacceptable ways to fill their time. These dogs will often lie down for a sleep as soon as you have gone so there will be a certain delay before their problem behaviour starts. Bored dogs are most likely to chew, although some will bark, usually at the slightest disturbance, just for something to do. If they chew, they are likely to select loose objects or they may choose items made

Leave plenty of things for
active dogs to do when you
leave them on their own.

Dogs are scavengers by nature. They will not think it is 'wrong' to raid the bin while you are out, but are following an innate drive to take food while they can.

from the same material, such as wood, plastic or upholstery.

Dogs most prone to these sorts of separation problems are young dogs with lots of energy, particularly those aged between six and 10 months. This is a time when dogs would naturally leave their nest site to explore their envirnoment. Keeping them confined at this time with little to do makes it likely that they will find their own ways to occupy themselves, often with their teeth around your house!

Breeds that were bred to work, and their crosses, often find it extremely difficult to lie down all day with nothing to do. They often have too much mental and physical energy for a sedentary life and some dogs can become quite disturbed if kept in such restricted conditions. Gundogs, especially labradors, were bred to use their mouths and are particularly likely to chew.

WHAT TO DO WITH BORED DOGS

Give energetic dogs much more mental and physical activity when you are at home. Plenty of off lead running is necessary for young, active dogs so teach them to come back when called and take them to a place where it is safe for them to run free at least twice a day. Equally important is the need to use up their mental energy. Do this by playing with toys as often as possible. Train them to respond to commands, to do tricks and to be useful around the house by fetching named items. Teach them to play games such as 'find the hidden toy' so that they can exercise while you sit back and relax. Rather than feeding them all their food in one dish, hide it in pots placed in different locations around the house so that they can search them out while you have gone. Try to be inventive about the things you do with your dog while you are at home and you will find that he is more content to lie down and do nothing while you are away.

THINK AHEAD

- Stuff strong toys and bones with food, such as biscuits, meat paste or cream cheese, to make them more interesting once the novelty begins to wear off. Toys are not much fun if a dog has to play with them by himself for long periods, so find ways to make them more interesting. A strong, solid ball can be drilled with small holes and filled with dry, pelleted food.
- Try to arrange for someone to visit your dog during the day if you can to break up the monotony.
- Exercise your dog well just before you leave and play with him so that he is both physically and mentally tired.
- Restrict your dog's access to valuable items or put them up out of his reach until he has learned to play with his toys and chews only.
- Put a low table or chair under a window for your dog to sit on. Some dogs are happier if they can see out of a window and watch what is going on outside and this will help relieve some of the boredom of a long day alone.
- You may like to find out if it would be possible to take your dog to work with you. This will give you added incentive to train him to behave well so that he would fit easily into your workplace.

You may have to introduce a new dog to a different routine from the one he was used to in the rescue centre. If you find your dog sleeps all evening and is active during the day, encourage him to be active when you are at home so that he is inactive when you leave him. Leave things for your dog to play with and chew while you are out. Gather at least 20 items together that he can play with and chew (there is an enormous range available in shops). Two different toys can be left down each day and not used again for a over week if you have 20. Pick toys up when you return home so that they stay interesting.

Dogs not used to living in houses

Some dogs will not be used to living in a house and will need to be taught how to behave before being left alone. Their natural tendency to explore can otherwise lead them into all sorts of trouble while you are not there to correct them. Do not leave them alone in a place where they can damage expensive items or chew through cables until they have learned how to behave.

To teach a dog how to behave well in your absence, keep him under close supervision during your early days together and correct him when he does something that is inappropriate. The best way to do this is to throw something soft and heavy, such as a cushion, so it lands on him just as he is beginning to engage in the undesirable activity. It should not hurt him, but it should unsettle him enough to put him off the activity next time. If the cushion appears to come out of the blue rather than from you, he is likely to connect the small fright with the activity itself rather than you. He is therefore unlikely to do it again even if you are not in the house at the time.

It is important to offer him something that he is allowed to chew a few minutes later. He will be in the mood for chewing or exploring and you can use this opportunity to teach him what he can chew. When he settles down to chew the offered item, praise him well. By repeating this procedure consistently during the first few weeks together your dog will gradually learn that it is not a good idea to chew anything other than the items you want him to chew.

Dogs can be taught to lie down and rest until you return. Make sure they are well exercised and comfortable before leaving.

CHAPTER

9

Curing Minor Behaviour Problems

It is likely that you will encounter some behaviour problems with your new dog as he adjusts to his new lifestyle. Some of these will be very minor and will cure themselves eventually as he settles in, but others will be more difficult and I have included a selection of the more common problems to give you some guidance on what to do.

If you cannot solve your dog's behaviour problem alone, a Pet Behaviour Counsellor can provide experienced, practical help and advice.

General rules

I have been able to include the basics of each cure only as space is limited in a book, but I hope some of it will be useful to help deal with those difficult teething troubles in the early days.

CHECK YOUR DOG'S HEALTH FIRST

Some behaviour problems are caused by an underlying medical problem and it is wise to take your new dog for a health check at your veterinary surgery before you do anything else. A dog that refuses to sit or lie down when asked, for example, or that is reluctant to move, is grumpy in the mornings or bites when picked up could have painful joints or be tender in a certain place. Some conditions, such as, epilepsy can cause mood changes that can result in erratic bad behaviour. Unusual behaviour is the first symptom for many ailments and, for a mild condition, it could be the only symptom. A health check will give peace of mind and is a necessary requirement before you see a professional behaviour counsellor.

FIND EXPERT HELP FOR SEVERE PROBLEMS

Many people profess to be experts when it comes to solving dog behaviour problems and you will receive advice from many quarters. You will need to find someone who has a considerable amount of both practical experience of dealing with dogs and the necessary academic training and knowledge to help solve behaviour problems. It is becoming easier to find such people now that pet behaviour therapy is becoming more widespread. Write to the Association of Pet Behaviour Counsellors (see page 158) or ask your veterinary surgeon for a referral.

WILL PUNISHMENT WORK?

If your dog is behaving in an unacceptable way, you will need to act to prevent it happening again. The natural human reaction is to punish. In some cases, it will be possible to inhibit a behaviour by the use of punishment, but in the majority the motivation behind the behaviour will remain and it is likely to be exhibited again, and maybe when you have less control.

If your dog tries an unwanted behaviour again you are likely to escalate the punishment and sooner or later you could be using severe punishment out of all proportion to the 'crime'. Worse still, punishment can quickly lead to resentment and a break-down of the relationship you were building up. Punishment is rarely as successful as we would like to think it is and a more intelligent approach will bring greater benefits and a quicker resolution to the problem.

Your dog may be behaving badly because one or more of his basic needs are not being met.

THE 'INTELLIGENT' APPROACH TO PROBLEM SOLVING

Try to find out why your dog does what he does. Finding the motivation behind a behaviour pattern is crucial for deciding on the correct course of action. Try to decide what is motivating your dog to do what he does. Think what it is about the bad behaviour that he finds rewarding. Once you know this, you can arrange for him to receive rewards in a different way so that he changes his behaviour.

SATISFY YOUR DOG'S NEEDS

Before attempting to cure a behaviour problem take another look at the special species needs in Chapter 5. Many problems arise because your dog's needs are not being met. If you suspect one of these needs is not catered for sufficiently, it will be easier to rectify this rather than focus on the problem itself. For example, if your dog barks excessively at every little sound in an attempt to 'entertain' himself because he is not receiving enough mental and physical exercise, it is easier to provide for that need than to attempt to stop the behaviour. Provide adequately for your dog's special species needs and the unwanted behaviour will be easily prevented or discouraged

In addition, look at the relationship you have with your dog before attempting to cure behaviour problems. Does your dog respect you? Is he willing to do things for you easily? Does he

Providing your dog with more play and exercise will help to ensure that he settles down more easily when he is inside the house.

look to you for support? Does he feel loved by you and part of your social group? If the answer to these questions is yes, you have a good basis for solving behaviour problems. If you are so cross with him because of his behaviour that you find you do not like him very much or you are thinking of returning him you are almost certainly doomed to fail unless you can change your attitude. Dogs know if they are loved and supported and those that are unwanted display all sorts of difficult behaviour that will not disappear until they feel part of the pack once more.

Dogs that are generally disobedient or do not pay attention often have a less-than-perfect relationship with their owners. Your dog will listen to you only if he respects you and if he wants to please you. Look again at the pack leadership rules (see page 69) and try to develop a more structured relationship with your dog.

Jumping up

Dogs jump up so that they can reach your face and have maximum social contact with you. This has its origins in puppy greeting behaviour which involves licking the muzzle of returning adults who might be bringing food for them. They consider it a compliment, whereas we, who get scratched, knocked over or covered in muddy paw prints, consider it a nuisance.

Turning away from a dog that is jumping up makes his behaviour less rewarding.

To cure this behaviour, you have to make it unrewarding and, when your dog offers an alternative greeting reward this instead. You either need to ignore the jumping up or prevent it from happening. Ignore the jumping up and turn away so your dog is presented with your back rather than your face to prevent him from being rewarded by this behaviour. Do not speak to, look at or touch him while he is jumping. Alternatively for a large, boisterous dog or one with a very bad habit, hold his collar as soon as you meet him and use it to hold him down as he jumps to prevent him coming up. As soon as your dog has all four feet on the ground and has stopped jumping, bend over or crouch down so he can greet you properly without needing to jump.

If everyone in your family acts consistently, you will find that he will eventually begin to realise that he can greet you more quickly by staying on the floor. At first, you may find that he tries harder to reach you if you are ignoring him, but if you persist, he will soon realise that this behaviour is no longer rewarding.

It is important to restrain your dog so he does not jump on children or visitors. Hold his collar and ask everyone to ignore him until he has settled. One way to make sure he is not going to jump is to ask him to sit. As soon as he is in the sitting position, they should greet him. If he gets up, they should remove their attention until he sits again.

For dogs with a very bad habit, it is a good idea to set up training times with family or friends. They come in through the front door, go through a training procedure with you and your dog where correct behaviour, ie sitting, is rewarded and leave through the back door and begin again. The excitement will gradually subside and it will become easier to teach him how to behave. Several of these sessions will be needed before he shows the new behaviour instead of jumping up and it will take many, many repetitions before you reach the final goal. Remember that dogs learn sets of associations and teaching him to greet people properly at the front door will need to be repeated in different places if it is to become second nature to him everywhere.

Problems at night

If your dog cannot be left alone during the day, he is unlikely to cope when left alone at night. Rather than risk sleepless nights, it may be better to let him sleep outside your bedroom until he feels more at home. This may seem like 'giving in' to him, but if the problem is caused by his anxiety about being alone there is nothing to be gained from forcing him to be alone too quickly. When he is more comfortable about being left alone during the day (see pages 116 to 120), you can begin to move him away from you at night until he sleeps where you want him to sleep.

NOT CLEAN AT NIGHT

If your dog is not house-trained, you will need to ensure you go through the training procedure at night (see page 136). If your dog is clean during the day unless you leave him on his own, you have a separation problem to cope with (see page 118). Dogs that go to the toilet soon after being left are more likely to have a separation problem than those that hang on until just before you get up in the mornings.

Some dogs are house-trained by day and confident about being left alone, but have got into the habit of going to the toilet inside at night. They may have developed this habit in kennels, they may be more relaxed at night or their feeding pattern is such

DRY FOOD

If you feed your dog dry food in the evening, soak it beforehand or feed it with added water. Otherwise your dog will be very thirsty and will drink a lot of water. This excess water will need to come out during the night so your dog will either end up disturbing you in an effort to go outside or will urinate on the floor.

INCONTINENCE

Some spayed bitches can become incontinent and may leak urine when lying down. If your female dog's bedding is wet in the mornings, seek advice from your veterinary surgeon who will provide appropriate treatment.

that they need to go at night. Other dogs will not go to the toilet outside for some reason and do not want to go to the toilet in front of you.

Whatever the reason, the easiest way to solve the problem is to take your dog into your bedroom at night and confine him to his bed so that he cannot get out. Few dogs will soil their own bed so if he wakes up in the middle of the night and makes a fuss take him into the garden and wait with him until he goes to the toilet. Praise him if he does, bring him back inside and put him back to bed. Going to the toilet in this way will be inconvenient for him and he will soon acclimatise his body to going in the morning instead. Continue this regime until you have a week of undisturbed nights before putting him back in his regular sleeping place. Confine him to his bed during the night for a further week, but leave doors open and go to him if you hear him making a noise.

House-training

Your new dog may not have lived in a house before or he may have forgotten about being clean in the house and will need reminding. If he has been kept in kennels for any length of time, he will be used to going to the toilet on a hard surface. Once in a home, he may try to use the kitchen floor or patio as his toilet and he will need to be taught to use an alternative place.

A dog that is not house-trained will select a few areas in the house to use as a toilet and will return to these sites again and again. He will usually sneak away to go to the toilet rather than go in front of humans because he will probably have been punished for going in the house in front of humans in the past. This type of punishment does not teach a dog to go outside, it simply teaches him that it is dangerous to go in front of humans. Such a dog will often go to the toilet inside after coming back from a walk, which will stimulate his body. This is particularly annoying, but in the dog's mind he is being very clean by waiting until he could use his toilet.

HOW TO HOUSE-TRAIN AN ADULT DOG

It is quite easy to house-train an adult dog and you will be able to establish new, good habits fairly quickly. Exactly how quickly, however, will depend on how well you can keep to a routine, how fast your dog learns, how old he is and his previous experiences.

STICK TO A ROUTINE

House-training will happen more easily if you keep to the same routine of feeding and exercising each day. A good routine will help your dog establish a regular toileting pattern, which will help you judge the best time to take him outside.

A new dog may take a few weeks to establish a new habit, especially if he has been in kennels for a long time.

Before beginning your new routine, clean all previously soiled areas with biological washing solution or a special cleaner available from your veterinary surgeon. This will remove smells that attract your dog back to the same place each time.

It is important that you keep your dog under constant supervision for a few weeks so he cannot go to the toilet in the house. When you cannot supervise him or when you are asleep he should be confined so he cannot get out of his bed. This will ensure he has no alternative but to go to the toilet in your presence and you can then begin to teach him where you want him to go. Very few dogs will soil their own bed and although it is unfair to confine them there for any longer than a couple of hours, it does prevent them from sneaking off when you are not concentrating and perpetuating bad habits. You will need to either put barricades around the bed or secure your dog so he cannot get out. Never use a check chain and ensure your dog cannot hurt himself when he is tied up. Keep him confined to his bed as little as possible and never for longer than two hours at any one time.

Take your dog outside and let him run around and sniff when you first wake up, last thing at night and every two hours during the day. Both movement and sniffing seem to stimulate dogs to

Reward any obvious sign that your dog makes when he wants to go outside and he will soon be asking to go whenever he needs to.

go to the toilet. Place any soiled newspaper or faeces where you want him to go so the smell will encourage him to go there.

Stay with him and be patient. If he starts to relieve himself, praise him quietly and reward him with a game or food treat when he has finished. If, after five minutes, he has not done anything, take him inside and try again later, but watch him carefully in the meantime.

Keep an eye on him when you are in the house at all times and be aware of what he is doing. If you see your dog about to relieve himself, shout a loud 'No!' and encourage him to run outside with you immediately. Praise him for doing so as it is essential that he associates going outside with a reward. If you catch him in time he will still need to go to the toilet so wait until he is relaxed and praise him well when he has been.

Do not punish your dog for an 'accident' you may discover too late. Consider it to be your fault for not supervising him enough. The easiest solution at night is to position your dog's bed just outside your bedroom door and confine him to it. If you hear him being very restless or if he begins to make a noise, take him outside (see page 136).

If you have to leave the house for longer than two hours during the housetraining period, do not confine your dog to his bed. Instead, ensure he has a chance to exercise and relieve himself before you go out and cover as much of the floor as possible with a large sheet of polythene with newspaper on top. This will not teach him to be clean, but it will make any messes easier to clean up. Do not punish him if he goes to the toilet while you are out. Simply put him in another room until you have cleared it up and try not to leave him for so long in future.

HOW LONG WILL IT TAKE?

You will need to continue this routine for at least two weeks. During this time, your dog will develop a new habit of going outside and will begin to want to go outside whenever he feels the need to go. After two weeks, gradually increase the time between visits to the garden and watch for any sign that he wants to go out. He may become more active or may wander over to the door. Reward this instantly by praising and taking him outside. Once you have reached this stage, you can begin to relax, stop confining him and give him more freedom in the house. Eventually, you will notice specific signals that indicate that he wants to go out, such as running to the door or standing beside it whining. Reinforce these by letting him out and he will soon be asking to go out whenever he needs to go to the toilet. If you always reward these signals with freedom to the garden, he will soon be asking to go out whenever he needs to go to the toilet.

OTHER HOUSE-SOILING PROBLEMS

As well as not being house-trained, some dogs are not clean in the house because of other reasons such as too much stress and tension in the household, anxiety about being left alone and because they are territory marking. Each of these problems will need a different solution other than basic house-training. Each problem will also have other distinct symptoms.

Stressed dogs, for example, will often leave piles of faeces in very obvious places rather than somewhere relatively hidden. They are also more likely to leave them at night. Dogs that are anxious when left will be unclean only when they are left alone. These dogs often produce many small, runny piles rather than one firm one and they may run about in it in their distress. Dogs that are territory marking will also soil in obvious places as they are trying to leave a smelly message for you, visitors or other animals. They will often mark prominent items in a room, entry and exit points and new objects. Curing such behaviour will depend on diagnosing the cause of the problem accurately. Once you have done this the treatment can be fairly straightforward. Seek further help from your vet or a pet behaviour counsellor if you are unable to work out why your dog is behaving in this way.

Excessive barking

Dogs that bark a lot are a nuisance to owners and neighbours. They give dogs a bad name and it is important that you stop the noise before you get complaints from others. There are many reasons why dogs bark too much. Many bark excessively because at some point in their lives all their species needs were not being met and they learned to bark as a way of coping with their frustration. Some will bark whenever they get excited, some may be trying too hard to protect the house and some will bark at their owners to attract attention.

BARKING THROUGH FRUSTRATION OR EXCITEMENT

To discover whether your dog is barking out of excitement or frustration, first ensure you are meeting all his species needs (see chapter 5). Check especially that he has an outlet for mental and physical energy if he is young or particularly active. Giving a dog a job to do in the form of play and other tasks can calm an excitable dog considerably. Teach a good immediate response to the 'sit' or 'down' commands – few dogs will bark when stationary and if your dog responds to these requests, he will often stop barking too, giving you two reasons to reward him well. If he continues to bark even when stationary, you can try teaching him to hold a toy in his mouth as it is difficult for a dog to hold something and bark.

Alternatively, you could teach your dog to bark and be quiet on command. This may seem counterproductive, but it is surprising how many noisy dogs are more quiet once they have learned to bark on command. It is as if they barked without thinking before, but once taught to do it when asked, they seem to be more aware of what they are doing and often stop. If you can teach your dog to bark on command, it is just as easy to teach him to be quiet. Your command may not work at first when he is very excited, but his response should get better in time, particularly if you reinforce your request with one hand on his collar and the other gently holding his mouth closed. Practise this command in different situations.

TERRITORIAL BARKING

Dogs that bark a lot because they are protecting the house and garden from every possible intruder need to meet more people so that they become more sociable. Take them out and about more often so that they do not see their little piece of territory as the end of their world. It is also important to prevent dogs that like to do this all day from running up and down the boundaries. If your dog does this, stop him quickly every time it happens by calling him to you and rewarding him well for coming. If you can, prevent it from happening in the first place and give him something else to do instead.

BARKING FOR ATTENTION

Some dogs will have learned that the only way to attract their owner's attention is to bark at them. These dogs will often stand directly in front of you while you watch TV or are engaged in

Dogs that show aggression when in the car often have a deep-rooted mistrust of strangers.

TEACHING DOGS TO BARK AND BE QUIET ON COMMAND

Fasten your dog to a solid object and step away from him, holding up something he wants. Wave it in front of him and try to generate as much excitement as possible. As soon as he makes any noise at all, even if it is just a whine, throw him his reward and praise him well. Some dogs make a noise more quickly than others, but persist and it is likely that you will eventually get some sort of noise from your dog. Repeat this exercise, gradually waiting for more and more of a noise before throwing the reward.

Introduce the word 'speak!' or 'talk' after a few sessions so that he begins to associate the word with the noise he is making. Continue to practise this for a while, until you can get him to bark on command in any location.

● To teach him to be quiet, again fasten him to a solid object and ask him to bark. This time, do not throw the reward but, instead, after a few moments, ask him to be 'Quiet!'. Use a hand signal to accompany this request to help him to

understand what you want. Wait until he is quiet, even if this takes a long time. As soon as he stops barking, throw him his reward and praise him. Repeat often and gradually build up as before until he responds at once to requests to bark and be quiet.
● Barking is more obvious and easier to reward than periods of quiet so be sure to spend more time asking for and rewarding quiet behaviour during your later training sessions since this is the behaviour you want to encourage.

something else and bark until you direct your attention to them. The only way to deal with your dog if he behaves in this way is to completely ignore him and never reward such behaviour. Everyone in your family needs to do this and you should warn your neighbours that you are about to try to break his habit.

Be prepared for an initial increase in the barking as your dog tries harder with a behaviour that used to work. Eventually he will give up and go and lie down. After a few moments of quiet everyone in the room must reward him with plenty of attention. If he begins to bark with excitement at this point, withdraw the attention again. He will gradually realise that barking does not work, but if he is quiet he will get all the attention he needs. This method needs perseverance, but it is guaranteed to work if you never reward your dog for barking for attention again.

Bad manners

Some dogs may not have lived inside a house before and will need to be taught how to behave properly. Sharing your home with a dog that has not lived as a pet before or with one that was allowed to get away with bad behaviour can be very difficult at first. These dogs will require an enormous amount of effort initially but you should begin to see results after a few days if you persevere.

Insist on good behaviour at all times. If necessary, physically prevent your dog from doing something wrong. Take control and show him what you want him to do so it does not become a continuous battle where you run around behind him telling him off. You can then reward him for doing the right thing and both of you will be satisfied. Initially, it may help to confine him to one room if his behaviour is very disruptive, but give him many outings into the rest of the house each day, whenever you are able to make a small amount of time available to teach him appropriate behaviour.

Make sure your dog does not barge through gates and doors ahead of you. Insisting on good manners from the outset will get your dog into good habits and make him more respectful.

ENVIRONMENTAL CORRECTION

As well as physically preventing bad behaviour, you can also use a technique called environmental correction to help him learn that there are some things he should not do. If your dog is about to jump up onto a table to eat from a plate of food, for example, throw something soft and heavy at him just as he is thinking about jumping up. The timing is crucial as once he has been rewarded by reaching the food, it is too late. If he is thinking about jumping and preparing to leap when the object lands, you will have got the timing just right. Throw the object so it makes him jump and move away from the area. It should not scare him so much that he runs away, but neither should it be so soft that he continues with what he is doing.

Alternative 'corrections' are to throw something that makes a loud noise towards him, such as a can with pebbles inside or a bunch of keys. It will be more effective if the 'correction' comes out of the blue so it should not appear to come from you. If you get it right and the 'correction' does not appear to come from you, it will be an effective deterrent from repeating the same behaviour even if you are not present. You will need several repetitions of this in different places before your dog decides that eating food from surfaces is not a good idea.

Car travel

Many owners experience problems when travelling in a car with their dog and if you intend to do a lot of travelling, how your dog behaves in the car is something you should check first. Problems can range from car sickness to frantic barking and ripping up seats. As with all problems, there is always a reason behind such behaviour and you will need to find out what it is before the problem can be solved.

CAR SICKNESS AND FEAR

Some dogs have genuine motion sickness – these dogs will often be fine on short journeys, but will become sick if they are in the car for longer periods. Many dogs, however, are just afraid of being in a car when it is moving and it is this fear that makes them sick. Such dogs will often begin to drool and look uncomfortable as soon as the car begins to move. They are likely to be sick quite soon after you have begun your journey. Other dogs may shake, whine or bark and some may even go the toilet in their distress. Dogs that bark because they are afraid will only

Dogs that leap around and bark when the car is moving are a nuisance and can be dangerous if they distract the driver.

do so when the car is moving. It will be worse if you are travelling fast, but it tends to settle down when on motorways.

If your dog is afraid of car motion, you need to desensitise him slowly. This will mean taking him on very short journeys at first, all of which end in a walk or a fun and rewarding event. The length of the journey should depend on your dog's fear levels. Gradually increase the journey times over the following weeks, taking care not to overwhelm your dog with too much too soon. If your dog barks because he is afraid, it will be easy to tell if you are taking things too fast.

Drive carefully, try to avoid bumps and take corners slowly. Placing your dog in a different part of the car may also help. If you have ever travelled in the dog compartment at the rear of an estate car, you will realise how bumpy it is and how it must be difficult for dogs, to keep their footing. Teach him to sit quietly in the front footwell or just behind the passenger seat. Be sure to confine him carefully at first so he cannot interfere with your driving and cause an accident.

CHASING

Some dogs have descended from dogs bred for herding and their desire to chase moving objects gets them into trouble when travelling in a car. These dogs will focus on objects coming towards them such as trees, people or other dogs, will bark frantically as they get closer and then spin round as they pass ready to 'chase' the next thing. In extreme cases, such dogs may also tear at upholstery in their frustration at not being able to run after the object.

These dogs will often bark only as the car speeds up and objects move past the car fast enough to trigger the excitement. To cure such a dog it is necessary to teach him to lie down so his head is below the level of the window or confine him to a covered travelling cage so he cannot see out. Ensure he has adequate opportunity to direct his chase energies into acceptable games with toys when he is outside.

FEAR OF THINGS OUTSIDE THE CAR

Dogs that are afraid other people, children, lorries or other animals will often bark at them when they see them from the car window. You will need to desensitise such as dog to his fear (see chapter 7), but a short-term solution is to restrict his view of the outside world using a covered travel cage so he cannot be scared by things passing by.

EXCITEMENT IN THE CAR

Some dogs will bark with excitement because most of their car journeys end in a walk or something else exciting. If your dog does this, take him on more boring journeys, which do not involve getting out, to lessen the excitement. It is also helpful to make him wait for 10 minutes or so at the end of each journey before allowing him out. When you do get him out, keep him walking to heel and doing slow exercises for a while before letting him free. Ensure that he is getting plenty of activity to use up his energies and play a long energetic game with him in the garden to use up any excess energy before loading him into the car.

ATTENTION SEEKING

Dogs that bark to attract their owner's attention at home are likely to do it in the car too, especially if they are prevented from reaching their owners by a dog guard. These dogs will look at the back of their owner's head and bark continuously until they are spoken to. Cure this problem at home (see page 140) before confining yourself in the car with him where you will find it hard to ignore the behaviour.

CAR TRAVEL TIPS

- Keep trips short at first.
- Follow up car journeys with a pleasurable walk or game if your dog dreads journeys or tire him out with a walk or energetic game beforehand if he gets overexcited.
- Drive steadily and avoid bumps.
- Move your dog from the rear of the car to behind the front passenger seat or in the passenger well to see if this calms him.
- Make sure your dog is secure and cannot interfere with you or the car controls.
- Try putting your dog in a covered travelling cage if he is afraid of things outside or likes to 'chase' objects that pass by.

Running away

Your new dog may have run away from his previous home on a regular basis. This will have taught him about the benefits of exploring farther afield. He may run off to find other people or dogs to play with, he may go hunting or he may be looking for a mate. Ensuring he (or she) is neutered will help with the latter, but dogs that run away often do so because their species needs are not being met. They are probably not being given enough to do to use up their energy or may not be given enough social contact.

If you acquire such a dog, it is important that you keep him physically restrained until you have developed a stronger bond with him and he realises how beneficial it is to live with you. Unless you have very secure fences, keep a long line attached to a point near the door and attach the other end to his collar whenever you let him free in the garden. Pay particular attention to not letting him escape through the main door, ensure he has a collar and tag and have him microchipped just in case. Eventually, if you are being a good owner and meeting all his needs, he should have no need to run away and will be content to stay around you.

Dogs can get through suprisingly small spaces if they are really determined.

CHAPTER

10

Beau's Story

When I first acquired Beau, a labrador/weimeraner cross, he was 18 months old and had bitten at least eight people. He would threaten anyone who walked too close, was aggressive to all dogs and other animals, was very domineering, pulled hard on the lead and, generally, was a mixed up and difficult dog. At the time of writing he is now 11 years old. He has visited elderly patients in hospitals as part of the Pets as Therapy dog scheme, has competed in agility and working trial competitions, is loving with everyone he meets, good with other animals and children and is, generally, my perfect adopted dog. His story is included here to give hope to those of you who are experiencing behaviour problems with your new adopted dog.

Beau at 18 months old. A very worried dog who was confident his aggression would deter unwanted invaders from his territory.

Beau came to my attention soon after I had begun solving pet behaviour problems for The Blue Cross. He had been out to two homes, had bitten both new owners and had also been aggressive to kennel staff too. The general consensus of opinion was that he could not be homed again to risk another bite and, unless I could do something with him, he would have to be put to sleep. I knew the theory and had had lots of practical experience with difficult dogs over the years, but I had never had to deal with anything quite this bad. I had plenty of doubts about a successful outcome, but since even if I failed to cure him, Beau would have lost nothing, it seemed worth a try. In addition, many staff at The Blue Cross were sceptical about pet behaviour therapy at that time and the desire to prove I could completely change a dog's behaviour gave me added incentive. I also knew that I had one of the best advisors in the world to hand if I needed advice. John Rogerson, who was teaching me more about dog behaviour, was at the other end of the phone if I needed to call him for reassurance and guidance on what to do next.

I decided on the day I would take over Beau's care as I knew he would need to learn to depend on me totally. On the allotted Thursday morning, I stood in front of his kennel and watched his frenzied barking and frothing at the mouth for what seemed like

We used gradual desensitisation and plenty of titbits to overcome Beau's fear of men.

an eternity. If it subsided a little, I would make a movement towards the door and he would begin again in earnest. Rather more frightened of going back in defeat to the kennel staff who were watching with interest from the kitchen window, I decided I would just have to risk it. Going into his kennel that day took more courage than I knew I had. Once I had managed to attach a lead with trembling fingers, he proceeded to take me out for a walk. Half way round, I decided to take back some control so I tightened the lead and told him to sit. He rolled his eyes towards me, gave me a stare that made the hairs on the back of my neck stand on end and lifted his lip ever so slightly to show a sliver of white canine. Determined not to be outdone, I told him firmly to stand still, praised him for doing this and walked on swiftly!

After that we progressed on a daily basis. I put into action all the tricks I knew for subtly reducing a dog's status and avoided confrontation at all cost. I refused to let him beat me in all

Instead of rewarding his attention-seeking barking, I taught him to roll over instead. Now, if he wants attention he rolls on his back and waves his feet in the air. It's very funny and works every time.

encounters, insisting that he do something once I had asked, making sure I could physically make him do it without getting bitten before asking. Quite quickly he seemed to realise he had met his match and began to change his behaviour towards me. Since I was not using aggression of any sort, he quickly began to trust me and we developed a firm friendship. Staff used to comment that he seemed to get smaller after I took him on. This could have been because he was no longer such a threat to them, but I think it had more to do with his lowered tail and body carriage as his status declined to a more reasonable level. At home, his attitude was one of humility once he had been treated to a formidable display of strength and power by Winnie, my Rhodesian ridgeback, who was very definitely in charge of the dogs in the household.

Beau's aggression to other people and animals was more difficult to overcome. He had had quite a lot of rough treatment from previous owners and professionals who should have known better in their efforts to try to control him and, consequently, was afraid of people approaching him. He was more afraid of men than women, so we began with any women who were brave enough to volunteer. I will be forever grateful to the women who worked at The Blue Cross during that time, particularly Tina Kew who took the first brave step of sitting still, eyes averted, hand outstretched offering food. We tried not to hold our breaths during those early encounters, but gradually they began to like and trust each other and, in this way, I was able to gradually increase his circle of friends.

It took about two years before I was able to trust him fully with strangers. This time was not without incident. Once, quite soon after I had taken him on, I had left him in the office on a Saturday morning while I went to help with the Christmas bazaar. One of the men who worked at The Blue Cross went in to my office unexpectedly carrying a big box. Beau leapt up and took the front of the box out with one big bite. I prefer not to think of what may have happened if the box had not been there!

Having a stable home and an owner whom he could trust were as much a part of the cure as the work I was able to do with him with other people. I made sure he was kept away from aggressive, difficult people, and, gradually, he learned to trust again. People came to represent good time and food to him, rather than fear and pain. On one memorable occasion, a group of us were having a coffee break together and one of the temporary staff asked what had happened to that awful, aggressive black dog we had. We all laughed and looked at Beau who was leaning against her enjoying the experience of having his head stroked.

During Beau's rehabilitation, I discovered an interesting test for assessing a dog's level of fear. When I first had him, Beau would make the whole car rock as he threw himself at the windows barking and snarling whenever anyone walked past. Gradually, as he began to change his attitude to people, this behaviour subsided until a stranger would have to go up and put their hands on the car to make it happen. Eventually, he stopped worrying about people all together and now never barks at people unless we see someone particularly suspicious on a dark, quiet road. This concept of showing true feelings when within a small, easily defendable space is now used as part of our assessment of dogs in a kennel environment and we are able to tell a lot more about their true character in this way.

Beau's aggression to dogs was probably caused mostly by lack of early socialisation together with a few attacks that confirmed his impression that all dogs were dangerous. His way of dealing with fear was to try to make himself as large as possible to show the world just how powerful he was. This unfortunate attitude made other dogs react very badly to him, which added to the problem. At the time, I was competing in agility competitions with my spaniel, Sammy. These proved to be an ideal training ground as most agility dogs are used to other dogs and tend to ignore them, as well as being focused on their owners. I would park in the most remote spot in the car park and stay on the edge of the action. If I got too close, Beau would display aggression, but if I got farther away, this would subside to shaking and whining. Gradually, this was replaced with calm behaviour, which I would reward with favourite titbits and lots of praise. This regime was practised whenever we encountered other dogs over the next year and his behaviour began to improve, slowly at first and then more rapidly.

At times, it was tempting to get cross with Beau. Having him try to launch himself at other well behaved dogs was embarrassing and annoying. Sometimes, it was hard to remember that he was afraid, and I would begin to wonder if he was just being difficult. On a few occasions, I shouted at him in frustration and pulled him around to try to stop him. This confused him and made him worse, and I would go home defeated. Reasoning things out when I was more calm, and calling to mind how he shook and cried at agility shows made me more sympathetic and, with a change in my behaviour, we began to make progress.

At the same time, I was gradually introducing him to other friendly dogs that he learned to tolerate and eventually play with. As he slowly began to improve, I began to do agility classes with him too. One day we were waiting our turn to go into the ring. Beau was off lead beside me and I was concentrating on the route we were to take. Seizing the opportunity, a German shepherd dog that always liked to have a go at Beau if he could, lunged out of the waiting group and bit him on the bottom. Instead of spinning round and launching a counter-attack, Beau whirled round to the front of me and sat looking up at the pocket I kept the titbits in, preferring to concentrate on something happy rather than get into a fight. It was then that I knew we had nearly made it. Nowadays, he continues to be a bit awkward with other dogs, but he is never aggressive. If they are difficult with him, he will growl and back off, sometimes coming to find me if he feels things may get out of hand. Such a faith in my abilities is very touching, but perhaps he knows that I would risk serious injury to help him out if he was in real danger.

When I first took Beau home, we had a shy, timid cat. Beau would become transfixed by her whenever she was in the room and would watch her with an unblinking stare, trembling and drooling. Given the chance, he would chase her, but I kept him under very close surveillance so that he was not able to do so. A few weeks after I had begun taking Beau home, I accidentally let him into the room where the cat was without keeping him restrained as I normally did. Beau made a dash for the cat, who raced across the kitchen and jumped up onto the window sill out of danger. I heard Beau's teeth snap together as he sprang up to get her.

Beau grew up with young children and always enjoyed their company. During his early life, they were the only humans he could trust.

I was so angry with him for 'letting me down' that I chased him round the house until I cornered him in the living room. All my training forgotten in the heat of the moment, I raised my hand to smack him. He leapt up, standing on two legs against the wall, eyes tightly shut, making biting movements with his jaws. In an instant, I was ashamed of myself for bringing back all the memories of the terrors he must have experienced in previous homes, and I called him to me and cuddled him. This experience did nothing for his desire to chase the cat which continued for a few more months, but it strengthened the bond of trust between us and made me realise how easily people are driven to use aggression when things are not going according to plan. It is also very easy to ascribe human values to our rescue dogs and to think of them as being 'ungrateful' when they misbehave when in reality they have no such conscience. Gradually, Beau learned to stay put whenever a cat was in the room. If he sees one now, he will not chase it, but he will not take his eyes off it either.

To assist with his overall response to commands, I began to train him to compete in the sport of Working Trials. Since this was mostly for my own entertainment, I decided that I would use positive reinforcement only and never tell him off for doing the wrong thing. As a consequence, it took me a long time to get him good enough to qualify at the Companion Dog and Utility Dog level, but the rewards of working with a dog that loved every minute of the training were worth it. In addition, I learned how much easier and better it is to train using positive methods, which I am now able to pass on to other people to help with their dogs. One of the first things I had to teach him was to retrieve since many of the exercises require dogs to find hidden objects. When I first took him on, he would not play or pick up anything and I had to begin with a small film canister filled with favourite treats. Gradually, we progressed until he would pick up anything, including metal objects. Once, when out in the 'search square' where several objects were hidden, he stood stationary for a few moments, looking intently at the ground. He then leapt high in the air, pounced, and came running back to me looking particularly pleased. I held out my hands to receive the object as usual and he spat out his trophy – a freshly killed, still warm, but very dead mouse.

A few months after I began working with him, I decided not to keep him as I already had two dogs and did not really want a third. I advertised him locally and several suitable people came to look at him. I managed to find a fault with them all and, after a while, someone kindly pointed out that I would never find anyone good enough, no matter how long I looked for the 'perfect' owner. I realised they were right and adopted him officially soon afterwards. Staff at rescue centres have my admiration. They do an incredibly difficult job; looking after and caring for animals, growing attached to them and then letting them go.

Beau and I have come a long way together. He has accompanied me everywhere, particularly to talks and courses that I give where I use his story to teach people how it is possible to change a dog's behaviour. In the early days, when I used to become very scared at the thought of public speaking, Beau would begin to drool when I began to worry and would continue until the talk was over. This outward sign of my fear was a demonstration of our close bond and it was a relief to all when I became more confident. The strength of our relationship was a big factor in Beau's conversion into a good pet dog. It is important for anyone taking on a problem dog to realise how much he or she will need to rely on you during the early stages.

I was lucky because Beau was basically a good dog underneath. By that I mean that his genetic makeup gave him a temperament that was neither too reactive nor too prone to developing irreversible fears. Had he had more collie or herding dog genetics in his makeup, I may never have got him over the early damage his environment inflicted on him.

It is strange to look back on all of this and remember how he used to behave. We have had many problem-free years since that difficult time and it is now hard to imagine life without him. My experience with him has taught me so much about behaviour problems and made me very aware of the plight of other people who take on difficult dogs. If you are having problems with your new dog, or have taken on a challenging dog that is as mixed up as Beau was, I hope his story will give you hope for the future. Get expert help if the problems are severe and remember that changes only happen slowly. Persevere and do not expect good behaviour straight away. If you fail, then you were unlucky, but at least you tried. If you succeed, you will have the pleasure of knowing that you saved a dog from a very uncertain future and you will have a love and loyalty that no money can buy.

Beau during a coffee break at work enjoying the company of the staff at The Blue Cross Centre.

Useful addresses

Association of Pet Behaviour Counsellors
P O Box 46,
Worcester WR8 9YS
Email: apbc@petbcent.demon.co.uk
WWW.apbc.org.uk

Association of Pet Dog Trainers
Peacocks Farm ,
Northchapel,
Petworth,
West Sussex GU28 9JB

The Blue Cross
Shilton Road,
Burford,
Oxon OX18 4PF
01993 822651

The Dogs' Home, Battersea
4 Battersea Park Road,
London SW8 4AA
0171 622 3626

National Canine Defence League
17 Wakely Street,
London EC1V 7LT
0171 837 0006

Royal Society for the Protection of Animals
Causeway,
Horsham,
West Sussex RH12 1HG
01403 264181

The Kennel Club
(for details of breed rescue organisations)
1–5 Clarges Street,
London W1Y 8AB
0171 493 6651

Index

A
adoption, process 24-25
adoption, sources of dogs 18
advertisements 21
age 11
aggression 33, 98-111
    defensive 109-110
    dominance 108
    to other dogs 108
    to owners 107
    pain-related 107-108
    predatory 111
    reasons 98
    redirected 108
    to strangers 103
    warning signs 99
alone, leaving dogs 56, 114-129
animals, small 39-40, 53-54
anxiety 33
appeasement 33, 101
assessment of character 26-40
    in kennel 28-33
    outside kennel 34-39
Association of Pet Behaviour
Counsellors 103, 131
Association of Pet Dog Trainers 97
attention 72, 120
    barking for 140, 142, 147

B
barking 139-142, 147
bathing 56-57
behaviour 10
    bad 82, 115, 143
    good 67
behaviour problems 22, 41
    minor 86, 119, 130-149
bitches 10-11, 86
biting 101, 103
    warning signs 99
body contact 17, 29-30, 37, 46
body language 80-81
body maintenance 85-86
border collies 13
boredom 124-128
breed rescue organisations 20
breeds 12-13

C

car sickness 144-146
cars, travel in 43, 144-146
case study 150-157
castration 86
cats 39-40, 51-53
character 10, 17, 23
    assessment *see* assessment
of character
chase games 85
chasing 146-147
chewing 87, 124, 127
children 14, 38-39, 45-48, 75
choosing dogs 8-25
coat types 11-12
collar shyness 107
collies 40, 78, 83
    crosses 13
come when called 90-91
commands *see* training
confidence levels 63, 65
crossbreeds 12
cuddling *see* body contact

D

defence, physiological changes
    101-102
defence, strategies 101
departure routines 117, 120
diarrhoea 58
difficult dogs *see* behaviour
    problems
distractions 89
dobermanns 15, 33
dogs
    information about new 23
    other 15-16, 35-36, 40-41,
    49-51
    second 116
dogs' homes 19-20
donations 20
down command 95
dry food 135

E

emotional blackmail 26
emotions 27
energy levels 16, 33
environmental correction 144
excitement 139-140, 147

extended pack 56
eye contact 31

F

fear 85, 98, 103
    in cars 144-146, 147
    of children 106
    separation problems 121-123
    of strangers 105-106
feeding 72, 135
female dogs 10-11, 86
fights 50-51, 101
first nights 55
food, dry 135
fouling *see* house-training
freeze position 101
friend's recommendations 21
friendship 60, 87
frustration, barking 139-140
furniture 61, 70

G

games 85
genetic traits 13
gentle character 17
German shepherds 13, 78, 83
greyhounds 13, 40
grooming 37, 72-73

H

hand movements, sudden 30
hand signals 81, 89
handling *see* body contact
head high 81
health 131
hierarchies 50, 65
home
    introducing dog 42-59
    left alone 56, 114-129
    taking dog 42-44
home visits 25
honeymoon period 63-65
house rules 42, 44, 56, 61-62
house-training 43-44, 55, 57-
    59, 136-138
    accidents 58, 135, 138
    nights 135-136
houses, unfamiliar with 129

I

immune system 38
incontinence 135
independence 18
information, new dogs 23
introducing dog to home 42-59

J

jumping up 134-135

L

labradors 127
    crosses 13
lurchers 13, 40

M

ogs 10-11, 86
marking territory 85, 123
mongrels 12
muzzles 48, 104

N

names 62-63
needs 76-87, 132-133
    frustrated 86-87
neutered dogs 10-11, 86
nights, first 55
nights, problems 135-136

O

over attachment 118-120

P

pack leaders 50, 65-66
    human 66-75
pedigree dogs 12
pet behaviour therapy 131
pets, other 15, 39-40
physical attributes 9-12
play bows 81
playing 36-37, 70, 87
    frustrated 110-111
possession games 85
praise 44, 62, 90, 138
problem dogs *see* behaviour
problems
pulling on lead 92-93
punishment 67, 69, 115, 131

R

rehoming 21-22
relationships 61-75, 132-133
reproduction 86
rescue centres 19-20, 23
rescue dogs, sources 18-21
rewards 44, 61-62, 67, 89, 90, 138, 143
rottweilers 31
routines 57-59
    departure 117, 120
rules, house 42, 44, 56, 61-62
running away 101, 149

S

safety, need for 83-85
separation problems 115, 118-123
    treatment 123-124
sex 10
show dogs 12
shyness 98, 102-103
sight 78-79
sit command 94
size 9
sleeping places 69-70
small animals 39-40, 53-54
smell 76-77
sociability 31
social contact 82
socialisation 98
soiling problems 135-139
sound sensitivity 77-78
spaniels 13
spaying 86
squeaky toy games 85
Staffordshire bull terriers 13
staring 31
stay command 96-97
strangers 15, 29, 103, 105-106
strays 22
stroking see body contact
strong character 17
submission 115

T

tail down 81
tail wagging 81
temperament traits 12-18
terriers 40
    crosses 13

territorial barking 140
thunderstorms 121
toilet training see house-training
touch 79
toys 36-37, 70, 87
training 88-97
    barking 140, 142
    classes 97
    come when called 90-91
    down command 95
    environmental correction 144
    house rules 42, 44, 56, 61-62
    leaving alone 120, 129
    quiet 142
    response to commands 38, 67
    sit command 94
    stay command 96-97
    suitability 17-18, 32
    walking on lead 92-93
    walking without pulling 92-93
    trust 60

V

veterinary surgeons 58, 97, 103,131

W

walking, loose lead 92-93
water 135
wolves 65
working dogs 12

PICTURE CREDITS

Acknowledgements in Source Order
The Rescue Dog
Ardea 56, /John Daniels 17 Bottom, /Jean-Paul Perrero 68 Top
Anne Marie Bazalik 24 Top Left
Chris Barham 6
Gwen Bailey 150 Centre Left
John Daniels 13, 53, 57, 116, 125
David Key 43 Bottom Right, 54 Top
Octopus Publishing Group Ltd. 32 Top, /Rosie Hyde 19, /John Moss 17 Top, /Tim Ridley Front Cover, Front flap, 9 right, 10 Centre, 11 Top Left, 11 Top Right, 12, 16, 18, 20 Top Left, 21 Bottom, 22 Top Left, 26, 29 left, 30 Top Left, 30 Top Right, 31 Bottom Right, 34 Main Picture, 35 Main Picture, 36 Top, 37 Bottom, 38 Bottom Left, 39 Centre Right, 40 Top, 42 Bottom Left, 45 Main Picture, 46 Top, 47 Centre Right, 47 Bottom Left, 48 Top, 49 Bottom Left, 51 Top, 55 Bottom Right, 59 Top Left, 60 Top Right, 61 Main Picture, 63, 64 Top, 66 Main Picture, 69 Bottom Right, 71 Top Right, 71 Bottom Left, 73 Main Picture, 74, 76 Main Picture, 78 Centre, 79 Top Left, 80 Top Right, 81 Bottom Right, 82, 84 Top, 85 left, 86, 87, 89, 90 Main Picture, 92 Top Left, 92 Bottom Left, 93 Top Left, 93 Top Right, 93 Centre Centre Right, 93 Centre Right, 93 Bottom Right, 94 Bottom Left, 95 Top Left, 95 Top Centre, 95 Top Right, 95 Centre Right, 95 Bottom Right, 96 Top Left, 96 Centre Left, 96 Centre Right, 97 Top Left, 97 Centre Right, 97 Bottom, 98 Top Left, 98 Top Right, 99 Top, 101 Main Picture, 102 Main Picture, 104 Top, 105 Centre, 106 Top, 107 Bottom, 111 Top, 113 Bottom Right, 114 Main Picture, 117, 119 Main Picture, 122 Top, 126 Main Picture, 129 Bottom Right, 130 Main Picture, 132 Top, 133 Top, 134 left, 137, 138 left, 141, 143 Top, 145 Main Picture, 148 Main Picture, 151 Top, 152 Top Left, 155 Top, 157 Bottom Right
N.H.P.A./T. Kitchin & V. Hurst 67 Bottom, /Norbert Wu 14 Bottom
RSPCA Photolibrary/Angela Hampton 83, /Tim Sambrook 27
Warren Photographic/Jane Burton Back Cover, Back flap, 3